P9-AOG-372

# UNDERSTAND MY
# MUSLIM
# PEOPLE

*What people are saying about*
## UNDERSTAND MY MUSLIM PEOPLE

This is a powerful testimony of God's grace in a former Muslim's heart and a helpful, well-written guide for understanding and reaching Muslims for Christ.

**DR. NORMAN L. GEISLER**
*president, Southern Evangelical Seminary, Matthews, North Carolina;*
*author and coauthor of numerous books including* Answering Islam

*Understand My Muslim People* is a "must read" for all evangelical Christians who will share their faith with friends and coworkers who presently embrace Islam. The book's organization and development follow a logical pattern and make for ease of reading while being quite stimulating and informative. Sections three (Islamic beliefs) and four (Islamic practices) are especially helpful and enlightening given the author's own formative background in Bangladesh. The concluding section, detailing how Christians can relate positively and effectively in their outreach to Muslims is the book's particular strength and dynamic.

**DR. GARY L. HEARON**
*executive director, Dallas Baptist Association*

This book combines two important elements in the field of evangelization: Abraham Sarker's testimony and a thorough study of the Islamic faith as he compared it to the Christian basic doctrines. I found his insight, understanding, and experience helpful in revealing the truth as it is manifested in the Bible. It is a book worth reading and provides a spectrum of knowledge and clarity.

**DR. SAMUEL SHAHID**
*director of Islamic Studies Program*
*Southwestern Baptist Theological Seminary, Fort Worth, Texas*

With the ever-changing demographics of America, *Understand My Muslim People* is an essential tool for understanding the mind-set of our Muslim neighbors and what they believe. Dr. Sarker shares insights about this fastest-growing religion of Islam, how to intellectually discuss the differences between Islam and Christianity, as well as how to show the love of Christ to Muslims.

**NATHAN SHEETS**
*president, EvangeCube Global Ministries*

This book presents an informative, enlightening, and intriguing insight into Islam. The telling of his dramatic journey from the Islamic faith to Christianity not only lends tremendous credibility to Dr. Sarker's work, but to the greatness of the God of the Bible. Dr. Sarker has done an excellent job in presenting the similarities and differences between the two faiths, and in providing sensible and sensitive tools for sharing Christianity with the Muslim community.

MARK WALKER, ABD
*senior pastor, Mount Paran North*
*Church of God, Marietta, Georgia*

If personal testimony provides powerful validation for any claim, Dr. Sarker's pointers to the one who opened his blinded eyes give us confidence in our own efforts toward hard-to-reach audiences. Read this story, for in it you'll find comfort and counsel if you are burdened to reflect the True Light across the world.

RAMESH RICHARD, Ph.D., Th.D.
*professor, Dallas Theological Seminary;*
*president, RREACH International*

Particularly since the horror of 9/11, numerous books have been published to explain, explore, and express the religion of a billion earthlings. *Understand My Muslim People* has a very distinct advantage in view of the fact that Dr. Sarker was born in a Muslim country, raised by devout Muslim parents, and began studying to become a Muslim cleric. His book describes the facts and fictions concerning Mohammed, Islam, and traditional Muslim practices. Anyone who reads the book will be greatly rewarded, informed, and deeply encouraged to share the gospel with Muslims. Dr. Sarker is proof positive that the gospel of Christ is the power of God unto salvation to everyone who believes—especially Muslims.

DR. ANIS SHORROSH
*author of* Islam Revealed

*Understand My Muslim People* is one of the clearest, most compassionate glimpses into how God touched the life of a devout Muslim and drew him to Christ. This is must reading for anyone trying to understand and reach Muslim friends.

DR. MICHAEL POCOCK
*chairman and senior professor of world missions and*
*intercultural studies, Dallas Theological Seminary*

All of us at Dallas Baptist University have been inspired by Abraham's conversion story ever since he came here as a student in 1996. Abraham's miraculous story and his firsthand insights into the Muslim world are eye-opening. This message so desperately needs to be read by all Christians, especially in the midst of so much misunderstanding of the Muslim people in the Christian church today.

DR. GARY COOK
*president, Dallas Baptist University*

*Understand My Muslim People* is a must-read from among many books I've read on the subject. I would urge every Christian minister to carefully read and utilize the words of this book.

FREDA LINDSAY
*cofounder, Christ for the Nations, Inc.*

Conversion from Islam is a very serious, even potentially life-threatening commitment, one that impacts both personhood and identity. Abraham Sarker realized this first-hand, but was also convicted that Jesus' sacrifice of love on the cross of Calvary extends to everyone, including his own Bengali people. I find the book well-organized and informative, fulfilling the Great Commission in a beautiful way. May the Lord use it for the strengthening of souls that realize we get rescued from the bondage of Islam in order to bring others to our Lord Jesus Christ.

TIMOTHY ABRAHAM
*former Muslim from the Middle East*

Writing from personal experience and with thoughtful conviction, Abraham Sarker offers helpful insight into the ideology and practices of our Muslim friends. Rejecting simplistic notions of a monolithic Islam, he leads us into a deeper understanding of both the diversity and the common threads that characterize Muslims everywhere. Reading Sarker will help correct many Western stereotypes of the people who follow Mohammed, while also opening the way for Christians to develop new friendships borne of respect and a mutual search for enduring truth. Abraham gives us a look behind the veil of Islam through eyes of love and concern.

DR. JOHN P. WILLIAMS
*superintendent, Evangelical Friends Church—Eastern Region, Canton, Ohio*

# UNDERSTAND MY
# MUSLIM
# PEOPLE

*by a former Muslim*

## DR. ABRAHAM SARKER

**BARCLAY PRESS**

NEWBERG, OREGON

54244 NON FIC 297

UNDERSTAND MY MUSLIM PEOPLE
© 2004 by Abraham Sarker

Published by
BARCLAY PRESS
Newberg, Oregon 97132
www.barclaypress.com

The author shares his proceeds from this book
to support the ministry of
GOSPEL FOR MUSLIMS, INC.
P.O. Box 153882, Irving, TX 75015
www.gospelformuslims.com

All rights reserved. No part may be reproduced
by any method without permission in writing
from the copyright holders, except for brief quotation
in connection with a literary review.

Scripture text is from the *Holy Bible: New International Version.*
Copyright © 1978 by the International Bible Society.
Used by permission of Zondervan Bible Publishers.

Cover design by Dan Jamison
ISBN 1-59498-002-0
Printed in the United States of America

# DEDICATION

*To my loving wife, Amie,*
*my best friend*
*and lifelong companion.*

# Contents

**Charts and Illustrations**

# Foreword

The piercing, amplified voice carried through the din and clatter of the dusty streets. Men rushing and jostling through the crowds stopped suddenly. As one they turned to the mosque centered in the village. They removed their shoes and washed their hands and faces at fountains placed alongside the walls of the mosque. Then they disappeared, ornate rugs rolled under their arms. When they next appeared, I was shocked by what I saw. Several had prostrated themselves with such fervor on their prayer rugs that their foreheads were bleeding. I felt ashamed as I contrasted their religious passion with my own.

Such was my first encounter with the Muslim world. The college summer I spent doing mission work in East Malaysia was my invitation to a larger world. Like most American Christians, I had little exposure to Islam and even less understanding of its beliefs and spirit. Until September 11, 2001, most of us were content to remain ignorant of this remarkable spiritual and cultural movement. Since that tragic day, much of what we think we have learned has come through the distorted prism of caricature and second-hand expertise.

We can no longer afford such ignorance. Islam is the fastest-growing religion in the world, and in America. More Americans seek God through Islam than through Episcopal and Presbyterian churches combined. The Muslim faith has actually made great strides toward acceptance in our society *after* 9/11, as cultural influencers have legitimized this religion as simply another way to worship the same God. As Islam impacts our lives even more significantly in coming years, Americans and Christians desperately need an objective guide to this spiritual phenomenon.

The volume you hold is the most unique answer to this need available today. Dr. Abraham Sarker possesses remarkable qualifications as our guide to the Muslim faith and its significance. Abraham grew up in Islam, the disciple of his village's spiritual leader. His intellectual brilliance marked him as a future leader of great promise within the Muslim world. He came to America to spread the message of Islam within our culture. What happened next is a modern-day book of Acts miracle.

Today Abraham is dedicated to helping American Christians understand the Muslim world and relate our faith to its followers. He knows Islam not from world religions textbooks but from first-hand experience. He understands the Christian faith as one of its most passionate advocates. He is able to relate the Muslim culture to American society on a level possible only to one who has lived in both worlds. And he is a daily example of the gracious and compassionate spirit he advocates as our most effective witness.

Abraham is a faithful member of the congregation I pastor, and my dear friend. He has impressed our entire church family with his communicational brilliance and personal warmth. He has taught our people many of the insights you will discover in his book. We are far better equipped to understand our faith and to share its grace with our culture than we were before Abraham joined his ministry to ours.

When I served on the faculty of Southwestern Baptist Theological Seminary in Ft. Worth, Texas, world religions was one of my areas of responsibility. For several years I taught the biblical worldview in contrast to the worldviews of mankind's great religions. I have found Abraham's discussions of Christianity and Islam to be historically and biblically accurate, and academically brilliant. And his personal story makes his intellectual presentations compelling and unforgettable.

I pray that *Understand My Muslim People* finds its way into the hands and hearts of Jesus' followers across our nation and beyond. Abraham's work will equip us with crucial insight in understanding our post-9/11 world. His insights will guide us to our Muslim neighbors with the good news of Jesus' love. And his personal encounter with the grace of God will draw us closer to the one whose Son is the way, the truth, and the life.

*James C. Denison, Ph.D.*
*senior pastor, Park Cities Baptist Church*

# Acknowledgments

These dear friends and their valuable wisdom have been instrumental in my Christian life and ministry. Without them this book would not be possible.

- Peter Shadid led me to faith in Christ.

- Cliff and Marge Steele took me into their home and church.

- Peggy Tift helped me to know what it means to be a Christian, and was like a mother to me.

- Dr. Gerald Derstine gave me a scholarship to study the Bible at The Christian Retreat.

- Freda Lindsay has been my cheerleader in the faith, providing encouragement and support during my study at Christ for the Nations Institute and throughout my Christian life.

- Joyce and Bill Watkins were generous supporters of my Christian growth.

- Dr. Gary and Sheila Cook are wonderful Christian examples. Dr. Cook was my "best man" and mentor who believed in me.

- Rebecca Brown's love and prayers greatly impacted my life.

- Dr. Gary and Paula Hearon are remarkable Christian leaders who became like parents to me.

- Roy and Dr. Jinky Twaddell have impacted my life and ministry through their friendship.

- Dr. Norval Hadley was instrumental in my work with Evangelical Friends Mission.

- Jeff and Cindy Padgett are special friends with a shared heart for ministry.

- John and Ruth Hatton have blessed my wife and me with their godly example, loving prayers, and support.

- Dr. Jim Denison is my pastor and my dear friend.

- Scott and Carla Robinson are faithful friends in my life and ministry.

- Dr. Charlie Frazier is a great friend and supporter in the ministry.

- John and Claudia Kalmikov's genuine love and friendship mean a lot to my wife and me.

- Craig Walker is my Sunday school teacher and a generous friend.

- Art Alexander is a wise friend and encourager.

- My beloved wife, Amie: You are more than my best friend, you are my heart.

- I'm grateful for all who have allowed me to preach the gospel of Jesus Christ and share my testimony from their pulpits.

# A Quest to Understand

Shock. That's what most Americans felt on September 11, 2001, after witnessing the worst act of terrorism ever committed against the United States. The stunned people of this nation were left to ask the question, "Why?" Why would nineteen men willingly commit suicide in order to take the lives of thousands of innocent people? What religion, reward, or fear would motivate them to such a horrific act? What kind of intense loyalty to radical Muslim clerics could drive them to *jihad*? These questions have spurred heightened interest in and much discussion about the religion of Islam.

Approximately one fifth of the world's population is Muslim. By the end of the twenty-first century, that number is expected to increase to a full quarter of the earth's population.[1]

Yet, this "Eastern religion" no longer remains far distant from the people of America. The United States has witnessed its own Islamic population boom. More than six million Muslims and more than twelve hundred mosques now call America "home."[2] More Muslims live in the United States than Episcopalians and Presbyterians combined.[3]

While Islam is the youngest of the major world religions — the others being Hinduism, Buddhism, Judaism, and Christianity — it is the fastest-growing religion in the world (and in the

United States). Followers of Islam believe they have the absolute truth for mankind. Mohammed, Islam's most revered prophet, claimed to have received his message directly from the angel Gabriel. Clearly, if Christians are to effectively reach out to the Muslims of the world, they must first understand Islam and the Muslim mind-set.

I have relied on multiple sources for the content of this book, including the Qur'an, or Holy book of Islam; the *Hadith*, or commentary on the Qur'an; as well as scholarly works written about the Islamic faith. My own personal background—I was reared as a Muslim in an Islamic nation and intensively studied Islam—also naturally informs what I have to say.

I have organized the book into five sections. In the first section, I tell how Jesus Christ brought me from a life devoted to my Muslim faith to a search for truth and eventually to a new life in Christ. In the second section I present an overview of Islamic origins. Part III outlines fundamental Islamic beliefs, while Part IV considers basic Muslim practices. In the fifth section I suggest a Christian response to the religion of Islam, including how a Christian can effectively witness to a Muslim.

Both Islam and Christianity claim to be the one true religion, and in many ways they resemble one another. Yet because significant and undeniable differences exist between the two, further understanding must occur if meaningful relationships are to take place between Christians and Muslims. I hope this book contributes positively to such an effort.

*Abraham Sarker*
www.UnderstandMyMuslimPeople.com
author@understandmymuslimpeople.com

## *Part I*

# Story of a Miracle

I was born into a devout Muslim home in the Islamic country of Bangladesh. While training to become an Islamic leader, one night I dreamed that I was burning in a lake of fire. This unsettling dream led to my search for the true God and eventually brought me to the feet of Jesus. While the gospel was free to me, it has cost me everything to follow Him.

This is a story of a miracle.

## ∘ 1 ∘

# Dedicated
# to Allah

Did you know that Islam is the second largest religion in the world after Christianity? Until God opened my eyes to see the truth, I was one of 1.2 billion Muslims blinded by Islam.

I was born into a devout Sunni Muslim home in the green, fertile nation of Bangladesh. My father, an Islamic leader with a prominent Islamic political party, and my mother, an Islamic schoolteacher, together reared me to be a model Muslim boy and future Islamic leader. Their dreams for me seemed to be coming true until a "miracle" took place and their world came crashing down. This is a story about how God snatched me from the clutches of hell and introduced me to the eternal Savior, Jesus Christ.

### A Beautiful Land

About 130 million people live in Bangladesh, a country approximately the size of Wisconsin. Our cities overflow with people, apartment buildings, shops, industrial buildings, rickshaws, motorcars, and pollution.

Yet in the midst of our increasingly modern cities, one can still see hints of the exotic beauty of this ancient land, especially in the villages scattered across the countryside. Mahatma Gandhi said of his own beloved homeland, "India lives in the villages." The same is true of Bangladesh. The Bengali way of life can be best appreciated in the thousands of villages that dot the tropical landscape. The beauty of Bangladesh finds its highest expression in the colors of its land, people, and culture.

Many villages nestle so far into the tropical foliage that one can reach them only by crossing on foot over narrow bamboo bridges, weaving between rice and mustard seed fields on paths carved out of dense clusters of broad-leafed trees. All around, lush green reflects from leaves to the long irrigation canals. Women walking along a well-beaten path might skillfully balance large water pots upon their heads, their dark, thick hair tied back loosely in a long braid. As they pass, you hear the gentle jingling of jewelry and delicate swish of saris, richly designed in lavish, bold colors. Young men also pass by, bamboo sticks in hand, casually herding a small group of goats to the next village, less than a mile away. The aroma of curried fish and rice hangs in the air, floating up from an open fire pit.

Beneath such external beauty, however, there lies an emptiness and oppression. A disease of hopelessness plagues the nation from the inside out, holding captive the souls of its people and lining their faces with despair.

### A Varied Spiritual History

Many years ago, under British rule, the region now known as Bangladesh was called the East Bengal. Hinduism dominated the area's religious practice. West Bengal, on the other side of the Ganges River, provided the site for Mother Teresa's work in Calcutta.

In 1793, a Baptist minister from England named William Carey journeyed to this land to share the gospel. He accomplished many notable things, including the translation of the Bible into Bengali (and related dialects). Carey lived and died in the Bengal, winning many to the Lord and enjoying a fruitful ministry that improved the Bengali way of life. Today he is called "the father of modern missions." Yet after him not many others arrived to carry the light of the gospel to the Hindu Bengalis.

Years later, Muslim missionaries from other countries settled in present day Bangladesh. The religion of Islam offered a system the Bengalis eagerly embraced, such as abolition of the caste system. The people heard that once they became Muslims, they would be equal, not dominated or segregated by caste, regardless of their family background. Eventually Islam claimed a majority of the country's citizens, and in 1988 Bangladesh became an Islamic nation.

### Civil War Strikes

During the months of my birth and infancy, an intense civil war ravaged my country. East Pakistan fought for its freedom to live as Bangladesh (a "country of Bengalis"), hoping to sever its ties to West Pakistan, a country that shared little in common with Bengalis other than a framework of Islamic beliefs.

My father, grandfather, and uncles joined thousands of other brave men to fight in this conflict. Eventually the violence grew so severe that my expectant mother could no longer reside in the capital city, Dhaka. She, along with other female relatives, secretly rushed away at night through rice fields, thick tropical underbrush, and humid marshland to a tattered bungalow in a remote village. There, in a little hut made of bamboo and straw surrounded by canals and marshland, I was born.

Days, weeks, and months passed as my family waited to hear any word about our loved ones. My mother clung to me, her firstborn, as if to hold on to life itself. After nearly a year of such fear and anxiety, one day a thin, battered figure walked heavily toward our bungalow. As the fatigued man approached ever closer to our hut, tense silence gave way to a cry of joy. My father had survived and had finally returned home!

It was a bittersweet homecoming, however, as he delivered grim news of less fortunate family members. My grandfather had been among those who paid the ultimate price. I never had the opportunity to meet him.

As we nursed my father back to full strength, Bangladesh became its own nation. Soon we returned to the capital city and tried to resume normal life.

### My Childhood in Bangladesh

Although Muslims consider age seven to be the age of accountability, every child born into an Islamic household is automatically born a Muslim. When I reached age seven, my parents, wanting to make sure I was a Muslim, required me to repeat the *shahada,* or creed of Islam: "There is no god but Allah, and Mohammed is his messenger." The creed must be said in Arabic—"*La ilaha illa Allah, Mohammed rasul Allah*"—regardless of the native language of the speaker. After I recited this creed for the first time, my parents required me to practice the Islamic religion in full force. From that moment on, I recited the shahada at least five times a day in my prayers.

Visitors to a Muslim country will hear the ritual call to prayer announced over a loudspeaker five times a day from the city's mosques. The melodious Arabic chant floats through the air, inescapably reaching all parts of the community. Whenever faithful Muslims hear the chant, they stop their daily activities, prepare themselves with ritual washing, and complete their required set of prayers, including special motions and positions on their prayer rugs.

In addition to these prayer rituals, I also memorized much of the Qur'an, a book that contains messages reportedly given by Allah to Mohammed, the supreme prophet of Islam.

Devout Muslims also are expected to fast during the entire month of Ramadan. As a young boy, I remember how much I struggled with this fast, especially during the stiflingly hot days of summer in which the month of Ramadan sometimes fell. If we wanted Allah to accept our fasting, we were told we could take no food or water from sunrise to sunset. (Some teach that you cannot even swallow your own saliva during this holy month.) Hence, my mother would not give me even a drop of water to drink.

I remember one particular day during Ramadan when I was seven years old. My friends and I had just finished playing a rigorous game of soccer under the hot sun. I rushed home desperately thirsty and said, "Mother, I am very thirsty. Please give me some water to drink."

"Son," she replied, "you must not drink until *ifter* [the breaking of the fast]."

"Mother," I complained, "if you don't give me water to drink, I will die!"

She had a simple answer: "You must complete your fast. You can do it, son."

Despite my pleas, she would give me nothing to drink until the sun went down. I remember lying on my bed, waiting in anxious pain for the moment when I could quench my burning thirst.

And so my parents determined to train me to live as a devout Muslim.

### My Devotion to Islam

Each adherent to Islam usually is assigned a mentor, someone who can disciple the young believer in the Islamic faith. As the firstborn son of my family, I had to set an example for my younger siblings; in particular I was expected to mentor my younger brother, Jamal. Since my father wanted me to have the best training, he hired the leader of our community mosque — our *imam* — to be my private mentor.

I was taught to memorize the *surahs*, or chapters, of the Qur'an, learned how to be a good Muslim, and became familiar with the origins of our religion as recorded in the Hadith, a commentary on the Qur'an. At times these teachings puzzled me, but I never questioned them. A good Muslim is taught to never question the Qur'an; it is the absolute word of God and cannot be questioned, for Allah will punish every disobedient, prideful individual.

At the age of thirteen, I joined the Islamic organization in which my father had become actively involved. There I received training to become an Islamic leader. Group members often traveled to remote villages to instruct the people on the teachings of Islam. They also greatly influenced our country's political system.

As a part of my involvement with this organization, I gave the prayer call from the local mosque. By giving the prayer call, I would remind all Muslims of their duty to pray to Allah. Five times a day I would climb the tall tower (called a *minaret*) and call out the melodious Arabic chant: "Allah is great, Allah is great. Come for prayer." The first call goes out at 4:30 A.M., before sunrise. At four other set times throughout the day I would return to the mosque to give the prayer call. For each prayer missed, a careless Muslim is condemned to many years in hell.

As a devout Muslim, I would have died for my religion. My heart was devoted to Allah and to His cause. Still, when I read the Qur'an, I would often fear Allah's severe punishment for any wrongdoing. I passionately taught others that, according to the Islamic faith, their only hope of attaining heaven lay in doing good deeds. Yet deep inside of me, I feared the capricious nature of Allah, as described in the Qur'an. I knew that no one could know whether he would go to heaven, regardless of his exemplary deeds. Allah was unpredictable, and one could only hope that he or she would find favor with the Almighty. To this point in my life, I had lived as a very devout Muslim, carefully trying to obey all of Allah's commandments. Yet even the most exemplary Muslim cannot be assured of his salvation.

## My Disturbing Dream

As I continued to grow in my service to Allah, one night I had a deeply disturbing dream. In my dream I had died, and when I went to heaven to face God, Allah threw me into a lake of fire. I knew very well from my study of the Qur'an that the lake of fire was, in fact, hell. All around me I could see nothing but blazing fire. I felt the searing pain of my body burning in that intense flame. The dream felt so real and so painful that I began screaming in my bed until my parents came rushing in to wake me.

Between sobs and gasps for air, I described my dream.

"Satan is trying to disturb you," my parents replied. "You're not to worry; you are a good Muslim."

Their words gave me no comfort, however, and the dream continued to trouble me for many days. As a devout fifteen-year-old Muslim, I could not understand what I had done that would bring Allah such displeasure.

A few nights later, I had the same disturbing dream. I had died, faced God, and He threw me into the lake of fire. Again I felt the sweltering pain of my body burning in the lake of fire. When I awoke, I decided to seek counsel from our imam, my private mentor. He gave me the same explanation that I heard from my parents.

"Satan is trying to disturb you," he said. "You're not to worry. You are a pious Muslim, and you do many good things for Allah."

I hoped I would feel better after hearing this message, but still the fear lingered; in fact, my troubled heart grew heavier. What had I done that would make God so displeased with me?

Several nights later, I had the same terrifying dream for a third time. Once again I had died, faced God, and was thrown into the lake of fire. Again I felt the intense agony of burning in those superheated flames. I awoke, feeling desperate. I saw only one thing to do: go to the mosque, pray, and ask Allah to reveal the meaning of my dream.

That next evening after finishing evening prayers, I remained in the mosque after the other worshipers took up their prayer rugs and went home. The beautifully painted tiles decorating the walls and inside of the huge dome had darkened with the dimming of the sun's rays, and a few electric light bulbs hanging from the ceiling and walls provided artificial illumination. Finally, night had come, and I was left alone on my prayer rug—the only item remaining on the clean, mosaic tile floor. Silence filled the large room, except for an occasional birdcall from outside and the gentle hum of insects in the warm night air.

I knelt down on my prayer rug with my head to the ground, the customary prayer posture for Muslims. As I desperately sought after God, my troubled heart had only one plea: "God, please speak to me and tell me the meaning of my dream. What have I done that You are not pleased with me?" I prayed with resolve, declaring, "I will not lift up my head until You tell me the meaning of my dream." I prayed with expectation, desiring to hear an audible voice from God, telling me what I had done wrong. I felt that by asking forgiveness of this sin, whatever it might be, I could still have hope of heaven, if God might choose to have mercy on me and forgive me.

Whenever I grew tired, I would stand up and walk around, and then return to my place on the prayer rug and plead to God, time after time. All night passed by. I did not hear from God.

Despondent, I sat in the middle of the huge, vacant mosque. I glanced at the clock—almost 4:30 A.M., time for me to give the morning prayer call. All night I had prayed, asking only one question, but God did not speak to me. My heavy heart ached with disappointment. I paused for a moment and closed my eyes as tears began to fall down my face. I cried out to God, "Why didn't You speak to me?"

Suddenly, something mysterious happened. At first, I heard a noise like a rushing wind. Drops like rain began falling where I sat, dousing my clothes, head, and hands. Immediately I opened my eyes and looked up to see if the ceiling was leaking, but saw no sign of it. The drops had fallen all around me, on my Muslim attire, on my head covering, and on my prayer rug. When I rubbed the drops on my hand, they felt like oil. The whole mosque filled with a sweet fragrance that I had never smelled, before or since.

Immediately afterwards, while I remained seated on my prayer rug, my imam walked in to lead the morning prayers. He immediately noticed the sweet fragrance permeating the room and witnessed the drops all around me. With astonishment in his voice he said, "I have never seen anything like this. Maybe Allah likes you!"

At that moment a tremendous peace came over me, such as I had never experienced. I still didn't know the meaning of my dream, but it no longer terrified me. My family and friends noticed an immediate difference in me and asked me what had changed. I didn't know how to explain my miraculous experience—but I still sought God's answer.

# ∘ 2 ∘

# From Muslim
# to Christian

A couple of weeks after the mysterious incident of the falling oil in the mosque, a second unusual event captured my attention.

After evening prayers, I walked alone to my home in the warm night air, the last person to leave the mosque. Suddenly I heard a voice in my own Bengali language say, "Go, and get a Bible." I looked around the deserted gravel road to find who had spoken, but saw no one; yet the voice had sounded as audible as if someone had been walking right behind me.

Before this moment I never would have considered even reading a Bible. I had been taught that even though it contained information about several of the Islamic prophets, Christians had corrupted the Book, and if a Muslim read it, he might be led astray from the truth. Muslims were not permitted to study it. Upon hearing this voice, however, an irresistible desire for a Bible came over me. I knew at once I would have to begin my search in secret, for how could I tell anyone about hearing this voice? They might become angry with me and perhaps even treat me cruelly.

For four years I looked for a Bible. I looked in bookstores and libraries, but never found one. I never saw a church and never met a Christian.

Then one day my father decided to send me to America. Often he had expressed a desire that the whole world believe in Islam, and now he said that America and the Western world had an especially great need. So he suggested I go to the United States, primarily to share my Islamic faith. I would become a witness among the infidels (non-Muslims). When I expressed some concern about my education, my father insisted I could finish my degree in America, if I so desired. I agreed to his proposal, and prepared to leave my beloved homeland of Bangladesh.

### My Journey to America

I still remember leaving my family in the Dhaka International Airport. My mother looked worried and told me, "I wish your father would send you to Saudi Arabia instead." At least, there her son would live among fellow Muslims. Now, with her son heading to America, she felt terribly concerned. She left no doubt about the cause of her concern: "Americans eat pork, and they drink alcohol!"

She needn't have worried about either concern, because I had always carefully followed the Islamic dietary laws. And besides, the very thought of eating pork made me feel almost queasy.

My mother gave me one last word of advice before I left on the plane: "Be careful, my son; Americans put pork in their cookies!" This bit of news especially disappointed me, because I do enjoy good cookies. With such wisdom ringing in my ears I flew to America.

By the time I arrived in the United States, I felt very hungry. As I waited in line at an airport fast food chain, I noticed a large sign beside me: "Special—Hot Dogs $1.99." This immediately confused me. *My mom forgot to mention that American peo-*

*ple also eat dogs!* I thought. Only after several months in the United States did I finally come to understand that hot dogs weren't really made from dog meat.

As I prepared to accomplish my religious mission in America, I joined with several fellow Muslims who had the same goal of representing Islam. Still, the desire for a Bible continued to grow within me. I simply could not forget the audible voice I had heard back in my homeland.

One day I visited a nearby university library and asked a young lady behind the front desk where I could find a Bible. She looked at me inquisitively, most likely because of my Islamic outfit, which I wore at all times. After a brief pause, she suggested that I go to one of the Christian organizations on campus, the Baptist Student Ministry (BSM), where they would give me a Bible.

After receiving her directions, I excitedly hurried off to this place on campus and asked the director where I might find a Bible. He directed me to some shelves across the room. I anxiously examined the selection of Bibles, and to my amazement saw a brand new Bengali Bible sitting on the first shelf. I quickly started looking through it, marveling how long I had been searching for a Bible—and here in America I found one in my own language!

I did not know at the time that this translation was the work of William Carey, the first Baptist missionary to my people. The director observed my enthusiasm and told me that I could keep the Bible. I thanked him and hurried back to my apartment. I waited until that night to read my new Bible in private, so as not to upset my Muslim roommates.

What I read astonished me. Many of the stories only briefly mentioned in the Qur'an were more fully explained in the Bible. In fact, I came to better understand many of the stories in the Qur'an when I read the Bible's account of the same incidents. I also discovered that not all the stories were the same. Consider the report of Abraham taking his son to be sacrificed, for instance. The Bible names Isaac as the son, while the Qur'an stresses that it was Ishmael.

I reflected back to what I had been taught in Islamic school. I had learned as a boy that the strength and core belief of Islam is its insistence in one God, the Creator of heaven and earth. As we studied in the Qur'an (Surah Al-Maida, verses 72-75), Mohammed specifically asserts that Jesus is not God, and that anyone who worships him as God blasphemes. Our Muslim teacher instructed us, "Christians worship three Gods: the father god; Mary, the mother god; and Jesus, the son god."

I remember asking my teacher, "So, are Christians like Hindus, who worship many gods?"

"If any religion teaches the worship of more than one god," he replied, "it is a polytheistic religion."

So it astonished me when I read in the Gospel of Mark that Jesus said, "Hear, O Israel, the Lord, our God is one" (12:29). Jesus, whom I considered the founder of Christianity, clearly taught that only one God existed! At this point I became convinced that Christianity was not a polytheistic religion, as I had been taught, but in fact, was a monotheistic faith. So I grasped that both Islam and Christianity were monotheistic religions, worshiping only one God—but what, then, was the difference between Islam and Christianity?

Inevitably I came to compare Jesus and Mohammed, the two central figures of Christianity and Islam. I discovered that Jesus was much greater than Mohammed. I found that Jesus was born without a human father, but Mohammed had a father named Abdullah. I found that while Jesus performed many miracles, Mohammed never did a miracle, apart from his claim to have received the Qur'an from Allah. Both the Qur'an and the Bible affirm the sinless character of Jesus, but the Qur'an records occasions when Mohammed had to repent of his sins (Surah Muhammad 47:19). Jesus died, was raised to life, and is living now in heaven, yet Mohammed died and is still in his grave, inside the prophet mosque in Medina, Saudi Arabia.

I became very confused. I knelt down beside my bed at night and began to pray. I held up my Bible in one hand and my Qur'an in the other and prayed, "God, if Jesus is greater than Mohammed, why should I follow Mohammed instead of Jesus? God, please lead me in the right direction." This searching continued for many days...until God answered my prayer.

### My Decision for Christ

One afternoon, in search of answers, I decided to visit the office of a professor on campus whom I thought to be a Christian. As I entered his office, adjacent to his classroom, he seemed both surprised and bewildered to see me. I introduced myself and asked him if he was a Christian.

He looked baffled, but he answered simply, "Yes, I am a Christian."

"Dr. Evans," I quickly asked, "What do you believe about Jesus?"

He paused and drew his right hand up to his chin in thought. Then he dashed over to the classroom area and faced the white board. I followed him and sat down at a desk. He turned to face me.

"There is a God," he began, "and He created Adam and Eve, the first human beings." Then he began drawing on the board to explain the basic story of the Bible.

I sat at that desk, thinking, *I really want to know about Jesus, not about Adam and Eve*. The Qur'an and the Bible tell quite similar stories of creation, and I felt very anxious to hear about the person of Jesus Christ. I wanted to know what Christians believed about Him.

At that very moment, a godly man named Peter had started to drive home after spending a frustrating day trying unsuccessfully to share Jesus with a Muslim student on campus. Peter had a burning desire to tell Muslims the good news of Jesus Christ. While stopped at a traffic signal, he suddenly felt an inexplicable urge to visit his old friend, Professor Evans.

Immediately he turned around and headed directly to Dr. Evans's office and to the classroom where I was seated.

As Peter walked in, Dr. Evans finished his thought and excitedly greeted his old friend. Dr. Evans introduced me and said that Peter would be able to answer my question about Jesus.

Peter suggested we take a walk together. It was late afternoon and students were walking busily around campus, moving from one class to another. As we talked, we sat on a bench beside some large trees, not far away from other groups of students. In a few minutes it became obvious that Peter was well educated in Islam. In fact, he had lived in an Islamic country for several years.

Peter opened our conversation with a question: "Did you realize that Jesus is greater than Mohammed?" Amazingly, this was the very focus of my personal struggle. It was this very issue that had brought me to Dr. Evans's office.

Just a year before, I would have adamantly defended Mohammed's superiority. But now, Peter's words spoke directly to my heart. As he described the person of Jesus, and how he is greater than Mohammed, my heart leaped. I can never forget what Peter told me that day.

"Our God is a personal God," Peter declared.

As a Muslim, I knew I could never have a personal relationship with almighty God. I saw Allah as distant, living somewhere far away in the heavens, aloof from humankind. I prayed five times a day in obedience to Allah, yet I never knew if He was listening. I also knew that He would not accept my prayers if my body, clothing, and prayer rug were not clean enough. Allah seemed like an angry, all-powerful king, quick to punish me if I made a mistake or failed to fulfill my duties as a Muslim. I felt fearful of God and could not fathom a personal relationship with Him. I could never call God my "Father."

Yet, deep inside, I longed for a personal God. He described a God who can talk to me, walk with me, understand me, and who wanted to have a close relationship with me. My heart filled with joy to think that I could have a personal relationship with my Creator. No longer did I have to live in fear of God, but I could commune personally with Him.

"Our God is a loving God," Peter continued. He insisted that God loved me unconditionally.

Peter spoke of a God who loved me so much that He had come down from heaven to earth and lived among us.

As a devout Muslim, I could never imagine that God, the Creator of heaven and earth, loved me unconditionally. From the Qur'an I knew that God might like me only when I loved him and fulfilled all of His commandments — a conditional love. The Qur'an asserts that, "Allah loveth not transgressors" (Surah Al-Baqara 2:190). So I lived in fear of making mistakes and failing to please Him. As a Muslim, I longed for a God who would love me and accept me as I was. Peter explained that Jesus came to earth and died on the cross for my sins because He loved me. What incredible news! And what a joy to know that God loved me and accepted me unconditionally!

"Jesus is the Savior," Peter further declared. He explained that Jesus came to give me the assurance of salvation, the hope of eternal life with God in heaven.

I reflected back to when I was a young Muslim boy. My father had explained that Mohammed was not the savior, but the Messenger of Allah: "Muhammad is.... the Seal of the Prophets" (Surah Al-Ahzab 5:40). He taught me that Mohammed did not come to save us. Instead, we have to save ourselves from eternal condemnation through performing good works. The only way we can go to heaven is by accumulating enough good deeds. If my good works came up short, then I would be sent to hell.

My father had emphasized, "You don't need a savior, son; all you need is a guide." Then he handed me the Qur'an. "This will be your guide."

I understood that I had to save myself by doing good works. As a Sunni Muslim, I knew that my good and bad deeds would determine my eternal destiny. I understood that on the Day of Judgment, Allah would weigh my good and bad deeds on a giant scale; if my good deeds outweighed the bad, I might have a chance of going to heaven. But I could never be sure of Allah's will for me until the Day of Judgment.

Peter explained that Jesus is the Savior of the world and that He came to save me from my sins and make a way for me to go to heaven. With all of my heart, I wanted to go to heaven. I felt such relief to know that I could be sure of my salvation while still on this earth, and that I could be sure of God's eternal destiny for me. My new friend quoted a verse from the Gospel of John: "For God so loved the world that he gave his one and only Son, that whoever believes in him shall not perish but have eternal life" (3:16). What tremendous news all of this was to me!

As Peter declared the good news about a personal, loving God who came to save me from my sins, my heart started beating faster. Deep inside I longed to have such a close relationship with the loving God Peter was describing to me.

I had been trained to defend my Islamic faith and to reason with a Christian about the superiority of Islam; but what Peter said about Jesus calmed my heart. I had no argument, but eagerly drank in each word, like a thirsty man who has found a spring in the desert.

Peter's next question startled me: "Will you accept Jesus Christ and receive His eternal salvation?" I had never considered such a thing. Converting to any other religion was unthinkable.

I explained to Peter why I could not accept his offer. "Peter, I am a Muslim. It is forbidden for me to become a Christian."

Peter paused, and then asked again, "Will you accept Jesus and receive His eternal salvation?"

I repeated my objection. "Peter, I cannot accept Jesus. If I do, my family and friends will be very angry."

Again Peter bowed his head and a few moments later asked, "Will you accept Jesus and receive His eternal salvation?"

"Peter, if I accept Jesus, my family will disown me. I will be alone with no family or friends."

Peter paused for a moment once again, and then asked me the same question: "Will you accept Jesus and receive His eternal salvation?"

I couldn't help but think, *This is the most stubborn man I have ever met!* Peter's persistence surprised me. He seemed eager for me to understand and accept the eternal salvation I could have in Jesus.

As we sat quietly on the bench, the sun began to dip below the horizon and the beautiful colors of sunset streamed across the sky. Suddenly the events of my life flashed before me as if I were replaying a movie in my mind.

My parents had reared me as a devout Muslim. By age seven I was praying five times a day and fasting the entire month of Ramadan. At age thirteen I joined an Islamic organization and had become so dedicated in my faith that I would die for my religion. When I was fifteen I had the same terrifying dream on three separate occasions: I had died and God threw me into a lake of fire. The dream disturbed me so much that I prayed all night, seeking to find out from God its meaning. Sweet drops of oil fell over me that night in the mosque and a tremendous peace came over my heart. Then, a few days later, I heard an audible voice tell me, "Go, and get a Bible." For four years I looked for a Bible in my country, but could find none. Then my father decided to send me to America to propagate Islam. Here I found a Bengali Bible at the Baptist Student Ministry. After carefully studying the Bible, I realized that it taught there is only one God. I also recognized the undeniable difference between Jesus and Mohammed. I prayed for several weeks, holding up my Qur'an and my Bible, asking God to lead me in the right direction.

And here, at this very moment, I felt that Peter was leading me in that direction. Could this be the answer to my earnest prayer?

I could not deny the Holy Spirit tugging on my heart. Though the arguments against accepting Jesus as my Savior tried to win in my head, somewhere deep inside of me I knew that Peter spoke the truth.

Finally, I enthusiastically told Peter, "Yes, I will accept Jesus Christ and receive His eternal salvation." Peter then knelt down with me underneath a shade tree and led me in a prayer to accept Christ.

It was April 14, 1992—the day a miracle took place. And my life would never be the same. Although the gospel was free to me, it cost me everything to follow Jesus Christ.

# ° **3** °

# Free,
# Yet Costly

The good news of Jesus Christ changed my life. Jesus has given this former Muslim hope and the assurance of eternal salvation. He has changed my life forever. As a Christian, I find life today full of wonder and surprise.

After I accepted Christ, my heart almost burst with joy, peace, and fulfillment. What a joy to know that I had a personal relationship with almighty God, who remains with me always! Now I could call God my Father. An overwhelming peace swept over me. God, the Creator of heaven and earth, loved me unconditionally!

I no longer lived under a burden of fear. I now knew that if I died, I would go to heaven. My salvation did not depend on my own self-righteousness, but on my faith in Jesus Christ.

### The Cost of Being a Disciple

The gospel was free to me—but it cost me everything to follow Christ.

I began going to church and attending a Bible study. My fellow Muslim friends grew quite angry with me once they found out about my decision, so I decided to find a new place to live.

A few weeks after my conversion, I settled into a mobile home that I rented by myself. One evening, in the dead of night, I heard a knock at my door. As I slowly opened the door, three of my Muslim friends rushed inside. They ran to my bedroom and took my passport and other important documents. Then they dragged me to their van and drove off.

One man started demanding, "Why did you become a Christian?" I made no reply. Then they began punching me in the stomach and shoulder.

"Why do you ridicule Islam and Mohammed?" They continued to interrogate me and intensified the beating, but still I said nothing.

"You should go back to your home country," they threatened.

When we arrived at some remote place, they stuck my face into the ground so hard that I could not breathe. I thought I was going to die. I just kept praying, "Jesus, help me. Jesus, save me."

After a couple of hours of interrogation and further beatings, they drove me back to a freeway near my home and stopped on a frontage road, where they shoved me out of the van and onto the ground. It was early morning, just before dawn, and I wearily walked back home, thanking God that He had saved me.

As soon as I reached my house, I once more thanked God for saving my life and prayed for God to somehow bring back my passport. I called my Christian friends and told them what had happened and asked them to pray for me, especially regarding my passport, because I needed it to stay legally in this country. I knew that God hears my prayers; and now I prayed earnestly for God to return my passport to me.

Amazingly, one week later, a stranger appeared at my door. "I found this on the highway," he said, "and thought it would be important to you." Then he handed me my passport and walked away. I felt so stunned that I just stood there, staring at my passport, unable to speak. I didn't even get the chance to say, "thank you," before the man had disappeared. At that moment I knew without a doubt that my God is a living God who hears and answers my prayers! I rejoiced in God's faithfulness.

### Troubles with Family

Even through my trials, God has remained faithful. But my faith in Christ has not come without a cost.

My family also became very angry with me because of my decision to follow Christ. One day I received a letter from my siblings. It read,

> Dear brother,
>
> We want to go to school, but people insult us. They call you an infidel, and they also call us infidels. Why did you become a Christian? Why are you giving us pain? Father is always angry, mother is always crying. Why can't you become a Muslim again?

This letter terribly disturbed me and brought great sorrow to my heart. I never meant to bring harm to my family.

Later, in 1995, while I attended a Bible college, my family officially disowned me. They cut off all communication and fellowship with me.

Reading their official pronouncement brought great grief to me. I cried out to God and sought comfort from Him. As I prayed and read the Bible, I came across a special text in the Gospel of Luke. It spoke of a large crowd following Jesus, when suddenly Jesus turned and said, "If anyone comes to me and does not hate [that is, love less] his father and mother, his wife and children, his brothers and sisters—yes even his own life—he cannot be my disciple" (14:26). I felt as though I were in that crowd, hearing Jesus address me personally. I knew that if I wanted to follow Him, I had to love my dear mother, father, brothers, and my sister, even my own life, less than I loved Him. I realized that it costs to become a disciple of Jesus Christ.

### God's Provision

I lost everything after I accepted Christ, but my faith in Christ remained firm. I still have a great desire to follow God and to study His Word. God miraculously opened doors for me, one after another, and He has blessed me in ways I never knew possible.

Where I lost my natural family, God gave me a spiritual family, and a few years later, a loving wife who shares my passion for the Lord and for the lost.

Where I lost the means of supporting myself financially, God provided for my education through bachelor's, master's, and doctorate degrees.

God has even begun to restore my natural family! Although my family disowned me, God enabled me to forgive them and to love them even more than I did before I became a Christian. I, along with my Christian friends, have faithfully prayed for my family to come to know Jesus personally.

Eight years after my conversion, I had the privilege of leading two of my brothers to Christ. Recently, my father and I were reunited after eleven years of separation. I explained to him how I found a way to have a personal relationship with almighty God, and that God loves us unconditionally. He stood amazed as I told him that I had found a Savior in Jesus Christ, and that He gives assurance of eternal salvation. My father saw the love and peace of God in my wife and me, and he felt moved by God's faithfulness to me throughout all these difficult years. He soon began reading the Bible for himself and the Holy Spirit touched his heart. He could not resist the truth about Jesus and finally also came to faith in Christ.

Truly, Jesus changes lives!

### The Call—Offering Hope to the Hopeless

God has given me a passion to share His love and the good news of the gospel of Jesus Christ with others, especially Muslims. He has led my wife and me to found the ministry Gospel for Muslims, Inc., to bring eternal hope and peace to these precious people for whom Christ died.

In these next few chapters, I would like to share with you what I have learned about the Islamic faith, knowledge acquired through twenty-one years as a devout Muslim, through study in Islamic and Bible schools, and through further independent research. I have sought to present an accurate understanding of the religion of Islam and the mind-set of its 1.2 billion adherents.

I still have Muslim family and friends whom I love dearly, so much that I want them to know the hope they can find in Jesus. My prayer is that you too might gain a love for Muslims, a burden to pray for them, and a longing to share the good news of Christ with them.

"That your ways [O, LORD] may be known on earth, your salvation among all nations" (Psalm 67:2).

## Part II

# A Brief History of Islam

Today, the religion of Islam, founded by Mohammed, is the youngest of all the major world religions, yet it is also the fastest-growing faith in the world. Islam began among the desert tribes of Arabia in A.D. 622, but the religion spread rapidly after its inception, and continues to grow in global influence and significance. How and why has this religion spread so rapidly? This section will address the historical development of this powerful world religion and the very critical role of its founder, the prophet Mohammed.

# ∘ **4** ∘

# The Early Life
# of Mohammed

Mohammed's impact on Islam is monumental. The religion cannot be fully understood without examining the life of its founding prophet, Mohammed.

Prophet, politician, and powerful warrior—Mohammed was all three. Islam's fundamental teachings and guidelines all came through this man. One cannot understand the religio-political system of Islam without coming to grips with his role in the religion's formation.

### Mohammed's Place in Islam

Orthodox Islam does not claim Mohammed to be divine, but his example gets lifted up throughout the Muslim world as the perfect model for mankind. Islamic scholar Ajijola acknowledges that "(Mohammed's) life became a source of inspiration to his followers. Even minute acts and deeds of him have been recorded by his companions and contemporaries for the benefit of mankind."[1] The esteemed twentieth-century Muslim scholar of India, Iqbal, expresses the love the Muslim people have for their venerated prophet: "Love of the Prophet runs like blood in the veins of his community." Iqbal even asserts, "You can deny God, but you cannot deny the Prophet!"[2]

Vedantism - Hinduism

Ancient Israel
Abraham

Judaism
Moses

Buddhism

Christianity

Islam

Historical Development
of the World's Religions

2500 BC  2000 BC  1500 BC  1000 BC  500 BC  0  AD 500  AD 1000  AD 1500

© Abraham Sarker 2004

*Figure 4.1*

This deep commitment to the cherished prophet of Islam became clear in recent times with Ayatollah Khomeini's *fatwa* (legal/religious sentence) for the execution of the British author Salmon Rushdie in response to his book, *The Satanic Verses*, which denigrated the prophet Mohammed and his revelation.

Kamal ud Din ad Damiri wrote in a respected Muslim classic the following reverential description of Mohammed:

> Mohammed is the most favored of mankind, the most honored of all apostles, the prophet of mercy, the head or Imam of the faithful, the bearer of banner of praise, the intercessor, the holder of high position, the possessor of the River of Paradise, under whose banner the sons of Adam will be on the Day of Judgment. He is the best of prophets, and his nation is the best of nations...and his creed the noblest of creeds.... He was perfect in intellect, and was of noble origin. He had an absolutely graceful form, complete generosity, perfect bravery, excessive humility, useful knowledge... perfect fear of God and sublime piety. He was the most eloquent and the most perfect of mankind in every variety of perfection.[3]

Clearly, Mohammed's place in Islam rises above any other human being. But why do Muslims regard him with such great esteem? Did his life truly exude all of these qualities? Can Christians accept him as a prophet too? Some answers should start to become clear as we briefly examine the life of this significant historical figure.

### Origin of Islam

Islam considers Mohammed "the seal of the prophets," the man who brought the best and final revelation from Allah to mankind. The Islamic calendar (and essentially Islam itself) began in A.D. 622, twelve years after the initial revelation Mohammed said he received. It is therefore the youngest of all the major world religions, as illustrated in figure 4.1 on the facing page. The religion of Islam came well after Judaism and nearly six hundred years after Christianity—a critical truth to keep in mind, as these two religions play a vital role in the development of Islam.

### Arabia at the Time of Mohammed

About fourteen centuries ago, Islam sprang up among the desert tribes of Arabia. In Mohammed's day, the Arab people were primarily nomadic shepherds, or Bedouins, although some had settled permanently in villages and towns. Most of these city dwellers had acquired wealth through their occupations as businessmen.

Trade was a popular and profitable family profession. Caravans of merchants traveled along the dry desert paths on camels loaded with merchandise, accompanied by cattle and slaves to trade. These caravans would travel for months into faraway countries, bringing back wealth and knowledge of other cultures and religions.

### The Role of Christianity and Judaism

Byzantine Christianity had exercised a slight influence on these merchants, as Judea, the home of Christianity, lay fairly close to Arabia. Christian princes ruled from the cities of Damascus, Antioch, Caesarea, and Alexandria, not far from the key Arab cities of Mecca and Yathrib (Medina). Yet Christian influence on the Arab people was not as strong as it might have been due to a couple of factors.

First, Byzantine leaders disagreed among themselves on certain issues regarding Christian theology. Second, on several occasions Byzantine rulers had treated Arab Christians with a measure of hostility and cruelty. Therefore, Arabs remained largely cool to Christianity.[4]

Arab people of the seventh century A.D. had contact with Judaism through the various Jewish tribes that had settled in Arabia. In fact, when Mohammed entered Medina in 622 A.D., many Jews resided in the city.[5]

Although many people from the monotheistic religions of Christianity and Judaism lived nearby, the people of Arabia remained primarily polytheistic. Every household commonly had several household idols, with shrines housing these deities. The word *Allah* simply means "the God" in Arabic. Allah was understood to be the supreme god over all the other gods. Apart from idolatry, the Arab people of this time followed no particular religious doctrine.[6]

### The Ka'ba in Mecca

The prominent city of Mecca, located on the central western coast of Arabia, lay directly on the major caravan route running north to Syria and south to Yemen. This affluent city was considered a very holy site to the Arab people of Mohammed's day, tracing back to the belief that a meteorite had fallen there centuries before the founding of the city. This black stone became an object of veneration, and by the time of Mohammed, pilgrims had constructed an enclosure around it, called the *Ka'ba*. Islam claims that this sacred black stone fell from heaven during Adam and Eve's day, and that Abraham and his son Ishmael built a house of worship there.[7]

Although the Arabs were not generally a very religious people, they considered this shrine at Mecca and the ritual practice accompanying it precious as an integral part of their cultural heritage. The Ka'ba gradually became an abode for various idols, relics, and paintings. Each tribe contributed its own deities to the shrine, and as many as three hundred sixty idols were housed there. One report even asserts that it contained a picture of Jesus and Mary.[8]

Arabs set aside a certain several month period each year for warring tribes to declare a truce in order to allow pilgrims safe travel to Mecca. During this annual pilgrimage, pilgrims would go to the Ka'ba to worship the idols, circle around it seven times, and touch or kiss the sacred black stone. Naturally, the Meccans took great pride (and a considerable profit) from

# Origin of the Arab People (Mohammed)
## GENEALOGICAL BACKGROUND

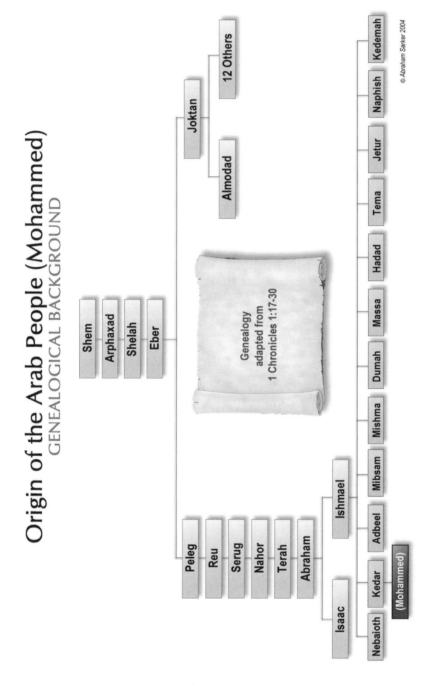

*Figure 4.2*

the keeping of this stone. The tribes continually struggled over which one would control the Ka'ba.[9]

It is significant that Mohammed was born into the prominent Quraish tribe, which at the time controlled the Ka'ba. Mohammed's distinctly cross-cultural message, "there is no God but Allah," at first brought ridicule, but now is embraced by nearly a fifth of the world's population.[10]

### Mohammed's Childhood

Little reliable information exists regarding Mohammed's early years, and varying traditions (Hadiths)—including some that originated long after his death—make it hard to gain an accurate picture of his life's work as an adult. This section therefore takes most of its information from the Qur'an, as well as from accounts on which most non-Muslim and Muslim writers agree.

Mohammed was born around A.D. 570 into a poor Quraish family of the Hashim clan living in Mecca. As an Arab, he is said to be a descendant of Abraham and Ishmael. Mohammed was the son of 'Abdu'llah, literally "servant of Allah," the son of 'Abdu'l-Muttalib, a leading citizen of Mecca. Just before Mohammed's birth, his father died while on a trading trip. His mother, 'Amina, had to raise Mohammed without the support of her husband. When news of the infant's birth reached the grandfather, 'Abdu'l-Muttalib went to 'Amina's house, gathered the newborn child into his arms, and called him Mohammed, or "The Praised One."[11]

### Lineage of Mohammed

While the Bible does not mention Mohammed's name, most believe that Mohammed descended from the tribe of Kedar.[12] As figure 4.2 on the facing page indicates, Mohammed came from the lineage of Abraham, but through the line of Ishmael, not Isaac. Through the lineage of Isaac comes the Jewish nation, and significantly, Jesus Christ; through the lineage of Ishmael comes the Arab people. One will understand Mohammed's message better if one realizes that Mohammed believed that his forefather, Abraham, was a monotheist.

### Mohammed Orphaned

When Mohammed was six, his mother died and he became an orphan. Before Mohammed's grandfather died, the young boy came under the guardianship of his uncle, Abu Talib. While Abu Talib deeply loved Mohammed, he never accepted Mohammed's religion of Islam. Yet Abu Talib, as chief of the Quraish tribe, extended protection to Mohammed from the rest of the tribe when it reacted against Mohammed's message.

Despite Abu Talib's prominence in the community, he was not wealthy. Mohammed therefore had no opportunity to attend school, but worked as a shepherd in the desert for much of his youth. He is often portrayed as illiterate, which explains why his recitation of the Qur'an is considered miraculous.

At twelve years of age Mohammed traveled with his uncle in the merchant caravans that journeyed to far-off nations. Through these trips he may have met Christian monks and heard the teachings of the Scriptures, which influenced him greatly later in life.

One significant incident reported in Mohammed's biographies concerns an encounter between Mohammed and a Syrian monk named Buhaira. The monk recognized the young boy as a prophet and warned Mohammed's uncle to "guard him (Mohammed) carefully against the Jews, for by Allah! if they see him, and know about him what I know, they will do him evil."[14]

In years to come, Mohammed would in fact have many problems with the Jewish community, one member of which would try to poison him. To this day, relations between the followers of Islam and the followers of Judaism remain hostile.

### What Did Mohammed Look Like?

Mohammed so abhorred idol worship that he forbade anyone to make any portrait or image of him, for fear that his followers might attempt to worship him. Therefore, the only information we have about the prophet's appearance comes in written form. Consider the following:

> Muhammad was sturdy and thickset, of medium height, with heavy shoulders and a thick black curling beard. He was beetle-browed, and long black silken lashes, which he painted with kohl, fell over eyes which were very large, dark and piercing, and often bloodshot. His skin was rosy, "soft as a woman's," and he had a Roman nose, thin and aristocratic, with flaring nostrils. He had dazzling white teeth, but was gap-toothed towards the end of his life. When he laughed, which was often, he opened his mouth wide, so that the gums were visible, and when he spoke, he turned his whole body, not only the head. It was a good head, with a high forehead and a little too large for the body, and his thick hair glistened and fell in waves to his shoulders. What people remembered most was the sweetness of his expression, and sudden opening of the enormous eyes....Of his voice they say it was very low and deep, but when he shouted, it was like a blare of trumpets, frightening everyone in sight...and with that strange quick walk of his he resembled more than ever a bull about to charge. His hair never turned gray, but was thick and lustrous at the end as in his youth.[15]

The youngest of Mohammed's wives, 'Ayisha, described his mannerisms as follows:

> He was a man just such as yourselves; he laughed often and smiled much. At home he would mend his clothes and cobble his shoes. He used to help me in my household duties; but what he did oftenest was to sew. He used to eat with his thumb and two forefingers; and when he had done, he would lick them, beginning with the middle finger. He had a special liking for sweetmeats and honey. He was also fond of cucumbers and undried dates. When a lamb or a kid was being cooked, Muhammad would go to the pot, take

out the shoulder, and eat it. He never traveled without a toothpick.[16]

The prophet also loved three things, 'Ayisha used to say: women, scents, and food.[17] We also know some of his other likes and dislikes:

> ...he hated dogs, lizards, people with yellow teeth, painters and sculptors, costly silks and embroideries, the smell of garlic and onions. He loved children, honey, cucumbers, dates, pumpkins, and every kind of perfume. He liked to go about the house mending furniture, cobbling shoes, and patching his own clothes; and he milked his own goats. He had a sweet tooth, and there was some softness in him.[18]

### Marriage to Khadija

When Mohammed reached his early twenties, Abu Talib recommended that he work for the wealthiest woman in Mecca, Khadija, a beautiful widow merchant and owner of a caravan. For three years Mohammed served her faithfully, and as Khadija heard of his faithfulness and honesty, she entrusted to him the entire caravan of her merchandise. He transacted her business effectively and earned Khadija a huge profit. She felt so pleased with his services that upon his return, she extended to him a proposal of marriage. Khadija was fifteen years older than the twenty-five-year-old Mohammed, but Mohammed readily accepted her offer, and in the year A.D. 595 Mohammed married this beautiful, rich widow.

Their marriage proved fulfilling to both partners, and although men commonly took other wives, Mohammed married no others for the length of their twenty-five-year marriage. Together they had two sons and four daughters, although both sons died in infancy and only one daughter, Fatima, survived her father.[19]

One may wonder, if Khadija and Mohammed had never married, would Islam exist today? Khadija provided the love and wealth Mohammed had never known as an orphaned child. She became the first convert to Islam and Mohammed's strongest supporter. Through this marriage, Mohammed found relief from the worry of economic hardship and won greater esteem from the local Meccans. With the financial freedom provided by Khadija's wealth, Mohammed had time to consider theological questions.

### Revelation from the Angel Gabriel

The polytheistic religion of the day did not satisfy the few individuals who desired to know God. A small group of these intelligent and discontented individuals, known as *Hanifs*, reportedly met to discuss the religious and political problems of their Meccan society. As Mohammed became increasingly concerned about the idol worship and immorality of his people, his soul longed to know the true religion. Mohammed may have fellowshiped with the Hanifs and gleaned some understanding of one God from them.[20]

In the years following his marriage to Khadija, Mohammed began retreating to the hills around Mecca to meditate. He often meditated at Mount Hira, walking the three-mile distance from the city of Mecca, through the barren black and gray hills rising through the white, sandy valleys of the desert. Some have even suggested that he would go for the entire month of Ramadan to meditate, living on meager rations of food and drink.[21]

During his search for truth, he is said to have committed himself to such deep meditation and worship that at times he went into a trance-like state and even had convulsions. Because of these occurrences and his struggle against idolatry, people began calling him one possessed by a spirit, a soothsayer, a poet, and even a madman (Qur'an, surah 81:22; in surahs 52:29-30 and 69:41-42, however, Allah is believed to have refuted these allegations).

Finally, at age forty, Mohammed described a most unusual and life-changing experience that took place during a time of meditation. He believed that he received a prophetic call from an angel (later identified as Gabriel, the same angel mentioned in the Jewish and Christian scriptures). Tradition states that while Mohammed meditated in a cave on Mount Hira during the month of Ramadan in A.D. 610, the angel came to him, commanding him to be the messenger of Allah. Ibn Ishaq, the earliest biographer of Mohammed, relates the following account:

> When it was the night on which God honored him with his mission and showed mercy on His servants thereby, Gabriel brought him the command of God. "He came to me," said the apostle of God, "while I was asleep, with a coverlet of brocade whereon was some writing, and said, 'Read!' I said, 'What shall I read?' He pressed me with it so tightly that I thought it was death; then he let me go and said, 'Read!' I said, 'What shall I read?' He pressed me with it again so that I thought it was death; then he let me go and said 'Read!' I said, 'What shall I read?' He pressed me with it the third time so that I thought it was death and said, 'Read!' I said, 'What then shall I read?'—and this I said only to deliver myself from him, lest he should do the same to me again. He said: 'Read in the name of thy Lord who created, Who created man of blood coagulated. Read! Thy Lord is the most beneficent, Who taught by the pen, Taught that which they knew not unto men' [96:1-5]. So I read it, and he departed from me. And I awoke from my sleep, and it was as though these words were written on my heart."

The tradition asserts that with each of these commands, the angel Gabriel squeezed Mohammed with such great force that he thought he would die, and afterward he felt completely exhausted. Mohammed then awoke, with the words of the angel inscribed on his heart. After he left the cave and stood on the hill, he heard a tremendous voice say to him, "O Mohammed. You are the messenger of Allah and I am Gabriel."[22]

At first Mohammed felt very distressed, believing an evil spirit had possessed him. He felt deathly afraid of the source of this new revelation. Respected modern Muslim biographer, M. H. Haykal, describes Mohammed's fear:

> Stricken with panic, Muhammad arose and asked himself, "What did I see? Did possession of the devil which I feared all along come to pass?" Muhammad looked to his right and his left but saw nothing. For a while he stood there trembling with fear and stricken with awe. He feared the cave might be haunted and that he might run away still unable to explain what he saw.[23]

But when Mohammed told his wife, Khadija, about his frightening encounter, she comforted and encouraged him. Reportedly she consulted her cousin, Waraqa, a Hanif who had converted to Christianity. Waraqa declared that Mohammed's revelation, in fact, came from the same source as that of Moses, and that Mohammed would become the prophet of his own nation. Ibn Ishaq, the noted biographer of Mohammed, offers the following story:

> And I came to Khadija and sat by her thigh and drew close to her. She said, "O Abu'l-Qasim [Mohammad], where has thou been?"...I said to her, "Woe is me, poet or possessed." She said, "I take refuge in God from that...God would not treat you thus...This cannot be, my dear. Perhaps you did see something." "Yes, I did," I said. Then I told her of what I had seen; and she said, "Rejoice, O son of my uncle, and be of good heart. Verily, by Him in whose hand is Khadija's soul, I have hope that thou wilt be the prophet of this people." Then she rose and gathered her garments about her and set forth to her cousin Waraqa B. Naufal...who had become a Christian and read the Scriptures and learned from those that follow the Torah and the gospel. And when she related to him what the apostle of God told her he had seen and heard, Waraqa cried, "Holy! Holy! Verily by Him in whose hand is Waraqa's soul, if thou has spoken to me the truth...he is the prophet of his people."[24]

From this account we see that both Khadija, Mohammed's wife, and Waraqa, the Christian cousin of Khadija, believed

Mohammed to be the next prophet of the Arab people, similar to Moses' prophetic role for the Jewish people.

After this first revelation there came a long period of silence, lasting about three years. Mohammed consequently sank into a deep despair, feeling forsaken by God. Thoughts of suicide began to trouble his mind. After this period passed, he resumed receiving messages from the angel.

When receiving a revelation, Mohammed would often break out in a sweat, and sometimes fall down to the ground, even foaming at the mouth. Islamic tradition teaches that the revelations came like the painful sound of a bell. At times Mohammed received his messages through dreams, visions, or as thoughts in his mind.[25]

Haykal even records Mohammed to have spoken with the dead: "the Muslims who overheard him [Muhammed] asked, 'Are you calling the dead?' and the Prophet answered, 'They hear me no less than you do, except that they are unable to answer me.'" Haykal concedes that "Muhammed's spiritual and psychic power of communication with the realms of reality and his awareness of spiritual reality...surpasses that of ordinary men."[26]

With each revelation, Mohammed became more convinced that he was the "seal of the prophets" and that the prophets before him, namely Abraham, Moses, David, and Jesus, had received only incomplete revelations (see surah 33:40). Mohammed believed passionately that Allah had chosen him to give the final and most complete revelation. Therefore his message began to include not only, "there is no God but Allah," but also, "and Mohammed is His messenger [or apostle]."

Mohammed declared idol worship an abomination to Allah. He taught his followers that he was continuing the revelation already received in the Scriptures, including the Pentateuch of Moses (Torah, or *Tawrut*), the Psalms of David (*Zabur*), and the Gospel of Jesus (*Injil*). "It is He Who sent down to thee (step by step) in truth the Book confirming what went before it;

and He sent down (the) Law (of Moses) and the Gospel (of Jesus) before this as a guide to mankind and He sent down the Criterion (of judgment between right and wrong)" (surah 3:3). Mohammed also predicted a Judgment Day in which each person would be evaluated by his or her deeds (surah 82:14-15).

*Summary*

Mohammed's place in Islam is central to understanding the origins and traditions of this vast world religion. Mohammed was a very religious man who abhorred idol worship and passionately believed in one God, Allah. He claimed to receive unique revelations from the angel Gabriel, which he believed confirmed his place as the "seal of the prophets." But how was his ministry received by his contemporaries, and what is the biblical evaluation of his message and prophethood? These issues are addressed in the following chapter, "The Ministry of Mohammed."

## ∘ 5 ∘

# The Ministry
# of Mohammed

How did Mohammed start his ministry? Christianity has been named after Christ and Judaism after the tribe of Judah—yet Muslims are not "Mohammedans."

The term *Islam* developed from the idea of submitting one's self to Allah. The word *Islam* simply means "submission to Allah." Therefore Muslims are those who have submitted to Allah's will. Some contemporary authorities claim that Islam means "peace," yet in Arabic the word for peace is *salaam. Islam* means surrender, or submission.

### The Spread of Islam

The heart of Mohammed's message is that only one God exists (Allah), and that as God's slave, man must submit to and obey God before all else. A day of judgment is coming in which each man will be judged and sentenced to heaven or hell. In order for one to become Muslim, one must confess the shahada, "There is no God but Allah, and Mohammed is His messenger."

After declaring that he had received angelic messages, Mohammed began preaching this message, quietly at first, and then with greater boldness. After hearing the revelations of

Mohammed, his followers committed them to memory and later recorded them on bits of cloth, leaves, stones, or whatever material might be handy. Later this compiled revelation would come to be known as the Qur'an or "Recitation."

At first, Mohammed proclaimed his messages only among his close family and friends. His wife, Khadija, became his first convert. A few other family members soon followed her example. 'Ali ibn Abu Talib, Mohammed's cousin, was the next to accept Islam. He later succeeded Mohammed as the fourth caliph (leader of the Muslim community) and became Mohammed's son-in-law by marrying the prophet's only surviving daughter, Fatima. Zaid bin Haritha, a slave given to Mohammed by Khadija, became the third convert. Mohammed later not only set him free, but adopted him as a son.[1]

At this same time, Abu Bakr, a close friend of the prophet, also embraced Islam. The wealthy Abu Bakr was an influential member of the Quraish tribe. He succeeded Mohammed as the first caliph. After Khadija's death, he gave 'Ayisha, his daughter, to Mohammed in marriage. The girl was betrothed at seven and the marriage consummated when she was nine (some sources say ten) years of age. 'Ayisha became Mohammed's favorite wife.

Over the next three years, about fifty individuals converted to Islam. The third caliph, 'Uthman, also belonged to this small first group of believers.[2] Most of Mohammed's own people did not appreciate his message, however, and began to persecute his followers.

### Mohammed's Followers Face Persecution

Soon Mohammed began to get bolder in his preaching and public ridicule of idol worship. He tried to persuade the elite of Mecca to believe in one God. Idol worship had not only become a pillar of Meccan culture, however, but also involved the livelihood of the Meccan people. The importance and attention to the Ka'ba could not be compromised, or the Meccans would lose profit from the pilgrims who came to worship the idols there. Meccans rejected Mohammed's message and began persecuting his followers, yet Mohammed himself remained unharmed due to the prominent position of his uncle, Abu Talib.

In A.D. 615, fifteen Muslim families fled to Ethiopia, or Abyssinia, a Christian country where they could escape persecution. As more individuals considered conversion to Mohammed's message, the prophet tried to comfort them by giving assurance that their persecution was not in vain, and that they were being persecuted just as the prophets described in the previous Scriptures had been.[3]

Two great setbacks in Mohammed's life and ministry occurred in A.D. 619. His beloved wife, Khadija, and his uncle, Abu Talib, died within months of each other. This devastated Mohammed not only emotionally, but also politically. With Mohammed's two greatest benefactors gone, the prophet lost his protection from the people of Mecca.[4]

### Mohammed's Invitation to Yathrib (Medina)

A significant event occurred in A.D. 620 when Mohammed was fifty years of age. Six men from Yathrib (later Medina) traveled to Mecca during the annual pilgrimage; they listened to Mohammed's message, felt impressed by his powerful personality and sense of honesty and justice, and accepted Islam. Their city of Yathrib had a large and wealthy Jewish majority that continually strove with the resident Arabs. These new converts believed that Mohammed could be a wise and impartial judge, which their community badly needed.

The next year, twelve delegates from Yathrib came to Mecca to extend an invitation to Mohammed to become the ruler of their city. Ten of these twelve delegates were Jewish, some of whom believed Mohammed might possibly be the Messiah. Mohammed promised to come, but as soon as news of the treaty reached Mohammed's enemies, they began plotting his assassination. Mohammed's followers covertly made their way to Yathrib, but Mohammed remained behind until he could secretly escape with his friend Abu Bakr.[5]

### The Night Journey (Mi'raj)

While Mohammed awaited the command from Allah to flee to Yathrib, it is recorded that he dreamed he was taken from the Ka'ba in Mecca to Jerusalem's Holy Temple (the general site of modern day Dome of the Rock). From there, in the blink of an eye, he was carried into heaven, where he received a majestic welcome in the presence of the former prophets and Allah's messengers. Here he received further revelation and his faith grew. Of the prophets he visited, he said he found Jesus in the second heaven, Moses in the sixth, and Abraham in the seventh, the highest heaven. Ultimately he was taken into the very presence of Allah, where he received specific instructions as to the procedures for Islamic worship in prayer.[6]

Some traditions call this night journey an actual bodily ascension, but if so, the journey must have been very quick, because upon his return, his bed felt as warm as when he left it. His wife, 'Ayisha, asserts that he never actually left his bed, but rather, slept there soundly until morning.[7] Most modern Muslim writers consider this event a purely spiritual phenomenon.[8]

### Migration to Medina (Hijra)

By A.D. 622, Mohammed finally could escape secretly from Mecca. His enemies almost assassinated him, yet he hid for a short period in a cave until his pursuers had left the area. He and Abu Bakr made the 280-mile journey on camels.

Muslims call this journey from Mecca to Yathrib (Medina) the *hijra*, or migration. It is a significant turning point in Islamic history:

> The migration of the Prophet...has been with justice taken
> by Muslims as the starting point of their chronology, for it

forms the first stage in a movement which in a short time became of significance in the history of the world.[9]

This event marks the beginning of the Muslim calendar, with subsequent dates listed as A.H., or *anno hegirae*. Once Mohammed arrived in Yathrib, the city became known as Medina.

Once in Medina, city officials granted Mohammed political authority, although by no means did his religion find wide acceptance. They considered Mohammed's Muslim community just one clan among many others. With three Jewish tribes, one Christian community, and one Muslim contingent in the city, a treaty that allowed freedom of religion was soon developed. The legal document that directed the various tribes to coexist peacefully and unite against outside attackers also named Mohammed as the final authority in settling civil disputes.[10]

So Mohammed's role changed from that of a religious figure ("a warner" of the truth), to a political leader as well. With this intertwining of religion and politics, the foundation for the religio-political system of Islam was laid.

Mohammed at first tried to gain the favor of the Jews in and around Medina and made some concessions by conforming to several Jewish customs. It appears that Allah did not, at this time, issue a command to use force in making converts for Islam: "Let there be no compulsion in religion" (surah 2:257). Yet this time of law and order in Medina did not last.

### Conflict with Jewish Tribes

In Mecca Mohammed had met with resistance only from the polytheistic citizens of the city. In Medina, however, he began to encounter opposition from the monotheists as well. The Jews became disillusioned with this self-proclaimed prophet and realized he could not be the Messiah, as he was not of the lineage of David, but of Ishmael. They did not accept Mohammed's claim that their holy Scriptures foretold his role as prophet. Mohammed insisted that they misinterpreted and concealed revelations from God.

> And (remember) when Allah laid a charge on those who
> had received the Scripture (He said): Ye are to expound it to
> mankind and not to hide it. But they flung it behind their
> backs and bought thereby a little gain. (surah 3:187)

Eventually a serious division developed between Mohammed and the Jewish community. Mohammed began threatening the Jews. Many Jews died as a result of this conflict, and much of the rest of the Jewish population was expelled under the pretext of breaching the city covenant.[11]

Although the Jews refused to accept Mohammed's religion, to this day Islam continues to honor many Jewish traditions. Islam still considers Jerusalem its third holiest city, after Mecca and Medina. Mohammed originally instructed his followers to pray in the direction of Jerusalem; but after his conflict with the Jewish community, he commanded his disciples to pray toward Mecca, by command of Allah. In the same vein, Muslims originally fasted on the Jewish Day of Atonement; but Allah then commanded fasting to occur in the month of Ramadan.

This conflict in Medina (and subsequent change of procedure) indicated a significant abandonment of the Jewish-Christian tradition and an initiation of a new spiritual course related to, yet in conflict with, many essential teachings of the Bible.[12]

Mohammed gradually organized the Medinans into a politico-religious community (*umma*), of which he became the ruler, law-giver, and reformer. Although Mohammed possessed an incredible ability to win and maintain human allegiance, he began to place political advantage, and at times personal preference, above the ethical and moral principles that he taught to others. An example can be seen in his marriages.

### Mohammed's Wives

At fifty-three years of age, Mohammed married 'Ayisha, the nine-year-old daughter of his best friend, Abu Bakr. In the last thirteen years of his life, Mohammed married additional wives,

Forgiveness and Mercy. For Allah is Oft-Forgiving Most Merciful. (surah 4:95-96)

So those who fled and were driven forth from their homes and suffered damage for My cause, and fought and were slain, verily I (Allah) shall remit their evil deeds from them and verily I shall bring them into Gardens underneath which rivers flow. A reward from Allah. And with Allah is the fairest of rewards. (surah 3:195)

In compliance with this new command, Mohammed sent out a party to capture a caravan belonging to Mecca. This occurred during the "sacred months" when the Arabs customarily refrained from warfare; yet the Muslims justified their action because of the new revelation from Allah. Their mission succeeded, they divided the goods among themselves, and then planned for the next attack.

At first Allah had commanded his followers to honor the sacred months in which fighting should not occur:

The number of months in the sight of Allah is twelve (in a year) so ordained by Him the day He created the heavens and the earth; of them four are sacred; that is the straight usage. So wrong not yourselves therein and fight the pagans all together as they fight you all together. But know that Allah is with those who restrain themselves. (surah 9:36)

In light of the circumstances, however, Allah insisted that it was the Muslims' duty to fight, even during the sacred months.

Fighting is prescribed for you and ye dislike it. But it is possible that ye dislike a thing which is good for you and that ye love a thing which is bad for you. But Allah knoweth and ye know not. They ask thee concerning fighting in the Prohibited Month. Say: "Fighting therein is a grave (offense); but graver is it in the sight of Allah to prevent access to the path of Allah to deny Him to prevent access to the Sacred Mosque and drive out its members. Tumult and oppression are worse than slaughter.(") (surah 2:216-217)

## Battle of Badr

Encouraged by his first victory, Mohammed, along with 350 fighting men, attempted to take on a larger caravan. They met and defeated the army sent to protect the caravan, a force about one thousand men strong. While forty-nine of the Meccan army died in the battle, only fourteen of Mohammed's army were lost, despite being outnumbered three to one.

This famous Battle of Badr (A.D. 624) assured Mohammed that God was with him, and it set precedent for how booty was to be divided in future raids. Mohammed kept one fifth of the valuables, to be used to help the needy.[15]

This attack alarmed the Quraish tribe, which feared that Mohammed would eventually defeat them as well. After this incident, many pagans came to Medina to submit to Mohammed's leadership. One can infer that the sword was more effective than words in drawing converts to Islam.

## Battle of Uhud

In response to their humiliating defeat, the Meccans prepared for another confrontation with Mohammed's forces. One year after the Battle of Badr, the two forces met at the mountain of Uhud, near Medina. The Meccans again outnumbered the Muslims, three to one; three thousand Meccans faced one thousand Muslim fighters. This time, Mohammed's forces lost the battle and had to withdraw to a secure position, while the Meccans returned home, rejoicing in their victory.

Despite this setback, Mohammed continued to lead or authorize additional attacks on neighboring tribes, "which seems to have aimed at extending his own alliances and at preventing others from joining the Meccans."[16] And so his power steadily grew.

## Meccan Attack on Medina

The Quraish returned in A.D. 627 to capture Medina, fielding an army of ten thousand men. Mohammed had prepared for their attack, however, by digging a trench around the unprotected areas of the city—a strategy suggested by a Persian disciple, but new to the Arabs. In two weeks this large army had surrounded the city of Medina and attempted to cross the trenches. Yet with exhaustion of supplies, unfavorable weather conditions, and secret negotiations between Mohammed and various tribes, the besiegers lost their resolve and wearily began to withdraw.[17] After this silent victory, Mohammed's position grew even stronger.

Soon after, Mohammed attacked the last Jewish tribe in Medina. In times past when Mohammed had attacked the Jews, they were expelled, not exterminated. But in this case, all of the men were beheaded and all the women and children sold into slavery. Tor Andrae offers a noteworthy perspective to this merciless slaughter:

> One must see Mohammad's cruelty toward the Jews against the background of the fact that their scorn and rejection was the greatest disappointment of his life, and for a time they threatened completely to destroy his prophetic authority. For him, therefore, it was a fixed axiom that the Jews were the sworn enemies of Allah and His revelation. Any mercy toward them was out of the question.[18]

One hears this disdain for Jewish people in the Qur'an: "Strongest among men in enmity to the believers wilt thou find the Jews and pagans" (surah 5:82a). Mohammed's belief in their eternal damnation is found in surah 98:6: "Those who reject (Truth) among the People of the Book and among the Polytheists will be in hell-fire to dwell therein (for aye). They are the worst of creatures."

### Mohammed Is Poisoned

A Jewish woman who lost her husband, father, and brother in the massacre tried to poison Mohammed. She cooked a goat and placed it before the prophet for his evening meal. Mohammed thanked her, took his favorite piece, the shoulder, and distributed the rest to his other friends. After tasting the first mouthful he spat it out and shouted, "Hold, this shoulder has been poisoned." A friend who had already swallowed a portion of the meat soon died. Excruciating pains gripped Mohammed, and although he survived, the bit of poison he consumed affected him until his death years later. The woman defended herself with this response:

> Thou hast inflicted grievous injuries on my people, and slain, as thou seest, my husband and my father. Therefore, said I within myself, If he be a prophet he will reject the gift, knowing that it is poisoned; but if only a pretender we shall be rid of our troubles.[19]

Although Mohammed faced several setbacks during this period, his power and position in Arabia continued to grow, until finally he would conquer all of Arabia.

### Mohammed Conquers Mecca

In A.D. 628 when Mohammed attempted to travel to Mecca with his followers to perform pilgrimage at the Ka'ba, the Quraish Meccans barred their way. A peace treaty (Treaty of Hudaybiah) was then forged, in which both sides agreed not to fight for the next ten years. In exchange, the next year the Muslims would be allowed to enter Mecca, unarmed, to make the pilgrimage. The prophet's followers considered this a defeat, but Mohammed assured them it was in fact a great victory.[20] A revelation came to Mohammed that Islam, as the true religion, would be "exalted above every religion" (surah 48:27-28). Mohammed therefore believed that Islam superseded both Judaism and Christianity.

Mohammed continued to win victories over other rebel tribes, and in A.D. 629 he and two thousand followers came to Mecca, unarmed, for the Lesser Pilgrimage. The Quraish vacated the city upon hearing of their approach, and Mohammed and his followers performed the pagan ritual of kissing the

Black Stone, offering sacrifices, and circling the idol-filled Ka'ba seven times. Later, this same ritual would become a pillar of the Islamic faith. On this trip he married his eleventh wife and won the allegiance of several of his former foes.

Although the treaty proscribed war for ten years, Mohammed became convinced that the time had come to conquer Mecca and complete his control of Arabia. When he returned to Medina from the Lesser Pilgrimage, he gathered an army of ten thousand men and returned to Mecca.

By A.D. 630, Mohammed's forces had become so strong that when they entered Mecca on their pilgrimage, no one dared to stop them. Abu Sufyan, the Quraish leader and bitter enemy of Mohammed, realized the futility of resistance and went out to meet Mohammed in order to become a Muslim. This action signified the surrender of the entire Quraish tribe and ultimately, the submission of Mecca.[21]

### Mohammed Destroys Idols in the Ka'ba

Mohammed soon marched to the Ka'ba and destroyed all of its idols and images, but left the Black Stone intact. Through his cleansing of the Ka'ba, Mohammed reversed the pagan religious practice of his people for hundreds, even thousands of years. In this symbolic act, Mohammed became virtually the sole leader of the Arabian people. Mecca became the center of his religion when just eight years before, he had been forced to flee the city.

Mohammed declared general amnesty for the people of Mecca, except for a few individuals executed for particular crimes. Large portions of booty acquired through victory over rebel tribes were given to the new believers in Mecca as a reward for their submission. Some of the earlier believers grumbled at this decision, yet many tribes continued to submit to Mohammed's leadership, realizing they could no longer resist. As the new leader of the Arab people, Mohammed sent Qur'an reciters to convert the surrounding communities to Islam.[22]

### Converts Taken by Force

At this time a revelation came that force should be used to make converts: "When the sacred months are past, kill those who join other gods with God wherever ye shall find them, and seize them, and lay wait for them with every kind of ambush; but if they shall convert and observe prayer and pay the obligatory alms, let them go on their way" (surah 9:5). Through this command, Mohammed intended to put an end to idolatry, and outwardly he certainly seemed successful. With the sword he forced both pagans and Christians to convert to Islam. It may be inferred that Mohammed considered Christians polytheists because of their worship of Christ.

Under a different policy, however, some Christians—such as those in Nejran—were allowed to keep their faith. After meeting for three days, the prophet invited them to accept Islam. They refused to accept the new religion, but Mohammed allowed this group of Christians to keep their faith, provided they pay a high tribute.[23]

One example of Mohammed's direction for the treatment of "People of the Book" is found in Qur'an surah 9:29:

> Fight those who believe not in Allah nor the Last Day nor hold that forbidden which hath been forbidden by Allah and His apostle nor acknowledge the religion of truth (even if they are) of the People of the Book until they pay the Jizya (compensation) with willing submission and feel themselves subdued.

### Mohammed's Final Sermon

In the tenth year after the hijra, in A.D. 632, Mohammed took all of his wives, along with a hundred thousand followers, to Mecca for the Greater Pilgrimage. He performed all of the ancient pagan customs associated with the Ka'ba, thus incorporating them into Islam and setting the example for all future pilgrims. At the end of the pilgrimage, Mohammed stated, "this day I have perfected your religion for you" (surah 5:5).[24]

Before leaving Mecca for the last time, Mohammed preached his final sermon in the Uranah Valley of Mount Arafat. This sermon is not recorded in the Qur'an, but appears in other traditional sources. The sermon appears here so that the reader may understand Mohammed's persuasive preaching and teaching. A brief reflective commentary follows this sermon.

Mohammed exhorted his followers with these final instructions:

O People, lend me an attentive ear, for I don't know whether, after this year, I shall ever be amongst you again. Therefore listen to what I am saying to you carefully, and take these words to those who could not be present here today.

O People, just as you regard this month, this day, this city as Sacred, so regard the life and property of every Muslim as a sacred trust. Return the goods entrusted to you to their rightful owners. Hurt no one so that no one may hurt you. Remember that you will indeed meet your Lord, and that He will indeed reckon your deeds. Allah has forbidden you to take usury (interest), therefore all interest obligation shall henceforth be waived....

Beware of Satan, for the safety of your religion. He has lost all hope that he will ever be able to lead you astray in big things, so beware of following him in small things.

O People, it is true that you have certain rights with regard to your women, but they also have right over you. If they abide by your right then to them belongs the right to be fed and clothed in kindness. Do treat your women well and be kind to them, for they are your partners and committed helpers. And it is your right that they do not make friends with any one of whom you do not approve, as well as never to commit adultery.

O People, listen to me in earnest, worship Allah, say your five daily prayers [Salah], fast during the month of Ramadan, and give your wealth in Zakat [almsgiving]. Perform Hajj [pilgrimage] if you can afford to. You know that every Muslim is the brother of another Muslim. You are all equal.

Nobody has superiority over other except by piety and good action.

Remember, one day you will appear before Allah and answer for your deeds. So beware, do not stray from the path of righteousness after I am gone.

O People, no prophet or apostle will come after me and no new faith will be born. Reason well, therefore, O People, and understand my words which I convey to you. I leave behind me two things, the Qur'an and my example, the Sunnah, and if you follow these you will never go astray.

All those who listen to me shall pass on my words to others and those to others again; and may the last ones understand my words better than those who listen to me directly. Be my witness oh Allah that I have conveyed your message to your people.[25]

### Commentary on Mohammed's Final Sermon

Many find Mohammed's final sermon contradictory to earlier revelations found in the Qur'an, as well as to other examples in the Hadith. Therefore a certain amount of uncertainty attaches to its meaning.

One example of this obscurity is found in Mohammed's admonition to "hurt no one so that no one may hurt you." Earlier, however, Mohammed was instructed in the Qur'an surah 9:5 to:

> ...kill those who join other gods with God wherever ye shall find them, and seize them, and lay wait for them with every kind of ambush; but if they shall convert and observe prayer and pay the obligatory alms let them go on their way....

These apparently contradictory instructions lead the reader to infer that Mohammed's directions vary by the situation or context.

Another example comes in Mohammed's final exhortation to treat Muslim men and women equally and with respect. Yet, surah 4:34 reads, "Men are in charge of women because Allah hath made the one to excel the other....As for those from whom ye fear rebellion, admonish them and banish them to beds apart, and scourge them." Surah 2:228 also reads, "And they [women] have rights similar to those [of men] over them in kindness, and men are a degree above them."

The initial revelations asserted the superiority of males over females, and directed that women should be punished if they showed the possibility of rebellious behavior. Islamic teaching also allows men only to divorce their wives, not wives to divorce their husbands.[26] Yet in his last sermon, Mohammed asserts that women and men should be treated equally. A certain amount of ambiguity remains as to what idea of equality he had in mind. The ideals of equality and respect expressed by Mohammed in his last sermon are admirable, yet these principles are not always accomplished in contemporary Muslim nations.

### Final Days of Mohammed

After his last sermon, Mohammed and his followers returned to Medina. The *Shiite* sect of Islam insists that on the final return journey to Medina, Mohammed stopped and appointed his son-in-law, Ali, as his successor. Other Muslims reject this tradition.[27]

Just after Mohammed returned to Medina, he became terribly ill. Afraid that his followers would quarrel after his death, the prophet admonished his leaders to obey his successor and to be loyal to each other. Mohammed then directed Abu Bakr to lead the worship in his absence; some took this as an indication that Abu Bakr was to succeed Mohammed.

Finally, on June 8, A.D. 632, Mohammed died while resting on the lap of his favorite wife, 'Ayisha. It is believed that followers dug his grave on that very spot and buried the prophet of Arabia there. Believers later built a mosque over the grave, and the prophet's final resting place became a place of pilgrimage. Today, this mosque in Medina is known as "The Prophet Mosque."[28]

Tradition states that at Mohammed's funeral, Abu Bakr summed up the Islamic view of the prophet with this comment: "O ye people, if anyone worships Muhammed, Muhammed is dead, but if anyone worships God, He is alive and dies not."[29]

### Evaluation of Mohammed's Life

How are we to evaluate Mohammed's life? Clearly, he was a man of determination and great ability who achieved remarkable success in the face of tremendous adversity. Mohammed was a very religious man who abhorred idol worship and passionately believed in one god, Allah.

Through Mohammed, the fundamental teachings and guidelines of the Islamic faith came into being, along with the religio-political system that grew up along with it. The Muslim community continues to hold him in high esteem as their revered prophet.

Although he appears to have begun his mission as a sincere proclaimer of the truth as he perceived it, somewhere along the way he went astray. According to the Bible, the revelations of a prophet of God must agree with all of God's previous revelations. Mohammed's message contradicts the Word of God at several points, and he cannot therefore be considered as God's prophet. Rather, to Christians, he is one of the false prophets foretold by Christ in Matthew 24:24-25, men who would lead many astray.

Although Mohammed claimed he continued God's revelation as contained in the Torah, Psalms, and Gospel, he omits the very heart of Jesus' gospel. The New Testament declares that Jesus Christ, the Son of God, came among us, ministered among us, died on the cross for our sins, and was buried and rose again so that humankind might have eternal life through faith in Him. Mohammed rejected Jesus' death and resurrection and the plan of salvation through Christ alone. He accepted Jesus as merely another prophet.

Several centuries before the birth of Mohammed, the apostle Paul warned believers in Jesus Christ against those who would try to persuade them to accept another gospel:

I marvel that you are turning away so soon from Him who called you in the grace of Christ, to a different gospel, which is not another; but there are some who trouble you and want to pervert the gospel of Christ. But even if we, or an angel from heaven, preach any other gospel to you than what we have preached to you, let him be accursed. (Galatians 1:6-8, NKJV)

To a different group the apostle gave another warning about the deceptiveness of Satan. "Satan himself masquerades as an angel of light," he warned (2 Corinthians 11:14).

Could Mohammed's revelations have come from one "masquerading as an angel of light"? Mohammed himself wondered whether a demon might have inspired his experiences. And in fact, descriptions of how Mohammed received his messages sound more like demon possession than biblical accounts of how God reveals His will. Followers of Mohammed even consider him psychic and able to communicate with the dead — a practice considered cultic according to the Bible (Deuteronomy 18:9-14).

In light of all these things, the message of Mohammed must be considered a "different gospel" and therefore unacceptable to Christians as God-inspired. Sadly, Mohammed and the millions of Muslims who followed his teaching never knew how much God loved them, nor His plan of salvation for them.

### Summary

Through Mohammed, the founder of Islam, the fundamental teachings and guidelines of the Islamic faith and religio-political system are defined, and the Muslim community holds him in high esteem as their revered prophet. Yet he was more than just a prophet; Mohammed also became a politician and powerful warrior for Islam, and his example has been followed for centuries since. Although this great leader was passionate about what he believed to be the one true God, Allah, he appears to have been swayed to proclaim a "different gospel." Most importantly, his revelations significantly contradict the previous scriptures of the Bible, and therefore his message is unacceptable for Christians.

Mohammed was able to conquer the whole of Arabia in his lifetime, and his followers would spread the religion even farther. Today, Islam is the fastest-growing faith in the world. How and why has this religion spread so rapidly? The next chapter will address the historical development of Islam subsequent to Mohammed.

## ◦ 6 ◦

# The World's
# Fastest-Growing Faith

With 1.2 billion adherents,[1] Islam is now the second largest religion on the globe.[2] Islam dominates nearly half of the continent of Africa, much of the Middle East, a large percentage of Asia, and an increasing minority in the Western world. It is also the fastest-growing religion in America. Approximately one fifth of the world's current population is Muslim, and that number is expected to reach a full quarter of the earth's inhabitants over the course of the twenty-first century.[3] This rising religion of Islam commands our interest and attention.

How and why has this religion developed so rapidly? This chapter seeks to convey a brief history of the development of Islam, subsequent to the death of its founder, the prophet Mohammed.

### The Rule of Caliphs

As soon as Mohammed died, a crisis in leadership occurred. Who would govern the rising Islamic community? Mohammed, the "seal of the prophets," finalized and perfected divine revelation. Therefore, the role of the new ruler would be to guard the prophetic legacy as a religious and political leader.

Four caliphs ruled from Medina from A.D. 632 to 661. *Caliph* literally means the "successor" in Arabic, but came to refer to the role of the religious and political leader who would govern the Muslim community.

Even if Ali had been appointed by Mohammed as the prophet's successor (as the Shiite branch of Islam claims), the surviving Muslim leaders chose Abu Bakr as the first caliph. He ruled for four years, during which time he sent Khalid to subdue several tribes that had rebelled after the death of Mohammed. A military force of 18,000 attacked Palestine and Syria in A.D. 634 and defeated the Byzantine armies in A.D. 636, while forty thousand additional Muslims marched on North Africa.

After the death of Abu Bakr, Umar ibn al Khattab was chosen as the second caliph. Umar accepted the peaceful surrender of Jerusalem, yet was assassinated in the Medina Mosque in A.D. 646.

Uthman ibn Affan became the Muslims' third caliph. During his period of leadership, the Qur'an was compiled and recorded on various objects, largely from the memory of faithful followers of Mohammed. At the age of eighty, Uthman was murdered in his own palace while reading the Qur'an.

After Ali ibn Abu Talib won election in A.D. 656 as the next caliph, the governor of Syria, Muawiya, refused to recognize his authority. A five-year civil war ended with the assassination of Ali.

Muawiya became the next caliph, ruling from Damascus. His Omayyid dynasty ruled the Muslim world for the next ninety years. The Omayyids brutally killed Mohammed's grandson, Husain, in A.D. 680. This significant event split the Muslim world into the two denominations that still exist today, the Sunni and the Shiite (sometimes pronounced Shi'a).[4] While the Islamic community often presents itself as a united force, hostility between these two major denominations has caused internal strife that lingers to the present day.

### Sunni and Shiite (Shia) Denominations

The Sunni sect encompasses nearly ninety percent of the Muslim population. In general, Sunnis maintain that leadership in the Muslim community should be based on leaders with the appropriate qualities elected by the majority, not necessarily someone from Mohammed's bloodline.

The Shiite sect, which makes up most of the remaining ten to fifteen percent of the Muslim population, holds that inspired and infallible interpretations of the Qur'an are passed through the bloodline of the Prophet Mohammed. Therefore, from the Shiite perspective, Ali — the cousin, adopted son, and eventual son-in-law of Mohammed — and Husain, Mohammed's grandson, were the rightful successors to Mohammed. Shiites believe that future leaders should also come from Mohammed's lineage. The fruits of this belief system have produced many subgroups within this branch, such as the modern day leadership of the Aga Khan (Seveners) and others.

Many Shiites reside within the countries of Iran, Iraq, Afghanistan, and Pakistan. The tendency toward the terrorist *jihad* mind-set generally arises more from radical extremists within this branch of Islam, although fanatical militants have surfaced from both groups.

While Christianity's many denominations sprang primarily from minor theological differences, their core beliefs remain the same across the theological spectrum. Sectarian division in Islam, on the other hand, arises not because of theological differences, but over the issue of leadership. Additionally, the Sunni branch bases its belief and practice solely on the teachings of the Qur'an, while the Shiite branch puts greater emphasis on historical figures and their claims to divine inspiration, as well as the traditions of Mohammed (Hadith). Several smaller denominations have arisen within both denominations, with some variance in beliefs and practices.[5] The major sects within these two denominations of Islam are explained in figure 6.1.

# Denominations Within Islam

## Sunni
**85-90% majority worldwide**
Government by community consensus based on traditions of law.

### Hanafi
Founded in Baghdad, the oldest and most open to modern ideas. 30% of Muslims worldwide, including Sunnis in the Indian subcontinent, Turkey, and Egypt.

### Maliki
Founded in Mecca, in the mid-eighth century, traditionally Arabic, dominant in North Africa with approximately 25% of Muslims worldwide.

### Shafi
Originating in Baghdad, a liberalized form of Maliki, 15% of Muslims worldwide, found in Indonesia, Malaysia, and Philippines.

### Hanbali
Founded mid-ninth century, the most strict, predominantly in the Arabian Peninsula. Less than 5% of Muslims worldwide.

## Shiite
**10-15% worldwide**
Usually focused around a historical figure and his claims to inspiration.

### Twelvers
Largest Shiite group, found mostly in Iran and Iraq. Believe that the twelfth imam of Ali's lineage will return as al-Mahdi — the chosen one.

### Seveners
Ismailis are the largest sect of the Seveners, headed by Aga Khan. They differ with the Twelvers on the issue of succession.

### Druze
Originated in Syria and Lebanon in 1021, deriving their name from Darazi, an Iranian mystic.

### Zaydis
Most conservative of the Shiites, mainly found in Yemen, the nearest to the Sunnis in their theology.

### Alawites
Found in Syria, they accept some elements of Christianity including Jesus' resurrection.

© Abraham Sarker 2004

*Figure 6.1*

Despite internal conflicts, however, Muslim armies went forth to conquer much of the known world. They believed their success proved that Allah was with them.

### The Spread of Islam

Within twelve years of Mohammed's death, Muslims had occupied Egypt, Syria, and Iraq, and were advancing westward into Libya and eastward into modern-day Iran. Muslim armies were able to conquer quickly partly because of a power vacuum in the region. The two great powers of the day, the Persian and Byzantine empires, had been at war for half a century, and found their forces exhausted when the Muslims arrived.

Many "people of the book," including Jews and Christians, and other monotheists such as Zoroastrians, were spared from the sword, but had to pay a high tax as "protected minorities." After conquering these regions, Muslim armies set up forward camps from which they conquered additional territory.

Explosive Muslim expansion continued for a century. Eastward, after occupying all of Afghanistan and Persia, the military crossed over the Indus River and penetrated central Asia, including modern day Pakistan. Northward, Muslim forces raided as far as Constantinople, yet could not occupy Turkey (Asia Minor). Westward, the Muslims occupied north Africa all the way to the Atlantic, and into Spain and southern France. The Muslim advance was finally halted in A.D. 732 by the French army at the famous battle of Tours.[7]

### Prosperity Age of Islam

By A.D. 750, the Damascus-based Omayyid dynasty ceased and was replaced by the Abbasid dynasty, which ruled from Baghdad for the next five centuries. During this period, science, art, and culture flourished, as well as the development and elaboration of Islamic law (*shari'ah*). The Arabs developed algebra and contributed to the science of astronomy. In the fine arts and architecture, Islam imprinted its cultural inheritance upon the

# Christianity and Islam:
## The Ebb and Flow

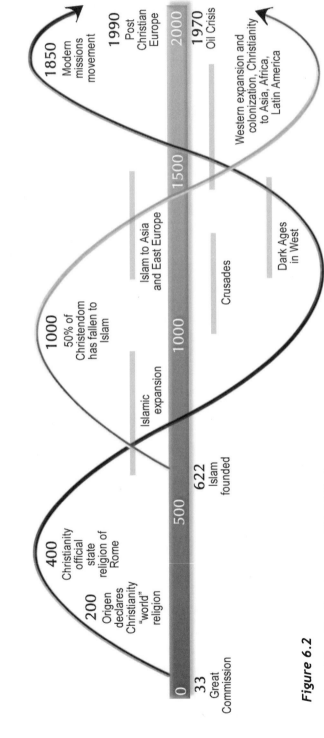

**0**
33
Great Commission

**200**
Origen declares Christianity "world" religion

**400**
Christianity official state religion of Rome

**622**
Islam founded

Islamic expansion

**1000**
50% of Christendom has fallen to Islam

Islam to Asia and East Europe

Crusades

Dark Ages in West

**1850**
Modern missions movement

**1990**
Post Christian Europe

**1970**
Oil Crisis

Western expansion and colonization, Christianity to Asia, Africa, Latin America

*Figure 6.2*

Adapted from *The New Context of World Mission*
by Bryant Myers (Monrovia, CA: MARC, 1996), page 13.

lands it conquered even as it absorbed the influences of the many nations it controlled.

Muslim medical science built upon knowledge gleaned from ancient Persia, including the concept of blood circulation and the practice of painless operations through the use of anesthetics. The wisdom gained during this period, referred to as the *Avicenna*—named for the great Muslim physician and philosopher, Ibn Sina—informed the great universities of Europe until the seventeenth century.

After A.D. 750, virtually the only further expansion by the Muslim military occurred in India. Islamic power reached its zenith under the Mogul emperors from 1556 to 1707, when Muslims dominated the majority of the Indian subcontinent. Amazingly, the far-flung Islamic Empire conquered more land area than the whole of the Roman Empire.

The religio-political system of Islam spread by peaceful methods as well. Muslim traders traveled to West Africa by camel caravan, to East Africa by sea voyages, and to the east along trade routes from India to Malaysia, Indonesia, and the Philippines. Local people, impressed by Muslim high culture, allowed Muslim traders to settle and marry local women. Eventually Muslim families emerged, and a trickle of converts joined the fold of Islam.

With the Mongol invasion in 1258, the caliphate in Baghdad fell, along with further development in Islamic culture, science, and art.[8]

### The Legacy of the Crusades

One tragic period in history caused the greatest breach in the relationship between today's three major monotheistic faiths. Some recall the era as valiant, while others refer to it with disgust. Wounds inflicted during this disastrous age remain raw for many, even after nine hundred years.

Several crusades from the West into the Holy Land occurred from the eleventh through thirteenth centuries, during

# Map of the Muslim World

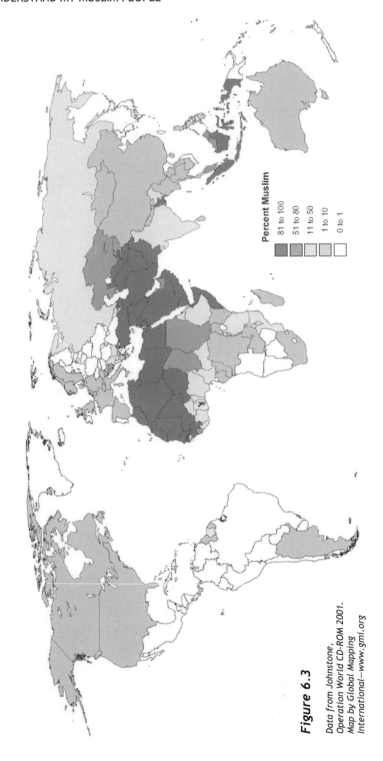

Percent Muslim

81 to 100
51 to 80
11 to 50
1 to 10
0 to 1

*Figure 6.3*

*Data from Johnstone,*
*Operation World CD-ROM 2001.*
*Map by Global Mapping*
*International—www.gmi.org*

Islam's cultural and scientific height. These events, although centuries in the past, remain significant to the Muslim world, as the Arab historian, Amin Maalouf, remarks in his work *The Crusades Through Arab Eyes:* "The Arab world—simultaneously fascinated and terrified by these Franj (Crusaders), whom they encountered as barbarians and defeated, but who subsequently managed to dominate the earth—cannot bring itself to consider the Crusades a mere episode of the bygone past."[9]

No single person or circumstance can be held responsible for these bloody marches into the Holy Land, but the strongest motivating force clearly was the church, which at that point in history could not be separated from the state. Papal authority had sharply risen and popes had discussed the idea of a crusade against the infidels (non-Christians) for centuries.

In one crusade after another, Western Christians and Muslims exchanged immense amounts of carnage and cruelty. These battles, fought in the name of Jesus, denigrated the name "Christian" in the eyes of Muslims and Jews alike. Even to the present day, this unfortunate series of campaigns has greatly injured the Muslim-Christian relationship.[10]

### European Impact on Islam

The Ottomans had restored the caliphate in the eastern part of the Islamic world after its initial collapse in 1258, and over the fifteenth and sixteenth centuries, the Ottomans conquered large portions of southeastern Europe, as well as the southern coast of the Mediterranean. So the Muslim world came into military, diplomatic, and commercial contact with several European states.

But a new era in Islam's history began around 1500 after Europeans contacted the eastern part of the Islamic world. The 1498 voyage of Portuguese explorer Vasco da Gama, around the Cape of Good Hope and on into India, disrupted Muslim trade on the east African coast. The major thrust of European impact, however, was not felt until after the Industrial Revolu-

# Rate of Growth for Islam

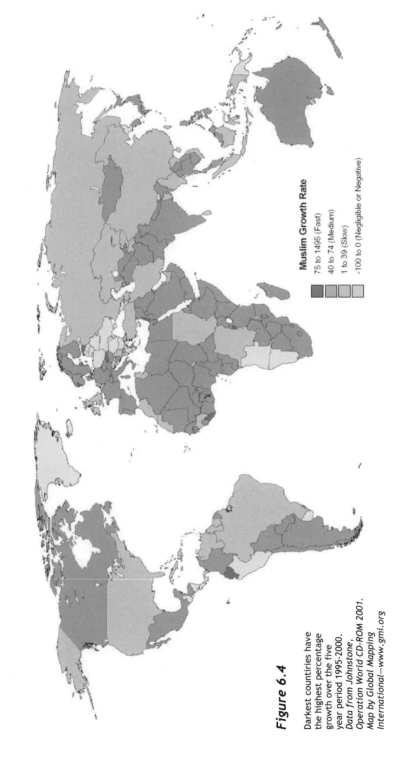

**Muslim Growth Rate**

- 75 to 1495 (Fast)
- 40 to 74 (Medium)
- 1 to 39 (Slow)
- -100 to 0 (Negligible or Negative)

## *Figure 6.4*

Darkest countiries have
the highest percentage
growth over the five
year period 1995-2000.
*Data from Johnstone,*
*Operation World CD-ROM 2001.*
*Map by Global Mapping*
*International—www.gmi.org*

tion. Napoleon's 1798 invasion of Egypt especially propelled the winds of change.

This European influence on the Muslim world involved economic, political, religious, and intellectual components, not unlike what occurred in Asia and Africa. It began through sea trade, but soon expanded to political influence and eventually, to colonization. As nineteenth-century European technology developed, so did the desire for modern conveniences in the Muslim world.

By the early twentieth century, movements for political independence increased and eventually bore fruit. Today, more than forty Islamic countries with Muslim majorities dot the planet. Countries with large Muslim populations are indicated in figure 6.3. Middle East oil has become a weapon in world politics. Although Muslim countries remained united against Western colonialism through the Second World War, splits have occurred since then between conservative and progressive groups.[11]

### Why Is Islam Growing So Fast?

The annual population growth rate for the Islamic world currently stands at 2.9 percent, ahead of Christianity's 2.3 percent growth rate. Within Christianity, however, the growth rate of evangelicals is more than double the average rate, at 5.4 percent. Pentecostal Christian groups are growing at well over triple the average rate, with an 8.1 percent increase each year.[12] Nevertheless, one out of every five individuals on the planet is Muslim. Figure 6.4 (facing page) indicates the rate of Islamic growth by individual country across the globe.

And why is Islam growing so fast? Several reasons appear to explain its rapid growth.

One major reason for Islam's growth is the high birth rate among Muslim families, which is higher than that of other people groups. Every child born into a Muslim home is automatically a Muslim. Chicago writer Deb Conklin gives several other reasons for Islam's rapid growth:

1. "Islam is an uncomplicated religion." There are only five (some sources say six) major doctrines to believe and five duties to perform, and guidelines exist, set for every part of life.

2. "Islam is an adaptable religion. It has contextualized itself into hundreds of cultures." Combinations of Islamic and animistic practices have produced the "folk Islam" practiced by many in the Muslim world today.

3. "Islam is a zealously 'evangelistic' religion." Muslims plan to and are in the process of taking the Western world into the fold of Islam. Consider the many Christian strongholds already captured by Islam in the Middle East, such as Istanbul (formerly Constantinople), Damascus, and Alexandria—formerly thriving Christian cities now controlled by Islamic governments.

"With evangelistic zeal backed by oil dollars," Conklin writes, "Muslims are willing to go anywhere and spend whatever it takes to win the world to Islam. In north Africa, the governments of Muslim countries in one recent year spent more to promote missionary activity in eight north African countries than the total Western missionary expenditure for the entire world. In countries with a Christian population, plans are to exterminate Christianity."[13]

Immigration accounts for the main method by which Islam is growing in the Western world. The World Jewish Congress reports that "Immigration has accounted for some 70 percent of the general population growth in the member states of the European Union over the past five years and the great majority of those who sought and seek a better life in Europe are Muslim." In fact, "at present, estimates of the number of Muslims in the European Union range from between 12 to 20 million—which means that there are more Muslims in Europe than there are Norwegians, Swedes, Danes, Greeks, Czechs, and Hungarians." Six to eight million Muslims live in France alone.[14]

While Islam has mounted a strong evangelistic presence and is successfully penetrating the Western world, many have nevertheless suggested that a crisis in leadership plagues the Islamic community.

### Leadership Crisis in Islam

As Islam expanded across Asia, Africa, and Europe, it adapted to the cultures it encountered. This strategy allowed it to blend in and spread rapidly. Yet this malleable characteristic has also created a crisis in leadership that has grown within Islam for centuries.[15]

The most recent manifestation of this crisis became apparent in the acts of September 11, 2001. Millions of Muslims condemned these acts, yet only a few have spoken out, and their voices were drowned out by the multitudes who kept silent.

R.W. Bulliet contends that today's crisis springs from the flexible structure of Islam.[16] With no organized denominations or centralized institutions, this religion has adapted to many cultures and regions. This lack of structure, however, makes it difficult for Muslims to join together and speak as one voice on important issues.[17] And this void of organization has allowed radical Muslims, such as Osama Bin Laden, to speak on behalf of the world's Muslims.[18]

Meanwhile, Islam continues to grow. And America itself is not exempt.

### Summary

After Mohammed's death Muslims spread the religion of Islam rapidly, at times through peaceful methods, but often by the sword. Since Islam's earliest days the religio-political system has had its share of struggles in leadership, resulting in the two sects of Sunni and Shiite that remain today. Many reasons have been offered for the religion's growth including a high birth rate and its uncomplicated, adaptive, and evangelistic nature. The religion of Islam has continued to grow in the Western world; in fact, it is the fastest-growing faith in the United States. The next chapter explores Islam's development in America as well as the "Nation of Islam" phenomenon, and how this facet of the faith differs from traditional Islam.

## ∘ 7 ∘

# Islam
# in America

Once a distant, unknown religion to most Americans, Islam is now the fastest-growing religion in the United States.[1] With more than six million American Muslims,[2] this nation houses the fifteenth largest Islamic minority in the world.[3] A 1994 statistic noted that eighty percent of the more than eleven hundred mosques in America at that time had been built in the previous twelve years.[4] The number of mosques since 1994 has reportedly increased by twenty-five percent.[5]

### Why Is Islam Growing in America?

Why is Islam increasing so rapidly in the United States? The three primary reasons echo the reasons behind worldwide Muslim expansion.

First, a large number of Muslim immigrants have come to America, hoping to make a better life for themselves. Second, the birth rate among Muslims is generally higher than that of other religious groups. Third, Islam is a religion of missionary zeal and is winning many converts in America, especially from the African-American community.

## 1. Muslim Immigration to America

While few verifiable resources indicate how the first Muslims came to America, Black Muslim Imam Nu'man insists that some of the "Native Americans" who migrated from Asia over the Bering Strait into the Americas were, in fact, Muslim.[6]

While the first black slaves to arrive in the American colonies came in 1619 to the Virginia settlement, by 1860 the enslaved African population in the United States had grown to 3,953,760.[7] Several of these African slaves brought with them their Islamic faith, such as Job ben Solomon, a Muslim literate in Arabic, and Omar ibn Said.[8] Yet slave owners suppressed the language and culture of their slaves, and no evidence exists to show that Muslim slaves propagated their religion.[9]

Some believe that a few Muslim Yemini immigrants came to America in 1869 to benefit from the Homestead Act of 1862.[10] Still more immigration between 1860 and 1918 integrated a few thousand more Muslims from present-day Syria, Turkey, Jordan, Lebanon, and Palestine. An estimated five to ten percent of this group was Muslim.[11]

In 1900 a group of Muslim homesteaders settled and performed the first communal prayers in Ross, North Dakota.[12] They built a mosque there in the 1920s, but within thirty years the building had been abandoned.[13] Syrian immigrants to Detroit formed their first Islamic association in 1912 (some sources say 1916), while the first mosque to be built in the United States appeared in Detroit in 1919.[14] One of the oldest established Muslim communities in the United States was founded in the early 1900s in Willows, California, just north of San Francisco.[15] Several thousand men from Punjab, India, came there to work as farmers, and of the 6,800 who emigrated from this region of India, over ten percent were Muslim.[16]

The first law restricting Muslim immigration was passed in 1921, followed by others that same decade. Institutionalized Islam did not begin in America until after World War II. The Federation of Islamic Associations formed in 1952, followed by the Muslim Students Association.[17]

The 1965 Immigration Act, signed into law by President Lyndon Johnson, caused an increase in the number of non-European immigrants, including many Muslims. Detroit serves as the largest port of entry for Arabs entering the United States; in fact, three-fifths of all immigrants entering Detroit are Arab.[18] Los Angeles alone has an estimated 200,000 individuals of Iranian descent.[19] And just a decade ago, America's universities educated an estimated 90,000 Muslim international students.[20]

The American Muslim Council in 1993 estimated the distribution of ethnicities among Muslims in the United States as noted in figure 7.1 below. It found that African Americans were 43 percent of the total; those from the Indian subcontinent (India, Pakistan, and Bangladesh) numbered 24 percent; Arabs accounted for 12 percent; Africans, 5 percent; Iranians, 4 percent; Turks, 2 percent; southeast Asians, 2 percent; white Americans, 2 percent (three-quarters female); and others, 6 percent.[21]

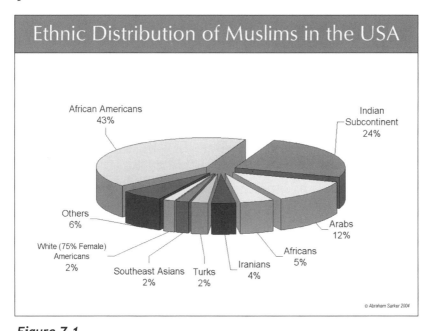

*Figure 7.1*

SOURCE: Steven Barboza, *American Jihad: Islam after Malcolm X* (New York: Doubleday, 1993), 9n.

Clearly, immigration has added many millions of Islamic background to the "melting pot" of America, and this American Muslim population continues to grow.

### 2. High Birth Rate Among Muslim Families

Many Muslims who immigrate to the United States retain their cultural practice of maintaining a large family. Reza Safa, a Middle Eastern Muslim convert to Christianity, writes, "Those from the Middle East enjoy large families as a cultural tradition. They do not think as much about the expenses of having children as people do in the West."[22] It is the duty of Muslim parents to train their children in the way of Islam.

### 3. Converts to Islam in America

Islam is a faith zealous to dominate the earth. Muslims view it as their duty to convert infidels to the "true faith" of Islam. Many Middle Eastern supporters have backed their commitment to evangelism with millions of dollars for building mosques in the United States. Saudi Arabia has spent $87 billion since 1973 in an effort to spread Islam to the Western Hemisphere, and particularly in the United States. Saudi Arabia's King Fahd specifically offered $7 to $8 million to construct a new mosque in the place of Masjid Bilal, the African American mosque in Los Angeles. [23] Even the countries of Iraq, Libya, Iran, and Kuwait have funneled millions of dollars to the West to propagate the religion.[24]

Interestingly, even though the Caucasian ethnic group accounts for the majority of the total U.S. population, only 1.6 percent of all U.S. Muslims are white American converts.[25] American converts to Islam occur primarily within the African American community. In fact, it is estimated that sixty to ninety percent of all conversions to Islam in the United States come from the African American community, and eighty percent of these converts grew up in the Christian church.[26]

To properly understand the development of Islam in America, a distinction must be made between orthodox Islam and Black Muslims (usually connected to the movement called

Nation of Islam). Many Americans are familiar with the famous Malcolm X and Louis Farrakhan—but what exactly does the Nation of Islam proclaim, and do orthodox Muslims consider them "true Muslims"?

### The Nation of Islam

A general lack of acceptance and justice for African Americans within the dominant culture fueled a hunger for dignity and significance. Writers on the subject of Black Islam insist that this sect—or separatist movement, as some consider it—had its roots in the teachings of Marcus Garvey and Noble Drew Ali.

In the 1920s, Marcus Garvey preached pride in African heritage and the necessity for racial separation. He insisted that blacks should worship a "Black God," "whose concern for the black man was prior to His concern for all other racial or national groups."[27] Although Garvey advocated black nationalism, he never promoted Black Islam.

### Noble Drew Ali and the Moorish Science Temple

While Garvey encouraged blacks to return to their African homeland to rediscover their roots, Noble Drew Ali (formerly known as Timothy Drew) took this concept one step further. He insisted that blacks return to their native religion as well.

In his work *The Holy Qur'an of the Moorish Science Temple of America*, Ali maintained that African Americans had to rediscover their Moorish and Asiatic roots. He claimed that Africans descended from ancient Canaanites, Ethiopians, and Moabites who espoused the religion of Islam. Ali established the Moorish Science Temple, featuring the core teaching—reaffirmed later in the Nation of Islam—that Christianity was the white man's religion and that Islam was the religion for people of color.[28]

### Wallace D. Fard, "Allah's Incarnation"

Building upon the teachings of Noble Drew Ali, Wallace Fard founded the Temple of Islam in 1930, one year after Ali's death. Fard worked out of Detroit and began proclaiming himself as "Allah's incarnation," or God in the flesh. His teaching became foundational to the Nation of Islam's theology. The organization even celebrates a unique holiday, recognizing February 26 as "Savior's Day," a commemoration of Fard's birthday.[29]

Fard believed that blacks should not only return to their native religion of Islam, but also to their original language of Arabic, so he encouraged them to change their given names to Islamic ones.[30] This charismatic stranger "denounced the iniquitous white man and exalted black Afro-Asians."[31] He disappeared mysteriously in 1934, to be succeeded by an early follower, Robert Poole, later known as Elijah Muhammad, Minister of Islam.

### Elijah Muhammad

Elijah Muhammad not only affirmed that Muhammad Fard (or Fard Muhammad, as he was also called) was Allah incarnate, but that he, Elijah Muhammed, was now the "Messenger of Truth." This leader established many of the core teachings of the Nation of Islam, including several that diverge with orthodox Islamic thought.

Orthodox Islam teaches, for example, that Allah has no partner and never came to earth as a human being. Elijah Muhammad denied this pillar of the Islamic faith when he asserted that, "Every race has a God looking like itself." Even more specifically, he insisted that the "Black God made the white god."[32] In contrast, orthodox Islam teaches that only one God has existed for all time and all people.

Elijah Muhammad claimed not only that, "All Muslims are Allahs," but also that "we call the Supreme Allah the Supreme Being. And He has a Name of His Own. This name is 'Fard Muhammad.'"[33] The idea that there is more than one God and that God came to earth to become a man is considered blasphemy in orthodox Islam.

Additionally, Elijah Muhammad discounted the second part of the Islamic shahada, believed passionately by orthodox Muslims all over the world, that "Mohammed is Allah's Messenger." This portion of the Muslim creed implies that Mohammed (of the seventh century) is the final and best prophet, and that no other prophets would come after him, since none were necessary.

Elijah Muhammad not only claimed that Fard Muhammad was Allah incarnate, but that he himself was the prophet from Allah, sent to proclaim this truth to the world. "Allah, in the Person of Master Fard Muhammad to Whom praises are due forever," he wrote, "has delivered to me whom He chose to deliver this Message of Truth....I say, Black Man, believe in Allah and come follow me."[34]

Ironically, centuries before Elijah Muhammad was born, Mohammed son of Abdullah, the founder of the Islamic faith, summed up the message of Islam in the same way: "Believe in Allah and follow me." This later became the fundamental creed of orthodox Islam. In his final sermon in Mecca, the original Mohammed claimed that no other prophets would come after him: "O People, no prophet or apostle will come after me and no new faith will be born."[35] Therefore, orthodox Islam cannot accept Elijah Muhammed as a prophet of Islam or Fard Muhammad as Allah incarnate.

The Nation of Islam grew as a powerful political and social force during Elijah Muhammad's regime, and the FBI kept its leadership and activities under surveillance. Elijah Muhammad's influence extended to a searching prison inmate who would become one of Black Islam's most distinguished converts, Malcolm X. Yet Elijah Muhammad's own power began to unravel as his famous protégé, Malcolm X, discovered and exposed his adulterous lifestyle.

### Malcolm X

Malcolm X initially accepted the radical racist teaching propagated by the Nation of Islam, but his life dramatically changed when he journeyed to Mecca to perform the Islamic pilgrimage (*hajj*). Through this experience, he realized how little he knew about orthodox Islam, especially how "true Islam" taught equality between the races. Alex Haley's autobiography of the Black Muslim leader recounts his experience:

| Comparison of Orthodox Islam and Nation of Islam | | |
|---|---|---|
| *Belief* | *Orthodox Islam* | *Nation of Islam* |
| God | Monotheistic, Allah is one and has no partner (surah 112), God is spirit (not man), infinite in time and space. | All Muslims are "Allahs," Wallace D. Fard came as God incarnate (God is man—not spirit), God and life itself are both material. |
| Prophet Mohammed | Prophet Mohammed of the seventh century is the final prophet, no others will come after him. | After Prophet Mohammed of the 7th century, Elijah Muhammad came as a prophet to tell about Fard's incarnation. |
| Race | Allah judges mankind on the basis of his / her righteous behavior rather than the color of his / her skin. All races are equal and should worship together. | The black race is superior to all others and the white race are devils. White people are not welcome in NOI (Nation of Islam) mosques. |
| Creation | Allah created the universe and Adam and Eve in the Garden of Eden. | Black scientists drew up the plan for history, and the cycle keeps repeating each 25,000 years.[37] |
| Qur'an | The Qur'an was dictated to Mohammed as the very Word of God through the angel Gabriel. | Black scientists who ordered history also wrote and revealed the Bible and the Qur'an to the rest of the human race.[38] |
| Shari'ah | Shari'ah is the sacred law with rules for all of Islamic life. It is based on the Qur'an and traditions of Prophet Mohammed (7th c.). For example, Muslims should not eat pork or drink alcohol, and should fast during the month of Ramadan. | Islamic traditions are not necessarily followed, but NOI created their own. For example, meals should be taken once a day between 4 and 6 p.m., and fasting should occur in December instead of Ramadan, Black Muslims shouldn't eat certain foods such as cake made with white flour.[39] |

*Figure 7.2*

There were tens of thousands of pilgrims, from all over the world. They were of all colors, from blue-eyed blonds to black-skinned Africans. But we were all participating in the same ritual, displaying a spirit of unity and brotherhood that my experiences in America had led me to believe never could exist between the white and the non-white.[36]

Malcolm's switch to a more orthodox Islam and his defection from the Nation of Islam outraged many in the Black Muslim community. On February 21, 1965, while beginning a speech at the Audubon Ballroom in Harlem, the zealous leader was assassinated by three gunmen.[40]

Meanwhile, Elijah Muhammad continued to lead the Nation of Islam until his own death in 1975. Elijah's son, Wallace D. Muhammad, publicly rejected his father's separatist doctrine and led a faction of the Nation of Islam toward the Islamic mainstream.[41] Louis Farrakhan, however, a protégé of Malcolm X and minister in the Nation of Islam, continued the vision of Elijah Muhammad in the dogma of racial separation.

Farrakhan met Elijah Muhammad in 1955 and soon joined the Nation of Islam, abandoning his musical career. With the split in the organization that occurred after Elijah Muhammad's death, Farrakhan officially declared in 1977 that he intended to reestablish the NOI on the same platform as Elijah Muhammad,[42] emphasizing that "Elijah Muhammad never intended for us to follow completely what is called orthodox Islam."[43]

### Louis Farrakhan

Farrakhan appeared most prominently in the national public eye through his support of Rev. Jesse Jackson's bid for the Democratic Party's presidential nomination in 1984 and again in 1988. Farrakhan's appeal to black empowerment and his charismatic leadership has attracted many within the black community.

### Nation of Islam vs. Orthodox Islam

How does the Nation of Islam compare to Orthodox Islam? Figure 7.2 on the facing page makes some telling observations.

Where orthodox Islam adheres to the beliefs in the shahada of Islam—that "There is no god but Allah, and Mohammed is Allah's Messenger"—Nation of Islam teaches that Allah is only the supreme God among others, and that Fard Muhammad was God incarnate. Orthodox Islam considers this idea blasphemous. Additionally, Elijah Muhammad insisted that the Prophet Mohammed of the seventh century was *not* the last prophet, but that he himself was a messenger of Allah, proclaiming the truth about Fard Muhammad. Other major differences include teaching on the order and creation of the world, as well as the interpretation and authority of the Qur'an and the shari'ah.

Ultimately, the Nation of Islam's black separatism contrasts sharply with orthodox Islam. The founder of Islam stated in his final sermon, "You know that every Muslim is the brother of another Muslim. You are all equal. Nobody has superiority over another except by piety and good action."[44] The Nation of Islam's view regarding the superiority of the black race directly contradicts the idea of equality taught in orthodox Islam.

With such fundamental theological divergences from orthodox Islam, what accounts for the attraction of the Nation of Islam?

### The Attraction of the Nation of Islam

One writer suggests that the attraction of the Nation of Islam is found not in the tenets of orthodox Islam, but rather that Black Islam "stands more as a rejection of Christianity as the white man's religion than as an embrace of the 'five pillars' of Islam."[45] The person who coined the term "Black Muslim" concurs that the draw of the Nation of Islam has more to do with race than religion:

> These Muslims are "Black Men," *black* as the antithesis of white. They do not subscribe to the familiar Moslem doctrine that a common submission to Allah erases and transcends all racial awareness. On the contrary, they do not

conceive the white man as capable of being a Muslim. "By nature he is incapable!"[46]

To further illustrate his point, Lincoln states in *The Black Muslims in America* that,

> The aegis of orthodox Islam means little in America's black ghettos. So long as the Movement keeps its color identity with the rising black peoples of Africa, it could discard all its Islamic attributes—its name, its prayer to Allah, its citations from the Qur'an, everything "Muslim" without substantial risk in its appeal to the black masses.[47]

The attraction of the Nation of Islam is found primarily in the ethnic unity it promotes, with particular emphasis on black pride and solidarity *against* the white race.

In his noted 1962 book on black nationalism, Essien-Udom succinctly states the attraction to this separatist movement: "The need for identity and the desire for self-improvement are the two principal motives which lead individuals to join and to remain in the Nation of Islam."[48]

Even black students from Christian homes at Clark College in Atlanta, Georgia, felt the lure of this movement. Why? Lincoln explains:

> Despite their Christian backgrounds, and despite the fact that they were even then attending a church-related college, these young men had despaired of Christianity as a way of life capable of affording them the respect and dignity they sought and deserved.[49]

### A Christian Response

Why has Christianity been unsuccessful in keeping these young African Americans within the church? Could it be that Christians have not shown enough of the Christlike non-racially skewed love necessary to show them the "brotherhood" they experienced in the Nation of Islam? Martin Luther King, Jr. highlighted this issue in a speech at the National Press Club in Washington, "The church is the most segregated major institute in America."[50]

Reza Safa, a former Muslim, stresses the need for Christians to show real love and acceptance in a society plagued with rejection and racism:

> If our love is not real, they will recognize it. It is time for us to make an effort and touch our cities with the love of Jesus. The church needs to proclaim Jesus and demonstrate His power. If we do not, the vacuum will be filled by men like Elijah Muhammad, Malcolm X and Louis Farrakhan.[51]

In my own experience as a former Muslim, I can attest to the power of the gospel and the genuine love of Christians who faithfully express God's heart. The love and acceptance of my new Christian "family" helped me to continue in my journey to follow Christ even in the difficult times when my natural family rejected me.

Similarly, the message of hope and acceptance that so many who are considering Islam desire is present in a relationship with Christ and the fellowship of believers. It is our responsibility as Christians to communicate this good news not only with our lips, but with our actions as well.

### Summary

Islam has seen tremendous growth in the United States and around the world. In America this is due primarily to floods of immigration, high birth rates among Muslims, and many conversions, particularly from the African American community. The establishment of Islam in America, initially most apparent in the twentieth century, shows a dichotomy in its study. The separatist movement of Nation of Islam (NOI), led by prominent Black Muslim leaders such as Elijah Muhammad, Malcolm X, and Louis Farrakhan, varies significantly from the teachings of orthodox Islam. While the NOI continues to gain converts through its emphasis on Black pride and identity, the strength of Islam as a whole lies in its core belief in one God, Allah. This and the other central beliefs of traditional Islam are discussed in the next section.

*Part III*

# The Fundamental Beliefs of Islam

Orthodox Islam holds to five fundamental beliefs, with belief in one God as its supreme principle. Mohammed indicates the importance of these five tenets in the Qur'an, surah 2:177, "...but righteous is he who believeth in Allah and the Last Day and the angels and the Scripture and the Prophets." This section will examine the fundamental Muslim beliefs in (1) Allah, (2) angels, (3) prophets, (4) Scriptures, and (5) the Day of Judgment. All Muslims, whether of the Sunni or Shiite sect, agree upon these five basic tenets.

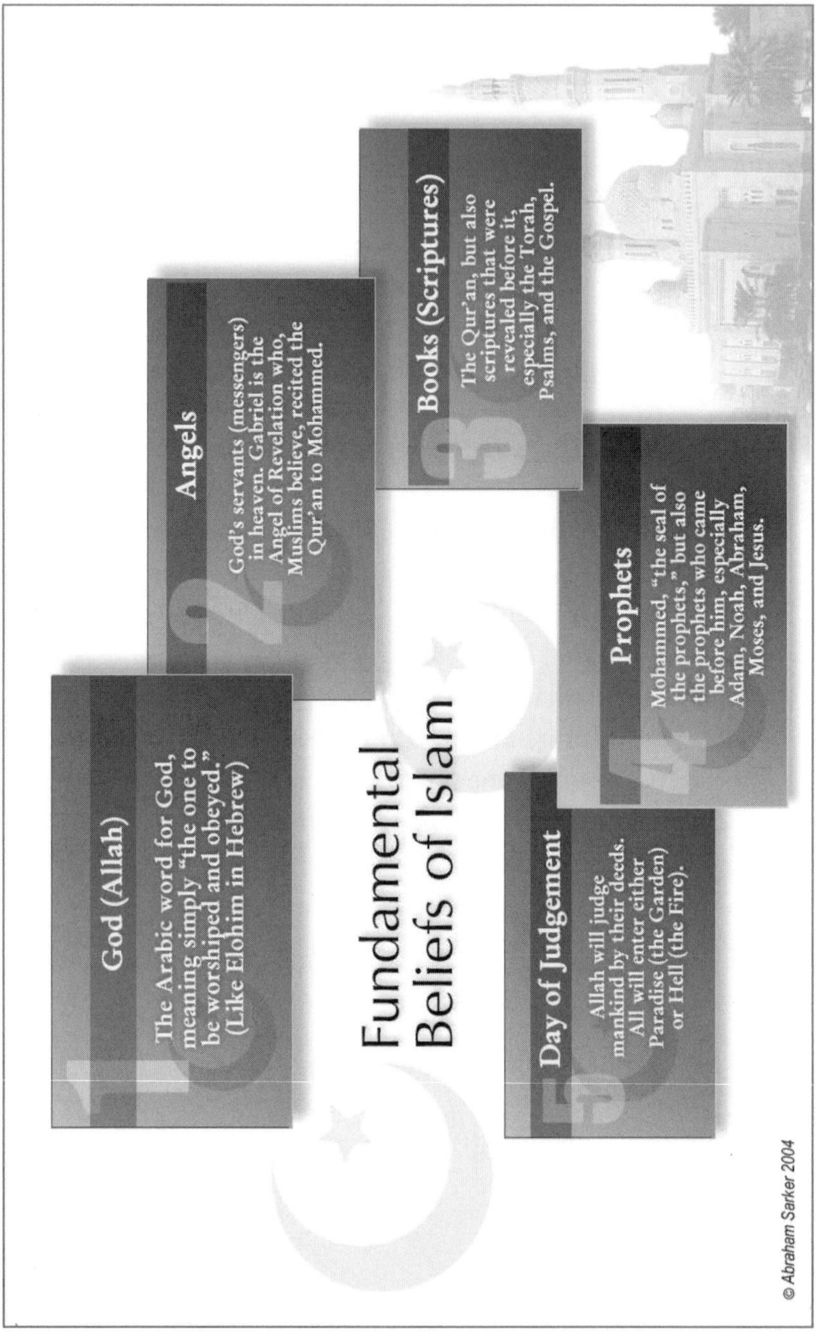

## Fundamental Beliefs of Islam

**1 God (Allah)**

The Arabic word for God, meaning simply "the one to be worshiped and obeyed." (Like Elohim in Hebrew)

**2 Angels**

God's servants (messengers) in heaven. Gabriel is the Angel of Revelation who, Muslims believe, recited the Qur'an to Mohammed.

**3 Books (Scriptures)**

The Qur'an, but also scriptures that were revealed before it, especially the Torah, Psalms, and the Gospel.

**4 Prophets**

Mohammed, "the seal of the prophets," but also the prophets who came before him, especially Adam, Noah, Abraham, Moses, and Jesus.

**5 Day of Judgement**

Allah will judge mankind by their deeds. All will enter either Paradise (the Garden) or Hell (the Fire).

© Abraham Sarker 2004

*Figure 8.1*

## ∘ 8 ∘

# Monotheism:
# The Strength of Islam

The strength of Islam lies not in its blueprint for Muslim conduct, nor in its detailed codes for morality, but in its central
commitment to one idea: monotheism. The power of Muslim
theology and philosophy lies in its brief, yet often repeated
creed: "There is no god but Allah, and Mohammed is Allah's
messenger." Millions of times each day this phrase proceeds
from the lips of devoted Muslims, and always in its mother
tongue of Arabic: *La ilaha illa Allah, Mohammed rasul Allah.*

### The Same God?

Many Christians who want to understand the religion of Islam
voice the question, "Is 'Allah' of the Qur'an the same as 'God'
of the Bible?" This question demonstrates a misunderstanding
of the real issue.

A better question might be, are "Yahweh" of the Bible and
"Allah" of the Qur'an the same? Here, the answer must be
"no," because the Allah described in the Qur'an exhibits many
characteristics unacceptable to Christians. Similarly, the attributes of Yahweh in the Bible are in some ways unacceptable to
Muslims.

Perhaps, then, the most appropriate question to ask is this: Did Mohammed teach, and does the Qur'an state, that the God revealed in the Bible is the same God that Islam proclaims? The answer here must unequivocally be "yes."

The Qur'an affirms in surah 3:3 that God spoke to Mohammed to confirm the earlier revelations He gave to the Jews and Christians: "He hath revealed unto thee (Mohammed) the Scripture with truth, confirming that which was (revealed) before it, even as He revealed the Torah and the gospel." Surah 29:46 of the Qur'an illustrates Mohammed's belief that the God of the "People of the Book" (Jews and Christians) is the same God that he proclaimed.

> And argue not with the People of the Book unless it be in (a way) that is better, save with such of them as do wrong; and say: We believe in that which hath been revealed unto us and revealed unto you; our God and your God is One, and unto Him we surrender.

Mohammed passionately believed that he was continuing the revelation begun with Abraham's declaration of one God. Just as Christians believe that the God who spoke to Abraham, Moses, David, and other Old Testament prophets is the same God who spoke through Jesus and the writers of the New Testament, so Mohammed believed this same God was speaking through him. Mohammed insisted, however, that he was bringing a final revelation that superseded the previous religions of Judaism and Christianity; this is why the Qur'an awards him the title, "Seal of the Prophets" (see surah 33:40).

### Etymology of the Term Allah

Where did the word *Allah* come from, and why did Mohammed associate Allah with the God of the Bible? The word *Allah* comes from the word *ilah*, a term related to the Hebrew word for God found in the Old Testament, *El* or *Elohim*. Both Arabic and Hebrew words carry the same meaning, "The Exalted One" or "the High One."[1]

Some authorities link the word *Allah* to the moon god of Arabia, and in fact, the theme of the moon does occupy a prominent place in Islamic decoration and culture.[2] Nevertheless, orthodox Muslim belief does not associate Allah with a moon god, or any deity other than the God spoken of by Abraham, Moses, Jesus, and ultimately and most significantly, the prophet Mohammed.

As a former Muslim, I never associated Allah with any type of idol. My Islamic schools informed me of the history of the Ka'ba, but I was never taught to associate Allah with anything but the oneness of God (*tawhid*).

When Christians sought to translate the Bible into the Arabic language, they found no other word but *Allah* to adequately describe the concept of God, the Creator of heaven and earth. The present day Arabic Bible therefore uses *Allah* for God. Today, when millions of Arab Christians pray to the God of the Bible using their native tongue, they use the word *Allah*. But while the word for God, *Allah*, remains the same for Muslims and Arab Christians, their respective understandings of God differ significantly.

### The Oneness of Allah

The unity and sovereignty of Allah form the cornerstone of Mohammed's message. And the heart of Mohammed's message was absolute monotheism.

The oneness of Allah (tawhid) is of supreme importance in the religion of Islam. It was the foundational teaching of Mohammed, clearly stated in surah 112: "Say: He is Allah the One and Only; Allah the Eternal Absolute; He begetteth not nor is He begotten; And there is none like unto Him."

This oneness of Allah is expressed continually throughout the Qur'an. The worst sin possible, and the only unpardonable sin for the Muslim, is *shirk*—which is associating anyone or anything with Allah. Surah 28:88 declares, "And cry not unto any other god along with Allah. There is no God save him."

This explains why Muslims have such a difficult time with the Christian doctrine of the Trinity. Muslims tend to misunderstand the Christian "Trinity" as the Father God, mother Mary, and Son Jesus. This belief, objectionable to both Christians and Muslims, originated in an early heretical sect of Christianity, the Choloridians, which flourished in the Middle East during the seventh through ninth centuries A.D. — during Mohammed's lifetime.[3] Surah 5:116 demonstrates how Islam rejected this doctrine:

> And when Allah saith: O Jesus, son of Mary! Didst thou say unto mankind: Take me and my mother for two gods beside Allah? he saith: Be glorified! It was not mine to utter that to which I had no right.

In surah 4:171, the concept of a Trinity is clearly unthinkable: "Say not 'Trinity': desist: it will be better for you: for Allah is One Allah: glory be to him: (for Exalted is He) above having a son." Interestingly, while the Bible develops the concept of a Triune God, it never uses the word "Trinity"; yet Islam rejects the idea of a Triune God in the Qur'an, while explicitly using the word "Trinity."

Surah 112 of the Qur'an also betrays a misunderstanding of the Christian doctrine of the Trinity, in that it asserts a natural father-son relationship rather than a covenant fellowship between Father God and Son Jesus. The belief that God would marry a human wife and have children is blasphemous both to the Christian and the Muslim.

### Ninety-Nine Names of Allah

Islam traditionally offers ninety-nine names to describe Allah's character, often called the "Ninety-nine Most Beautiful Names of Allah." Yet Arthur Jeffrey, the prominent European Islamicist, asserts that Islam actually ascribes many additional names to Allah: "the lists of these names as found in the texts vary greatly....Redhouse in his article in the *Journal of the Royal Asi-*

*atic Society* for 1880 collected from various lists no fewer than 552 different names for Allah."[4]

The Qur'an offers many names for Allah in surah 59:22-24:

> He is Allah, than whom there is no other God, the Knower of the invisible and the visible. He is the Beneficent, the Merciful. He is Allah, than whom there is no other God, the Sovereign Lord the Holy One, Peace, the Keeper of Faith, the Guardian, the Majestic, the Compeller, the Superb. Glorified be Allah from all that they ascribe as partner (unto Him). He is Allah, the Creator, the Shaper out of naught, the Fashioner. His are the most beautiful names. All that is in the heavens and the earth glorifieth Him, and He is the Mighty, the Wise.

The attributes mentioned here could equally describe Yahweh of the Bible — yet Islam and Christianity mean quite different things by the same terms, as we will see.

### Relationship of God to His Creation

Islam views Allah as the Creator and Judge of all mankind. The Qur'an teaches that Allah created the heavens and earth in six days (surah 32:4), and that all of nature abides by the laws He put into place. One Muslim author asserts,

> Everything in the world, or every phenomenon other than man is administered by God-made Laws. This makes the entire physical world necessarily obedient to God and submissive to His Laws, which, in turn, means that it is in a state of Islam [submission], or it is Muslim...the physical world has no choice of its own. It has no voluntary course to follow on its own initiative but obeys the Law of the Creator, the Law of Islam or submission.[5]

Islam teaches that only humans have the free will to choose to obey or reject God's commands. Yet God knows the destiny of each individual before he or she acts (see surah 9:51).

Islam teaches that God created Adam, the first human being, from clay. Allah created him to be a representative (viceregent) on the earth. The Qur'an gives this account in surah 2:30:

> "Behold thy Lord said to the angels: 'I will create a vicere-gent on earth.' They said 'Wilt thou place therein one who will make mischief therein and shed blood? Whilst we do celebrate Thy praises and glorify Thy holy (name)?' He said: 'I know what ye know not.'"

From this account, we see that Allah sent Adam to the earth as His representative, sometimes also referred to as God's *khalifa* (caliph). Adam and Eve (*Hauwa* in Arabic), the first two pure, sinless human beings, enjoyed continuous communion with their Creator until the "fall." When Adam and Eve ate of the forbidden tree, God cast them out of the Garden (in heaven) and down to the earth. Yet the Qur'an's version of this event illustrates a deep disparity between the Muslim and Christian positions.

### How the "Fall" Affected Humankind

Islamic theology considers the "fall" a minor slip by Adam and Eve, something entirely forgiven after they repented. No further effect on the human race occurred.

Islam teaches that all people are born true Muslims, pure and innocent (see surah 30:30). The disobedience of Adam and Eve actually was part of God's plan to bring them to the earth. One scholar highlights the differences between the Christian and the Muslim understanding of the fall like this:

> The Christian witness that the rebellion by our first parents has tragically distorted man, and that sinfulness pervades us individually and collectively, is very much contrary to Islamic witness. Islam teaches that the first phase of life on earth did not begin in sin and rebellion against Allah. Although Adam disobeyed Allah, he repented and was forgiven and even given guidance for mankind. Man is not born a sinner and the doctrine of the sinfulness of man has no basis in Islam.[6]

Since human beings, according to Islam, are not "fallen" or born with a sinful nature, there is no need to be "saved" and thus no need for a savior. One Muslim author, Faruqi, explains how the state of mankind is neither "fallen" nor "saved":

> In the Islamic view...because they (mankind) are not "fallen," they have no need of a savior. But because they are not "saved" either, they need to do good works—and do them ethically—which alone will earn them the desired "salvation"....Salvation is an improper term, since, to need "salvation" one must be in a predicament beyond the hope of ever escaping from it. But men and women are not in that predicament. Islam teaches that people are born innocent and remain so until each makes him or herself guilty by a guilty deed. Islam does not believe in "original sin"; and its scripture interprets Adam's disobedience as his own personal misdeed—a misdeed for which he repented and which God forgave.[7]

Since Muslims do not see themselves as sinful by nature, they don't perceive a need for a savior. They believe they earn their own passage to heaven through performing good works.

And how does a Muslim perform these good works? Submitting oneself to Allah is the only way to bring Him pleasure. The good works required are delineated in the five pillars (duties) of Islam (discussed in Part IV of this book). Significantly, according to the Qur'an, Allah never sent His Son, Jesus Christ, to save the world, but rather prophets into the world so humans could save themselves by doing good works.

And how does a Muslim perceive his or her relationship to Allah?

### Relationship of Humankind to God

The Qur'an pictures the relationship of humankind to God as slave-to-master. In Qur'anic language, this relationship is described as slave (*abd*) and master or lord (*rabb*).[8] As an example, Mohammed's father's name was Abd-Allah, which translates into "slave of Allah."

The duty of every human is to submit to the will of Allah in everything, as an obedient slave. In surah 51:56, Allah says, "I have created...men that they may serve me." Allah remains aloof from humankind, transcendent over all creation, and reigns as a king from heaven. He has sent prophets and books to guide men and women on the right path, and each individual must strive to stay on that righteous path, which includes submission to the will of Allah.

### Submission to the Will of Allah

A Muslim is quite plainly, "someone who submits to the will of Allah." But just what is the will of Allah?

Allah is sovereign and all-powerful; He created all that is and He wills all that happens. Qur'an surah 9:51 states, "Say: 'Nothing will happen to us except what Allah has decreed for us: He is our protector': and on Allah let the believers put their trust." Everything occurs by the will of Allah, and He guides some rightly and leads others astray.

> Whom Allah doth guide he is on the right path: whom He rejects from His guidance such are the persons who perish. Many are the Jinns and men We have made for Hell: They have hearts wherewith they understand not, eyes wherewith they see not, and ears wherewith they hear not. They are like cattle nay more misguided: for they are heedless (of warning). (Qur'an, surah 7:178-179)

This passage teaches that Allah has created some individuals to whom He gives no guidance, with the intent of sending them to hell. Others He guides to the right path, granting them the opportunity to earn heaven.

> So God (Allah) is the One Who leads astray, as well as the One Who guides. He is the One Who brings damage, as also does Satan. He is described also by terms like the Bringer-down, the Compeller, or Tyrant, the Haughty—all of which, when used of men, have an evil sense. In the Unity of the single will, however, these descriptions co-exist with those that relate to mercy, compassion, and glory.[9]

Islamic scholars admit that Allah's actions seem contradictory, at times bringing good, and at times bringing evil. As the great Muslim commentator, Goldziher, points out, "there is probably no other point of doctrine on which equally contradictory teachings can be derived from the Qur'an as on this one."[10]

Geisler and Saleeb further explain the unity of Allah's will:

What gives unity to all God's actions is that he wills them all. As willer he may be recognized by the descriptions given him, but he does not essentially conform to any. The action of his will may be identified from its effects, but his will itself is inscrutable.[11]

So why is Allah described as compassionate? He is so because He performs compassionate actions. His nature does not dictate His action, but rather, His actions demonstrate His will.

In Islam, Allah wills all that is; therefore an ambiguity remains within and without Islamic scholarship as to which aspect is stronger, predestination or the free will of humankind. The well-respected Muslim theologian, Al-Ghazzali asserts that:

He [God] willeth also the unbelief of the unbeliever and the irreligion of the wicked and, without that will, there would neither be unbelief nor irreligion. All we do we do by His will: what He willeth not does not come to pass.[12]

So where is the free will of humankind? If God has already decided each human action, where is there room for a person to choose? If God controls all of my thoughts and actions, then am I not acting like a robot? Can I do anything to change my life? Muslims who hold such a fatalistic mind-set may doubt whether it benefits them to try at all, since God already has determined if they will believe and so act rightly.

### Fatalism and Allah's Will

This resignation to fate, *kismet*, leads many Muslims to succumb to issues over which they feel they have no control.[13] This helps to explain fanatical self-sacrifice in war, resignation in disaster and bereavement, and inactivity in preventable evil, such as epidemics. All of these can be seen as the will of Allah, and therefore nothing should be done to stop them.

Any evil or good that comes along is sent from Allah, and humans should not strive to change them. This explains the common use of the phrase, "If Allah wills it," throughout the Muslim world. This fatalistic outlook leaves a void of hopelessness in the hearts of many Muslims.

At the same time, Islamic thought teaches Muslims not to question Allah, as that would be disobedience and result in punishment. Al-Ghazzali also acknowledges that:

> We have no right to enquire about what God wills or does. He is perfectly free to will and to do what He pleases. In creating unbelievers, in willing that they should remain in that state;…in willing, in short, all that is evil, God has wise ends in view which it is not necessary that we should know.[14]

### Is Allah Loving?

Both Muslims and Christians list love as an attribute of God. But how is this characteristic expressed in each faith?

Interestingly, all of the surahs in the Qur'an, except one, begin with the phrase, "In the Name of God, the Compassionate, the Merciful." In Islam, Allah is seen as loving—yet not with the unconditional *agape* type of love used to describe the God of the Bible. In surah 3:31-32, Mohammed emphasizes that Allah loves those who love and obey him, but not those who don't believe.

> Say, (O Muhammad, to mankind): If ye love Allah, follow me; Allah will love you and forgive you your sins. Allah is Forgiving, Merciful. Say: Obey Allah and the messenger. But if they turn away, Lo! Allah loveth not the disbelievers (in His guidance).

If a Muslim follows all of the decrees of Allah, he or she has opportunity to be loved by his or her Creator; but if an individual sins or does not believe, he or she will never receive that love and acceptance. On the contrary, he or she can surely expect to receive the due punishment. Consequently, love from Allah is conditional, based on how well an individual submits to Allah's will. While Muslims will speak the phrase, "In the name of Allah Most Gracious Most Merciful" before reciting any portion of the Qur'an, Allah's love extends only to those who submit to His will.

In Islam, Allah is said to be loving, not because of His inherent nature, but because He does loving things. He has the will to do whatever He pleases, and if He chooses not to be loving, then He is not bound to be.

### The Capricious Nature of Allah

It should come as no surprise that Muslims cannot call Allah their Father. He remains distant to His creation and has a capricious nature. One never knows if he or she will be forgiven and allowed admittance into heaven, because Allah may change His mind at any moment.

The nature of Allah can seem confusing, resulting in uncertainty about whether absolute right and wrong exists. Geisler and Saleeb assert that, in Islam, "an act is not intrinsically right or wrong. It is right only when God specifically declares it to be such according to his will."[15]

Therefore, certain actions may be unacceptable and sinful at one period, and yet later Allah may mandate that this same action is not only allowed, but required. Remember Allah's instructions concerning infidels? Initially in Mohammed's career as prophet, Allah prohibited the killing of infidels: "Let there be no compulsion in religion" (surah 2:257). Later, however, Mohammed was commanded to kill the infidels if they did not convert to Islam: "O Prophet (Mohammed), contend against the infidels and be rigorous with them" (surah 9:74). Allah may change His instructions as He deems necessary. He has power to change His laws and previous revelations, and has no need for consistency in either nature or action.

The Qur'an asserts that Allah changes His revelation in order to present something better: "None of Our revelations do We abrogate or cause to be forgotten but We substitute something better or similar; knowest thou not that Allah hath power over all things?" (surah 2:106).

Mohammed taught that the Qur'an continued what Allah said to the Jews and Christians earlier, but the Qur'an contains numerous contradictions to the Bible (see chapter 11). Allah may change His revelation at any time He so chooses.

This creates a particularly worrisome predicament for the Muslim believer as he or she considers the Day of Judgment. Even though he or she has completed many good deeds, Allah, the distant, unpredictable judge, may change His mind about that individual, or His will may have always been for that individual to go to hell. One never really knows if he or she will be granted heaven, because it is up to Allah whom He will choose. The capricious nature of Allah and the revelation supplied in the Qur'an give Muslims no real assurance of eternal bliss.

### Allah Is All

Despite the many uncertainties inherent in their faith, Muslims hold fast to their belief in one God, Allah. His name is on their lips throughout the day. When a Muslim promises to complete a certain task, he adds the condition, "If Allah wills." When a Muslim sneezes he or she is to say, "Praise Allah!" When a Muslim witnesses something beautiful or awesome, he or she is to declare, "Glory to Allah!" No matter the circumstance, a Muslim should utter, "Thanks be to Allah!"

Monotheism is the strength of Islam. Muslims proudly believe in one God and claim to follow the true religion—yet is belief in one God enough? As New Testament writer James stresses, "You believe that God is one; you do well. Even the demons believe—and shudder" (James 2:19). How does the Islamic teaching about Allah compare to the Bible's concept of God?

### A Picture That Gives Hope

While God of the Bible and Allah of the Qur'an share many characteristics, they also diverge in many important ways.

The Bible, like the Qur'an, teaches the oneness of God: "The LORD our God, the LORD is one. Love the LORD your God with all your heart and with all your soul and with all your strength" (Deuteronomy 6:4-5). The New Testament echoes this teaching, as Jesus declares: "the Lord our God, the Lord is one" (Mark 12:29).

Yet the Bible also teaches that this one God exists as three Persons, in complete unity of will, purpose, and action, each Person functioning in three different ways as a Trinity. The term *Trinity*, not used in the Bible, was coined by the church three centuries after Christ's ascension to express what Scripture declares about the three Persons of the Godhead.[16] Both the Old and New Testaments support the Christian belief in a Triune God consisting of the Father God, Son Jesus, and Holy Spirit—the Three in One. The relationship of Father God and Son Jesus does not imply a biological relationship, but a special covenant relationship or fellowship.

*The role of Jesus Christ.* The role of Jesus Christ is key to grasping the difference between the Muslim and Christian understandings of God. Muslims do not consider Jesus anything more than a revered prophet; they deny that He was God. Christians, on the other hand, believe that Jesus is God incarnate. God sent His Son, Jesus Christ, into the world to die on the cross as a perfect sacrifice for sin. Jesus fulfilled God's plan for the salvation of the world. Almighty God, out of love for His creation, humbled Himself to come to earth in the form of a human being in order to fulfill His plan of salvation through the death and resurrection of Christ.

*God's relationship to a fallen world.* This brings us to a second important divide between the Muslim and Christian views of God. In Christian theology, Adam and Eve's disobedience in the Garden is considered an important turning point in the human race's relationship to God. The "fall" resulted in all men and women being born with a sinful nature, separated from God by sin. Romans 5:12 explains, "sin entered the world through one man, and death through sin, and in this way death came to all men, because all sinned...." Therefore, every man and woman needs the Savior appointed by God, namely, Jesus Christ.

In the Bible, God did not create human beings merely to serve Him, but to display His glory. "Everything comes from God alone, everything lives by his power, and everything is for his glory" (Romans 11:36, Living Bible). All of creation declares the glory of God, including humankind. God does not keep aloof from the men and women He created, as does Allah. God loves mankind, His creation, so much that He sent His Son, Jesus, to die for them. And while He calls men and women to serve and worship Him, His love for them is so great that He grants them the opportunity to become a part of His own family: "How great is the love the Father [God] has lavished on us, that we should be called children of God!" (1 John 3:1; also see John 1:12-13).

The Yahweh of the Bible invites us to experience a personal relationship with Him through Jesus Christ, such as a happy father and child enjoy: "...you received the Spirit of sonship. And by him we cry, *Abba*, Father" (Romans 8:15).

The Muslim fatalistic mind-set also contrasts with the Christian witness that while God allows certain blessings and tragedies in our lives, He allows them for our ultimate good: "And we know that in all things God works for the good of those who love him, who have been called according to his purpose" (Romans 8:28).

God desires that everyone He has created will choose to love Him and walk in His ways. Second Peter 3:9 declares that God is "patient with you, not wanting anyone to perish, but everyone to come to repentance." Although God knows the future, He does not create some individuals for hell and others for heaven. Any individual who spends eternity in hell does so because of his or her own choices, not because God desired such a fate for them when He created them. God is infinitely righteous and holy and does not create or associate with evil: "Your eyes are too pure to look on evil; you cannot tolerate wrong" (Habakkuk 1:13; see also James 1:13).

*Unconditional love missing in Islam.* Finally, the God of the Bible loves unconditionally. His very nature is loving: "God is love" (1 John 4:16). Everything He does issues from His loving heart. Yahweh loves all of mankind, even those who sin and do not believe: "But God demonstrates his own love for us in this: While we were still sinners, Christ died for us" (Romans 5:8).

God loves because love is inherent in His unchanging nature: "I the LORD do not change" (Malachi 3:6). Because God's nature never changes, He acts in unceasingly loving ways: "For the LORD is good and his love endures forever; his faithfulness continues through all generations" (Psalm 100:5).

Not only does God's nature not change, but neither do His words: "Heaven and earth will pass away, but my words will never pass away" (Mark 13:31). Jesus promised that the Law of the Lord will never be changed or erased: "I tell you the truth, until heaven and earth disappear, not the smallest letter, not the least stroke of a pen, will by any means disappear from the Law until everything is accomplished" (Matthew 5:18). Therefore, the believer in Jesus Christ may have absolute assurance of salvation, knowing the certainty of God's unchanging promise: "For God so loved the world that he gave his one and only Son, that whoever believes in him shall not perish but have eternal life" (John 3:16).

### Summary

Included here is a basic understanding of the God of Islam, Allah. The monotheism of Islam is fundamental to understanding the core of Islamic thought and history. This belief in the oneness of Allah is reiterated through the Muslim creed spoken several times daily by faithful Muslims, "There is no god but Allah, and Mohammed is Allah's Messenger." Allah is not only the Creator, but a capricious judge who will evaluate humankind on the Day of Judgment, choosing to grant mercy to some and punishment to others, changing his mind at any moment. Allah is above all others and has no partner, yet He is unknowable and loves only the righteous, not those in sin and unbelief. Allah created man to serve Him, not to have a personal relationship with Him.

Mohammed taught that Allah is the same God that Jews and Christians worship (surahs 3:3 and 29:46); however, the attributes of Allah in the Qur'an vary significantly from those of Jehovah in the Bible. Interestingly, Mohammed still claimed that he received his revelation from the same source as prophets in previous scriptures. How does Islam explain Allah's methods in communicating His statutes to Mohammed as well as previous prophets? The important role of angels in Islamic theology will be considered next.

## ∘ 9 ∘

# Beings
# of Light

Muslims believe unswervingly in one God—but how do they believe God communicated His statutes to mankind? Let us now consider the vital position that angels occupy among the fundamental beliefs of Islam.

### Servants of Light

Angels are a very real and important part of Islamic teaching. According to Islam, they are sinless, genderless beings formed from light. They possess no free will, but follow every command of God. They spend most of their time worshiping Allah, but they also carry out duties for Him according to His command.[1] H. A. R. Gibb, the British Islamic scholar, writes:

> In the imagery of the Koran the angels are represented generally as God's messengers. They are...His creatures and servants and worship Him continually; they bear up His Throne, descend with His Decrees on the Night of Power, record men's actions, receive their souls when they die, and witness for or against them at the Last Judgment, and guard the gates of Hell. At the battle of Badr they assisted the Muslims against the vastly superior forces of the Meccans.[2]

Such are the general duties of angels as represented in Islamic thought. But four key angels have specific and vital responsibilities.

### The Four Archangels

Among the multitudes of angelic beings four prominent archangels stand out: Gabriel, Michael, Azrail, and Israfil.

Gabriel (*Gibra'il* in Arabic) is the angel of revelation; some Muslims also consider him the Holy Spirit. Since Allah is too exalted to speak directly with man, it is necessary for an angel to speak on His behalf. Gabriel brought the revelation of Allah to Mohammed, as well as to the other prophets throughout history. Muslims believe that the angel Gabriel dictated the words for the Qur'an, word by word, to Mohammed.

Surah 19:17 of the Qur'an also states that Mary, the mother of Jesus, received the news of Jesus' impending birth from the angel Gabriel:

> ...then We (Allah) sent to her Our angel and he appeared before her as a man in all respects.
>
> She (Mary) said: "I seek refuge from thee to (Allah) Most Gracious: (come not near) if thou dost fear Allah."
>
> He (Angel Gabriel) said: "Nay I am only a messenger from thy Lord (to announce) to thee the gift of a holy son."

Of the four archangels, Gabriel is given the most prominent position because of his duty to relay messages directly from Allah. Nevertheless, the other three archangels have significant duties as well.

Angel Michael (*Mika'il*) is considered the angel of providence and the guardian of the Jewish people. Angel Azrail (*'Izra'il*), or "the angel of death," is responsible for ending the lives of humans. Angel Israfil will blow the trumpet on the Day of Judgment to summon all people in the resurrection.[3]

### The Two Interrogating Angels

Two interrogating angels, *Munkar* and *Nakir,* black in color, are said to visit each body as it enters its grave in order to ask three questions: "Who is your Lord? What is your faith? Who is your messenger?"

If one answers correctly ("Allah," "Islam," and "Mohammed," respectively) these angels will depart the body and allow it to rest. If the individual answers incorrectly, however, these angels will torture the corpse until the Day of Judgment.[4]

### A Host of Recording Angels

Other angels are assigned to specific human beings, with the task of recording an individual's good and bad deeds. Their records will then be presented to Allah on Judgment Day.

These respected recorders are called *Kiraman Katibin* in Arabic.[5] Muslims believe that each person has two of these angels accompanying him or her at all times. The angel sitting on the right shoulder records all of the individual's good deeds, while the angel sitting on the left shoulder records all of the bad deeds. Surah 50:17-18 explains how every word and deed is recorded by these angels:

> Behold two (guardian angels) appointed to learn (his doings) learn (and note them) one sitting on the right and one on the left. Not a word does he utter but there is a sentinel by him ready (to note it).

On Judgment Day Muslims will be evaluated by all the good and bad deeds they have acquired on earth, as recorded by these angels. The Hadith explains the role of the recording angels in the following way.

Each person on the Day of Judgment will wait expectantly in a long line in heaven, waiting for his or her turn to be judged by Allah. When he or she comes to the throne of Allah, these angels will come to that individual's side and present the books of recorded deeds.

Then the moment of truth comes, when each individual's eternal destiny is revealed by those books. The angel recording the good deeds will place his book on one side of a gigantic scale. Then the angel recording the bad deeds will place his book on the other side of the scale. Allah weighs the books to determine which is heavier, the good or the bad deeds; then He will declare judgment for the human, either to an eternity in heaven or an eternity in hell. While on this earth, a devout Muslim will remember these angels with fear and trepidation as he or she dutifully completes obligations to Allah.[6]

### Satan and Jinn

Not all spiritual creatures have chosen to follow Allah's command. Allah created a species halfway between angels and men, called *jinn*. Some jinn are good and some are evil, but the doctrine of fallen angels is not generally accepted in Islam, since angels have no choice, but always follow the will of Allah.[7]

The creation of jinn is mentioned in the Qur'an, surah 15:26-27: "We created man from sounding clay, from mud moulded into shape; and the Jinn race, We had created before, from the fire of a scorching wind." The purpose for the creation of the jinn is stated in surah 51:56: "I have created only Jinn and men, that they may serve Me." Allah created humans and jinn to serve Him, yet Allah made jinn from fire before humankind came into being.

An interesting argument emerges concerning the identity of Satan (*Iblis*). Although Islamic theology asserts that Satan was of the jinn race, Qur'anic evidence seems to suggest that he was more of a fallen angel. Consider the account in surah 38: 71-78:

> Behold thy Lord said to the angels: "I am about to create man from clay. When I have fashioned him (in due proportion) and breathed into him of My spirit fall ye down in obeisance unto him."

So the angels prostrated themselves all of them together;
Not so Iblis: he was haughty and became one of those who
reject Faith.

(Allah) said: "O Iblis! What prevents thee from prostrating
thyself to one whom I have created with My hands? Art
thou haughty? Or art thou one of the high (and mighty)
ones?"

(Iblis) said: "I am better than he: Thou createst me from fire
and him Thou createst from clay."

(Allah) said: "Then get thee out from here: for thou art
rejected, accursed. And My Curse shall be on thee till the
Day of Judgment."

When Allah commanded all of the angels to bow down to
Adam, the first man, all but Satan obeyed. Satan proudly insisted that he was superior to the man made from clay, and as a
result was cast out of heaven.

In surah 18:50 this incident is again mentioned: "And
(remember) when We said unto the angels: Fall prostrate before
Adam, and they fell prostrate, all save Iblis. He was of the Jinn,
so he rebelled against his Lord's command."

Since Satan obviously disobeyed Allah, and angels always
obey God, the explanation is that he must have been of the jinn
race. But whether Satan is classified as a fallen angel or a jinn,
he played a key role in deceiving Adam and Eve into eating of
the forbidden tree in the Garden. He is considered the chief
enemy of humankind, as well as the leader of the evil jinn and
demons.

### Summary

Allah created angels and jinn with specific, structured duties to
complete as part of their worship and service to Him. Included
among them are the four archangels, the interrogating angels,
the recording angels, and the evil Satan (Iblis) and jinn. Since
Allah is high and exalted, unapproachable by human beings,

angels were necessary if communication was to take place between God and man.

But what of the human side of this chain of divine communication? Only a few human representatives were chosen to communicate with angels, and so to bring God's revelation to the rest of humankind. These are the prophets.

## ° 10 °

# The Role
# of Prophets

Abraham, Moses, Jesus, Noah, Adam, David — do these names sound at all familiar to you? They do if you know the Bible.

But they also will sound familiar if you have read the Qur'an, for these men are considered some of the most significant prophets of Islam (even though their messages differ significantly from the older accounts in the Bible).

Why does Islam insist that prophets were necessary, and why are so many of the Islamic prophets the same as those mentioned in the New and Old Testaments?

### The Purpose of Prophethood

Islam teaches that Allah communicated His guidance to frail, weak, and forgetful humankind through His chosen messengers, or prophets. This role of prophethood (*risalah*) is vital to Muslim life.[1]

Although the exact number of prophets is not stated in the Qur'an, the Hadith suggest that Allah has sent 124,000 prophets into the world to teach men to follow the right path.[2] The Qur'an claims that Allah's prophets have been sent to every nation at different times throughout history (see surahs 10:47; 13:7; 35:24).

Islam makes a distinction, however, between individuals who simply carry information and proclaim God's news—traditionally "prophets," *al nabbi* in Arabic—and those sent with divine Scripture to reform and lead mankind—called "messengers" or *rasul*. Consequently, not all of the many prophets (al nabbi) were also messengers (rasul) of divine Scripture.[3] One Islamic scholar summarizes the purpose of prophethood:

> Some of Adam's offspring who were righteous followed Allah's teaching, but others drifted into evil activities. They compromised the true guidance by associating Allah with other gods and objects. In order to provide man with firm and constructive guidance, God raised prophets among every people. The fundamental message proclaimed by all prophets was the same. They taught or reminded man of the unity of God, the reward of leading a good, pious, and peaceful life, the day of judgment, and the terrible punishment for unbelievers. All prophets brought this same message (Islam) from Allah.[4]

Islam insists that all of Allah's prophets proclaimed the same basic message: that God is one, and that He will reward the pious but punish the disobedient. In short, the prophets since the beginning of time urged people to submit to Allah (which is Islam).[5] Therefore, Muslims believe that all the previous prophets were also Muslims: "all those prophets...were Muslims, and...their religion was Islam, the only true universal religion."[6] That means Abraham was a Muslim, Noah was a Muslim, Jesus was a Muslim, and so forth.

### Who Are the Islamic Prophets?

Passages in the Qur'an retell stories of many Old Testament characters, their information apparently based on Old Testament narratives or adapted from Jewish apocrypha.

History tells us that Mohammed had frequent interaction with the Jewish community and so likely gleaned some understanding of the Hebrew prophets from them. Also, Mohammed's eighth wife, Maryam, is thought to have been a Christian slave girl from Ethiopia, sent by the governor of Egypt. She likely brought with her some type of Christian documents, possibly some early apocryphal fables containing stories similar to what is found in the Qur'an, yet not included in the Bible.[7]

All but four of the twenty-five prophets named in the Qur'an are also mentioned in the Bible.[8] The five most prominent Islamic prophets, recognized with the highest title of "*ulu'l-Azm*," or "people of the determination," include the following: Mohammed (the apostle of God); Noah (the preacher of God); Abraham (the friend of God); Moses (the speaker with God); and Jesus (the word of God). Some sources also include Adam (the chosen of God).[9]

Although Qur'anic stories about these prophets resemble biblical accounts, they vary from the original narratives in the Bible, which predates the Qur'an. The Old Testament account in Genesis 22, for example, reports that God tested Abraham with the instruction to sacrifice his only son, Isaac. When the Lord saw that Abraham truly loved God more than anything, even his own son, God miraculously provided a substitute animal for the sacrifice, thus sparing the boy's life. And so Isaac lived to become a forefather of the Jewish nation.

In the Qur'anic account of this story, found in surah 37:102, God instructs Abraham to sacrifice his son Ishmael, not Isaac. Although the name Ishmael is not explicitly stated in the passage, tradition asserts that Ishmael was indeed the son in question, and that Isaac was not born until after this incident. Ishmael is considered the forefather of the Arabic people and Mohammed's ancestor.

Why these alterations from the original narrative? Were the changes accidental due to the absence of authentic resources, or were they somehow intentional? No certain answer can be given.

Included below is a list of the twenty-five prophets specifically mentioned in the Qur'an, along with their biblical name, if applicable.[10] Some sources maintain that many of the Arabic names do not provide a clear correspondence to biblical characters, but instead refer to Arabian prophets or reformers.[11]

| Qur'anic and Biblical Prophets | |
|---|---|
| *Qur'anic Name* | *Biblical Name* |
| 1. *Adam* | Adam |
| 2. *Idris* | Enoch |
| 3. *Nuh* | Noah |
| 4. *Hud* | — |
| 5. *Salih* | — |
| 6. *Ibrahim* | Abraham |
| 7. *Isma'il* | Ishmael |
| 8. *Ishaq* | Isaac |
| 9. *Lut* | Lot |
| 10. *Ya'qub* | Jacob |
| 11. *Yusuf* | Joseph |
| 12. *Shu'aib* | — |
| 13. *Ayyub* | Job |
| 14. *Musa* | Moses |
| 15. *Harun* | Aaron |
| 16. *Dhu'l-kifl* | Ezekiel |
| 17. *Dawud* | David |
| 18. *Sulaiman* | Solomon |
| 19. *Ilias* | Elijah |
| 20. *Al-Yasa'* | Elisha |
| 21. *Yunus* | Jonah |
| 22. *Zakariyya* | Zechariah |
| 23. *Yahya* | John |
| 24. *'Isa* | Jesus |
| 25. *Muhammad* | — |

**Figure 10.1**

## Qualifications of a Prophet

Human. Male. Infallible. These three characteristics define all of the Islamic prophets.

*Human.* This belief negates the possibility that any prophet could have been God incarnate. Muslims see a conflict in associating anything with God, and cannot comprehend the possibility of God coming to earth in the form of a human being.[12]

Mohammed is highly revered as a prophet of Islam, and his lifestyle and teaching affect Islam more than any other prophet. However, although much adoration is ascribed to him, orthodox Islam asserts that he is not to be worshiped, because he is only a human being, not a deity.

*Male.* The Qur'an contains stories primarily about men, with the occasional report of a woman associated in some way with a prophet, or a story about a woman of outstanding character. Qur'anic evidence, as well as the traditions of Mohammed and rulings of Islamic Law, lead one to infer that no prophetic word could come from a female.

*Infallible.* The general Muslim populace believes that prophets were sinless, or at least innocent of any major sins. How could a prophet communicate the truths of God if he had committed serious sin? Many Muslims believe that since nothing happens outside of Allah's will, Allah prevented these special prophets from committing any major sin. Abdalati expands this idea: "All the prophets of God were men of good character and high honor....Their honesty and truthfulness, their intelligence and integrity are beyond doubt. They were infallible in that they did not commit sins or violate the Law of God."[13]

Many Muslims do not accept the biblical accounts of God's prophets because they cannot conceive that a genuine prophet would commit a serious sin. Recall David's (*Dawud*) adultery with Bathsheba and his virtual command to slay her husband, or Moses' (*Musa*) murder of an Egyptian, or Noah's (*Nuh*) drunkenness. All are unacceptable to Muslims. Islamic theology asserts that Christians must have corrupted the Bible

# Jesus Never Sinned
## (According to the Qur'an)

**ADAM**
"They said: Our Lord! we have WRONGED ourselves. If Thou forgive us not and have not mercy on us, surely we are of the lost!" (surah 7:23)

**ABRAHAM**
"And Who, I ardently hope, will forgive me my SIN on the Day of Judgement." (surah 26:82)

**MOSES**
"He said: My Lord! Lo! I have WRONGED my soul, so forgive me." (surah 28:16)

**DAVID**
"...and he sought forgiveness of his Lord, and he bowed himself and he fell down prostrate and REPENTED." (surah 38:24)

**MOHAMMED**
"...and ask forgiveness for thy SIN and for believing men...." (surah 47:19)

**JESUS**
**NEVER SINNED!**

© Abraham Sarker 2004

*Figure 10.2*

because it recounts occasions when important prophets committed some "major sins."

Even so, the Qur'an yet records several incidents when the Islamic prophets had to ask forgiveness for a sin they had committed! Even Mohammed is documented to have repented. In fact, the Qur'an records an incident of sinning for all of the major prophets, with just one exception: Jesus! It is very interesting that the prophet continually on the lips of Muslims was emphatically *not* sinless. As the Qur'an records in surah 47:19, Allah commanded Mohammed to "ask forgiveness for thy sin and for believing men." Yet according to the Islamic Holy Scriptures, the honored prophet Jesus never committed a single sin as demonstrated in figure 10.2 on the facing page.

Christian observers might well want to know, why then do Muslims believe that Mohammed held a superior role? Why do Muslims consider Mohammed the greater prophet?

### The Prophet Jesus in Islam

Muslims accept many fascinating details about the life of Jesus. Yet while the Qur'an and the Bible use several identical terms to describe Jesus, they mean distinctly different things.

If you were to ask a Muslim, "Do you believe in Jesus, the Messiah?" he or she will answer "yes," usually with great conviction. So if Muslims already believe in Jesus, then what makes Islam so different from Christianity? This issue has brought about much confusion for the casual observer, yet a deeper look into what these two faiths believe about Jesus Christ reveals an amazing and life-changing difference.

The name of Jesus ('Isa in Arabic) is mentioned ninety-seven times in the Qur'an. He is given such honorary titles as "the Messiah" (surah 4:171; 5:72), "the Spirit of God," and "the Word of God" (surah 4:169-171). He is considered a "Sign unto Men" and "Mercy from (God)" (surah 19:21), as well as "the Speech of Truth" (surah 19:34).

Christian theology connects such terms to the divine nature of Christ, whereas "to the Muslim they lack entirely the

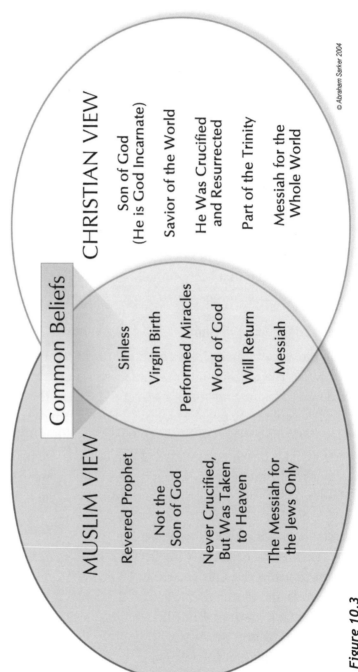

## Jesus
### (Muslim and Christian Views)

© Abraham Sarker 2004

**CHRISTIAN VIEW**

Son of God
(He is God Incarnate)

Savior of the World

He Was Crucified
and Resurrected

Part of the Trinity

Messiah for the
Whole World

**Common Beliefs**

Sinless

Virgin Birth

Performed Miracles

Word of God

Will Return

Messiah

**MUSLIM VIEW**

Revered Prophet

Not the
Son of God

Never Crucified,
But Was Taken
to Heaven

The Messiah for
the Jews Only

*Figure 10.3*

content of deity."[14] Islam claims that Jesus was nothing but a prophet of Allah and denies that He is the Son of God. It also denies His crucifixion and resurrection and His role as the Savior of the world. And yet it does not deny everything the Bible teaches about Him. Note the similarities and differences between the Muslim and Christian views of Jesus as illustrated in figure 10.3.

### The Virgin Birth of Jesus

Both the Qur'an and the Bible document the miraculous birth of Jesus through the Virgin Mary, although the Qur'an gives a briefer version with a few varying elements.

Surah 66:12 states that the Spirit of God breathed upon Mary: "And Mary, daughter of Imran, whose body was chaste, therefore We breathed therein something of Our Spirit. And she put faith in the words of her Lord and His Scriptures, and was of the obedient." The Islamic account asserts that the angel Gabriel delivered a message of the miraculous conception of Jesus to Mary:

> He [Gabriel] said: I am only a messenger of thy Lord, that I may bestow on thee a faultless son.
>
> She [Mary] said: How can I have a son when no mortal hath touched me, neither have I been unchaste!
>
> He [Gabriel] said: So (it will be). Thy Lord saith: It is easy for Me. And (it will be) that We may make of him a revelation for mankind and a mercy from Us, and it is a thing ordained. (surah 19:19-21)

Muslim scholarship insists that Jesus cannot be called the Son of God just because He had no earthly father. Ahmed Deedat, the illustrious Muslim apologist, argues, "If Jesus is God, and the very Son of God because He has no earthly father, then Adam is a greater God because he had no father and no mother!"[15]

Virgin born, certainly. But Son of God? Not to a Muslim.

### Jesus Is the Messiah

In eleven of the ninety-seven times Jesus is mentioned in the Qur'an, He is afforded the title, "the Messiah Jesus," or "*Al-Masihu-Isa*" (surah 4:171; 5:72). Still, the Qur'an insists that this Messiah is no greater than any of the other prophets.

Such a contention, of course, causes some confusion, for nowhere does the Qur'an explain exactly who or what the Messiah is. In some Islamic teaching, Messiah means "the anointed one," and therefore this title also applies to Mohammed.

Muslims also insist that Jesus was the Messiah for the Jews only; they limit His ministry to His own people group. Mohammed, on the other hand, was a messenger sent for all of mankind. Noted author on Islamic themes, Kenneth Cragg, writes that "Jesus had a specific—some would say limited—mission to Jewry....Only Muhammad as the 'seal of the prophets' belongs to all times and places."[16]

### Jesus Is the Word of God

While Muslims do not believe that Jesus was the Son of God, the Qur'an does call Him "the Word of God." Surah 4:171 declares, "the Messiah, Jesus son of Mary, was only a messenger of Allah, and His word which He conveyed unto Mary, and a spirit from Him."

Christian theology invests this title with far more meaning than does its Islamic counterpart. Muslims believe that Jesus spoke the words of God, but little else.

### Jesus Performed Miracles

Both the Qu'ran and the Bible agree that Jesus performed miracles. Surah 5:110 references a few of these miracles:

> Then will Allah say: "O Jesus the son of Mary!...Behold! I strengthened thee with the holy spirit so that thou didst speak to the people in childhood and in maturity....And behold! [Thou] makest out of clay as it were the figure of a bird by My leave and thou breathest into it and it becometh

a bird by My leave and thou healest those born blind and the lepers by My leave. And behold! [Thou] bringest forth the dead by My leave.

Of the miracles mentioned in this passage, the Bible makes no mention of Jesus speaking as a newborn infant or of His making a living bird from clay. Yet both books affirm that Jesus did miraculous deeds.

### Was Jesus Really Crucified?

Islam teaches that Allah protected all His prophets and never allowed any of them to be killed. This explains why Muslims deny the crucifixion of Jesus.

In surah 5:110, Allah describes how He prevented the Jews from killing Jesus: "And behold! I did restrain the Children of Israel from (violence to) thee when thou didst show them the Clear Signs and the unbelievers among them said: 'This is nothing but evident magic.'" The assertion that Jesus was not crucified is also made in surah 4:157: "they said (in boast) 'We killed Christ Jesus the son of Mary, the Apostle of Allah'; but they killed him not nor crucified him but so it was made to appear to them."

Much of Islamic scholarship follows an interpretation similar to that found in the *Gospel of Barnabas*, rather than the biblical record. Scholars believe that this pseudo-gospel was probably written after A.D. 1300.[17] In fact, no copy of the *Gospel of Barnabas* can be found dating to before the 1500s.[18] No writers, Muslim or Christian, ever referred to it until the sixteenth century. It even contradicts the Qur'an twenty times, and has Jesus denying that he was the Messiah, something unacceptable to either Muslim or Christian sources.[19] Still, it gives a unique slant on the crucifixion of Jesus:

> Jesus answered "...God in order that I be not mocked of the demons on the day of judgment, hath willed that I be mocked of men in his world by the death of Judas, making all men to believe that I died upon the cross. And this mock-

ing shall continue until the advent of Mohammed, the messenger of God, who, when he shall come, shall reveal this deception to those who believe God's law.[20]

Scholar J. Jomier's extensive research on this text showed "beyond any doubt that the G.B.V. (*Gospel of Barnabas*, Vienna ms.) contains an islamicised late medieval gospel forgery."[21]

Despite the historical evidence, Muslims generally believe that God miraculously saved Jesus from a mob of attacking Jews by miraculously changing Judas' face to look like that of Jesus, so that the mob really crucified Judas in Jesus' place. Jesus did not die, because Allah "raised him up" to heaven (surah 4:157-158). Therefore Jesus remains alive in heaven until the day he is to return to earth.

One ambiguity about the final events of Jesus' life remains in Islamic teaching. In surah 19:33, Jesus is recorded as stating, "Peace on me the day I was born, and the day I die, and the day I shall be raised alive!" Although this sounds similar to the New Testament prophecies Jesus made about His death and resurrection,[22] Muslims deny the passage has anything to do with crucifixion or resurrection. They maintain that the text relates to Jesus' second coming, when He will die and be raised to life again, like all other prophets on the Day of Judgment.

Islam teaches that Jesus did not die, but is alive today in heaven, and will return one day to earth. But why will He return? The purpose for Jesus' return differs significantly in the Christian and Muslim perspectives.

### Why Will Jesus Return?

Both Islam and Christianity affirm that Jesus will return to earth. But according to Islam, Jesus will return to earth just before the end times in order to accomplish several specific objectives. He will:

1. Kill the Antichrist (*al-Dajjal*)
2. Kill all the pigs

3. Destroy all the synagogues and churches

4. Break the cross

5. Establish the religion of Islam

6. Live for forty years

7. Marry

8. Die and be buried beside Mohammed in the prophet mosque of Medina.[23]

While the Bible would concur with only the first of these reasons for the Second Coming, Muslims hold passionately to all eight.

### Did Jesus Foretell Mohammed's Coming?

Muslims teach that in his role as prophet, Jesus foretold Mohammed's coming. Can Islam produce any biblical support for such a claim?

Many Christians recognize the passage in John 14:16-17 where Jesus says, "I will ask the Father, and he will give you another Counselor to be with you forever—the Spirit of truth. The world cannot accept him, because it neither sees him nor knows him. But you know him, for he lives with you and will be in you." The Christian would say Jesus is here speaking about the Holy Spirit, who would come at Pentecost to comfort believers.

Muslim theologians insist, however, that Jesus instead was foretelling the coming of Mohammed. They cite two reasons for this. First, the Greek word used for Counselor or Comforter is *paracletos*, similar to the word "*Ahmad*" in Arabic—another name for Mohammed.[24] Second, in surah 61:6, Jesus is said to have prophesied that Mohammed was coming next, in order to finish the work that He could not do: "[I give] glad [tidings] of an Apostle to come after me whose name shall be Ahmad."

Muslims simply cannot accept that Mohammed's coming is not prophesied in previous Scriptures, as they believe it should be.

### Mohammed, Seal of the Prophets

No discussion of the Islamic prophets would be complete without mentioning the central and greatest prophet of all, Mohammed. Surah 3 describes him as the "Seal of the Prophets" because his revelation supersedes all previous revelations. He brought the final and most complete revelation from Allah.

After Mohammed, Allah stopped sending prophets, because no others were necessary. Mohammed had received all of the revelation Allah planned to send to humankind until the end of time.

Islam reveres not only the Qur'an, dictated by Mohammed, but also the traditions (Hadith) of the sayings and the actions (*sunnah*) of the prophet. These collections were compiled two to three hundred years after Mohammed's death, yet the faithful heavily rely on them to interpret the Qur'an.

### What Does the Bible Say?

What does the Bible have to say about God's prophets, especially in regard to some of the claims and teachings of Islam?

First, the Bible has no problem with admitting the sin—even the vilest sin—of God's prophets, for these stories reaffirm that all human beings have a sinful nature. Yet it teaches that when a sinner repents, God forgives his or her sins and restores that believer to close fellowship with Himself. Even though David made some terribly poor choices as a king of Israel, Scripture could legitimately describe him as "a man after God's own heart" (1 Samuel 13:14) because of his repentant attitude, sincere faith, and passionate desire to walk in the ways of God. These stories illustrate the loving, forgiving nature of Yahweh and His redemptive plan for all who come to Him in faith. Humans don't have to be perfect to be used for God's glory.

Second, many prophecies about the Messiah given by earlier Hebrew prophets were fulfilled by Jesus Christ. The prophet Isaiah foretold the virgin birth of Jesus: "Therefore the LORD himself will give you a sign: The virgin will be with child and will give birth to a son, and will call him Immanuel [God with us]" (Isaiah 7:14). The first chapter of the Gospel of Matthew affirms that Jesus was "God with us," making possible God's plan of salvation for the world through the incarnation of Christ.

Luke 1:30-38 gives an account of Jesus' miraculous conception and Mary's obedience to God's plan. The angel Gabriel also affirms that Jesus will be called the Son of God. Christianity sees Jesus as the Son of God, not because of His biological relationship to almighty God, but because of His unique covenant fellowship with almighty God.

Third, the Bible agrees with the Qur'an that Jesus was sinless. Hebrews 4:14-15 declares, "Therefore, since we have a great high priest who has gone through the heavens, Jesus the Son of God, …one who has been tempted in every way, just as we are—yet was without sin." The sinless life of Jesus Christ is especially significant to the Christian because "God made him who had no sin to be sin for us, so that in him we might become the righteousness of God" (2 Corinthians 5:21). It is through sinless Jesus' sacrificial death on the cross that sinful mankind has a way to fellowship with a holy God.

Fourth, from the Jewish and Christian perspective, the title of Messiah, "anointed one," has enormous significance. While the "anointed one" could refer to a few special positions in Jewish history—such as the high priest (Leviticus 4:3), the nation's king (2 Samuel 1:14), and the prophets of God (Psalm 105:15)—the Bible gives several detailed prophecies of a unique Messiah from the line of David whose kingdom would never end.

The Bible prophesied that this coming Messiah would be born in Bethlehem (Micah 5:2) of King David's lineage (Isaiah 11:1-5). Yet as the "son of man," it insisted that He had existed from before time began (Micah 5:2) and that all people would worship Him forever (Daniel 7:13-14). The hands and feet of this Messiah would be pierced and people would cast lots for his clothing—details fulfilled during the crucifixion of Christ (Psalm 22; cf. Luke 24:39; Mark 15:24). Because Jesus fulfilled these and many other prophecies spoken about Him, Christians concluded that He was indeed the Messiah predicted by so many prophets of old.

Even John the Baptist, Jesus' contemporary, recognized that Jesus was the Messiah: "This was he of whom I said, 'He who comes after me has surpassed me because he was before me'" (John 1:15). Jesus Himself confirmed that His coming blessed not only Israel, but all people. He told the Roman centurion who had asked Jesus to heal his servant, "I tell you the truth, I have not found anyone in Israel with such great faith. I say to you that many will come from the east and the west, and will take their places at the feast with Abraham, Isaac, and Jacob in the kingdom of heaven" (Matthew 8:10-11). The gift of salvation through this Messiah is available to all, "because it is the power of God for the salvation of everyone who believes: first for the Jew, then for the Gentile" (Romans 1:16). Jesus as the Messiah benefits all of humanity, not just the Jewish nation.

Fifth, when the Bible refers to Jesus as the Word of God, it places tremendous significance in the fact that this Word existed with God eternally before the world began. Consider John 1:1-3, where Jesus' role is developed further: "In the beginning was the Word, and the Word was with God, and the Word was God. He was with God in the beginning. Through him all things were made; without him nothing was made that has been made."

This passage clearly presents Jesus, the Word of God, as fully God, the vehicle through which God created all things. Islam mentions this term only in passing without explaining its significance, but the New Testament uses it to describe the full deity of Jesus Christ.

Sixth, the Bible recounts numerous miracles of Jesus, including healing the blind[25] (something no Old Testament prophet ever did) and lepers,[26] and raising people from death to life,[27] similar to a few shorter references in the Qur'an. Yet Jesus performed many other miracles not described in the Qur'an, such as feeding five thousand people from one single lunch,[28] walking on water,[29] and casting out demons.[30]

The greatest miracle of all—Jesus' resurrection from the dead—is not recorded in the Qur'an. Yet the Bible provides strong historical evidence for the crucifixion and resurrection of Jesus, verified by many witnesses and confirmed by an abundance of ancient manuscripts (more than 5,000 copies of the New Testament date back to within 100 to 225 years of their first-century composition). Distinguished Christian apologist Norman Geisler asserts, "The New Testament is the most highly documented book from the ancient world!"[31]

Moreover, not only does the Bible proclaim the death and resurrection of Jesus, but several non-Christian historians of the first and second centuries attest to the events surrounding the death of Jesus. Among these recorders of Jesus' life and death are the Jewish historian Josephus; the Roman historian Cornelius Tacitus; and others.[32] Furthermore, the disciples of Jesus not only professed faith in the death and resurrection of Jesus, but they willingly gave up their lives for it.

Even though this evidence of Jesus Christ's death and resurrection was available at the time of Mohammed, he either ignorantly or purposefully denied the truths of the Scriptures given by the prophets he claimed to join.

And what of the Second Coming of Christ? Christianity proclaims that Jesus will come back suddenly, at a time no one knows, except God. He will return in the same way he ascended, in the clouds, visibly, with a loud command and a trumpet sound. Jesus will usher in the resurrection, the dead in Christ shall rise first, and the righteous still living will be caught up with Him in the clouds. At that time He will sort out the righteous from the unrighteous (Matthew 24–25; 1 Thessalonians 4:13-18). Pointedly, the biblical account does *not* include a time of marriage or building a physical, human family for Jesus.

Last, does the Bible really prophesy Mohammed's coming? The Islamic interpretation of John 14:16-17 simply does not align with the rest of the New Testament's description of the "Counselor." It cannot be Mohammed, for the Bible says this Counselor will be with the believers forever (John 14:16); he lives "with us and in us" (even within the believers of Jesus' day, 14:17); and he will convict the world of guilt in regard to sin (16:8). Mohammed could not have fulfilled any of these descriptions and could not therefore have been the one prophesied by Jesus. Rather, Jesus was describing the third person in the Trinity, the Holy Spirit, who came at Pentecost to indwell all believers, to comfort them and guide them into all truth.

### A Final Revelation?

Muslims insist that Mohammed presented to the world a perfect religion. To investigate this claim, one must consider the Qur'an revealed to this prophet.

Why does nearly one-fifth of the world's population hold so closely to his revelation? Its contents are accepted without question by those who call themselves Muslim.

### Summary

The role of prophets in Islam is significant as they were the only human beings able to receive information directly from Allah and His angels, and as such they were also responsible to communicate Allah's wishes to mankind. Muslims accept many of the prophets common to Judaism and Christianity; however, the stories and revelations associated with these previous prophets are not necessarily the same. Although Muslims highly esteem Jesus as one of their prophets they deny His crucifixion and resurrection, and they deny that His sacrifice for mankind is part of God's plan of salvation for all. In fact, Islam considers all previous revelations incomplete, which is the reason Allah had to send the final and best prophet, Mohammed. And how does his revelation measure up to the Bible? The next chapter considers the third fundamental belief in the Qur'an and other holy Islamic scriptures.

## ° 11 °

# The Qu'ran:
# Final Word from Allah

Muslims consider Mohammed the final prophet and his revelation, the Qur'an, as the purest and most complete revelation Allah ever gave to humankind.

But why is the Qur'an considered superior to the other Scriptures also accepted in Islam? And what other Scriptures do Muslims accept?

### Prior Scriptures of Islam

Islam teaches that the message of the Qur'an came directly from Allah in order to confirm the revelations given to prophets of the past.

"The revelation of the Scripture is from Allah, the Mighty, the Wise. Lo! We have revealed the Scripture unto thee [Muhammad] with truth; so worship Allah, making religion pure for Him (only)" (surah 39:1-2). The Qur'an avows in surah 3:3 that God gave Mohammed his revelation to confirm the earlier revelations given to the Jews and Christians: "He hath revealed unto thee [Mohammed] the Scripture with truth, confirming that which was (revealed) before it, even as He revealed the Torah and the Gospel."

While it is believed that the prophets of Islam each brought a revelation from God, Muslims maintain that the books revealed to Noah (Nuh) and Abraham (Ibrahim) no longer exist. Similarly, the Torah (Tawrat) containing the five books of Moses (Musa), the Psalms (Zabur) of David (Dawud), and the Gospel (Injil) of Jesus ('Isa) no longer exist in their original form. Muslims claim that the version now possessed by Jews and Christians has been altered, with sections eliminated. "The people of the Book know this as they know their own sons; but some of them conceal the truth which they themselves know" (surah 2:146). Surah 2:101 also affirms this assumption:

> And when came to them an Apostle from Allah confirming what was with them a party of the people of the Book threw away the Book of Allah behind their backs as if (it had been something) they did not know!

Muslims claim that the Bible now in existence must be corrupt, since it does not mention Mohammed and often conflicts with statements in the Qur'an.

### Importance of the Qur'an

Muslims hold the Qur'an in high esteem as the very Word of Allah, and it is treated with the utmost of care and respect. It is the most memorized book in the world, yet only recently has it become available in languages other than Arabic.[1] While Islam sees no need for a Savior, the Qur'an serves as the ultimate guide in helping one to attain eternal life.

Often the Qur'an refers to itself as "The Explanation" (*al-Bayan*), a "Clear Argument" (*al-Burhan*), or "Light" (*an-Nur*).[2] And because the Qur'an is revered as a direct word from Allah, the text is treated with the utmost respect. Anis Shorrosh explains the Muslim's conscientious handling of the Qur'an:

> The Qur'an is held in the greatest esteem and reverence among Muslims as their holy scripture. They dare not touch it without first being washed and purified. They read it with the greatest care and respect, never holding it below their

waist. They swear by it and consult it on all occasions. They carry it with them to war, write sentences of it on their banners, suspend it from their necks as a charm, and always place it on the highest shelf or in some place of honor in their houses. It is said that the devil runs away from the house in which a portion of the Quran, Surat al-Baqarah (The Cow) 2, is read.[3]

The importance of this holy book to Muslims can also be seen in their impressive effort to memorize its contents. Special schools are set up solely for the instruction of Qur'an memorization. Once a student has successfully memorized the entire Qur'an (roughly the size of the New Testament), he or she is granted the esteemed title, *hafiz* (one who knows the Qur'an by heart).

The Qur'an is always memorized in Arabic. Some orthodox Arab Muslims insist that God does not understand (or at least listen to) prayers in any language other than Arabic. Since the Qur'an is believed to have been originally given in Arabic, many Muslims resisted translating it into other languages, for fear that its meaning would be misconstrued. Hence, only very hesitantly has the Qur'an been translated into other languages, and many who memorize and read the Qur'an have great difficulty understanding its meanings. To become a hafiz, one does not need to understand what he or she is reciting, but merely be able to recite the Qur'an accurately.

### Origin of the Qur'an

The Qur'an is believed to have been in existence in heaven from eternity, "Nay, but it is a glorious Qur'an [on] a guarded tablet" (surah 85:21-22), yet it was not fully revealed to humankind until the angel Gabriel spoke it to Mohammed over a twenty-three year period.

According to Islam, the Qur'an had to be revealed because previous revelations were incomplete. The Qur'an confirms (and where necessary revises) the previous revelations in the Bible, and it supersedes all other texts.

The word *Qur'an* actually means "recite" or "read" in Arabic, and the first editions of the Qur'an relied heavily on disciples who memorized and recited Mohammed's own oral recitation.

The role of a prophet is to speak what Allah reveals. "It is not fitting for a man that Allah should speak to him except by inspiration or from behind a veil or by the sending of a Messenger to reveal with Allah's permission what Allah wills: for He is Most High Most Wise" (surah 42:51).

Thus, as portions of the Qur'an were revealed to Mohammed, he became the conduit to funnel them to mankind. Inspiration came to Mohammed in different ways, such as through dreams and visions, but also during seizure-like experiences in which he would fall to the ground, sweat, shiver, and hear a loud bell ringing in his ears. 'Umar ibnu'l Khattab, an early biographer of Mohammed, asserts that Mohammed roared like a camel and foamed at the mouth during these experiences.[4]

### Compilation of the Qur'an

Many devout believers memorized the surahs that Mohammed recited in their presence, and tradition asserts that scribes recorded some portions on pieces of paper, palm-leaves, bits of leather, stones, and bones, whatever was available at the time of revelation. Until Mohammed's death, the Qur'an existed only on scattered objects and in the hearts of loyal Muslims.

A year after Mohammed's death, however, many of the hafizes had died; many were killed in the battle of Yamamah in A.D. 633. Umar, the second caliph of Islam, ordered that the Qur'an be collected, lest it might be lost forever with the death of these reciters. So Zayd Ibn Thabit was appointed to the task of collecting the scattered parts of the Qur'an.[5]

Later, during the reign of Uthman, the third Muslim caliph, another predicament arose. Several conflicting versions of the Qur'an were circulating among various Muslim communities. Uthman feared doctrinal confusion might occur, and hence

Zayd was ordered to undertake a new project, this time revising and editing the Qur'an. Uthman ordered that all copies in the Islamic empire be sent to him, and ordered Zayd and his committee to compile the surahs into one manuscript.

When scribes discovered differences in the surahs, Uthman instructed Zayd to take out any text not in the Qur'aish dialect. Then, after production of a revised version, several copies were sent to each of the major headquarters of the Islamic empire. The remaining copies were recalled and burned.[6] In this way, all of the eyewitness accounts were destroyed, leaving only one edited copy as a witness to the Qur'an's authenticity.

Popular Orthodox Muslim theory tells a completely different story. It maintains that the Qur'an was assembled in the same form in which it exists today, under the direct supervision of angel Gabriel and prophet Mohammed.[7] Substantial historical evidence, however, shows that Uthman assembled and sent out his official copies some forty years after Mohammed started preaching, a full sixteen years after the prophet's death.

### Organization of the Qur'an

The Qur'an is not organized chronologically or thematically, but in general, from the longest to shortest surahs (except for the first surah, which acts as a brief opening prayer). A close examination of the Qur'an reveals substantial differences between the revelations given in the Meccan period (A.D. 611-615), and the Medinan period (A.D. 623-632).

The Meccan revelations are characteristically shorter in both verse and surah length, and they deal mainly with warnings against idolatry and impending judgment. They also include doctrines and stories taken and adapted from the Pentateuch.

In contrast, the Medinan revelations are longer both in verse and surah length. These surahs deal more with legislative rules for family and civil life, as well as the commands for jihad (holy war).[8]

### The Qur'an and the People of the Book

Mohammed insisted that the Qur'an confirmed the earlier scriptures, referring to the text of the "People of the Book." But how does the Qur'an view the "People of the Book"?

In the Meccan and early Medinan period, the Qur'an takes a friendly attitude toward Jews and Christians. "Lo! those who believe (in that which is revealed unto thee, Muhammad), and those who are Jews, and Christians, and Sabaeans whoever believeth in Allah and the Last Day and doeth right surely their reward is with their Lord, and there shall no fear come upon them neither shall they grieve" (surah 2:62).

Muslims were encouraged to live peaceably with the "People of the Book," even to accept their Scriptures:

> And argue not with the People of the Scripture unless it be in (a way) that is better, save with such of them as do wrong; and say: We believe in that which hath been revealed unto us and revealed unto you; our God and your God is One, and unto Him we surrender. (surah 29:46)

Mohammed even insisted that Muslims refer to the knowledge of the "People of the Book" if they had a question about their own Qur'an: "ask those who have been reading the Book from before thee" (surah 10:94). Not surprisingly, the majority of the stories in the Qur'an are based on Old and New Testament narratives.

After Jews and Christians in Medina rejected Mohammed, however, he took a different attitude toward these two religious groups, even admonishing Muslims not to become friends with them: "O ye who believe! [T]ake not for friends and protectors those who take your religion for a mockery or sport whether among those who received the Scripture before you [Jews and Christians] or among those who reject faith" (surah 5:57). His affirmation of the salvation of Jews and Christians also changed: "If anyone desires a religion other than Islam (submission to Allah) never will it be accepted of him; and in the Hereafter he will be in the ranks of those who have lost (all spiritual good)" (surah 3:85).

When the Jews and Christians refused to accept Mohammed as a prophet, he accused the "People of the Book" of concealing and misinterpreting Scripture. Surah 5:13-15 illustrates Mohammed's teaching on the corruption of the Jews and Christians and the necessity for the complete revelation of the Qur'an:

> But because of their breach of their Covenant We cursed them and made their hearts grow hard: they change the words from their (right) places and forget a good part of the Message that was sent them nor wilt thou cease to find them barring a few ever bent on (new) deceits: ...From those too who call themselves Christians We did take a Covenant but they forgot a good part of the Message that was sent them so We estranged them with enmity and hatred between the one and the other to the Day of Judgment. And soon will Allah show them what it is they have done: O People of the Book! there hath come to you Our Apostle revealing to you much that ye used to hide in the Book and passing over much (that is now unnecessary): There hath come to you from Allah a (new) Light and a perspicuous Book.

Yet if Allah's words never change, and "no change can there be in the Words of Allah" (surah 10:64), then how did the Jews and Christians manage to possess only a corrupted version of the original, perfect copy of the Gospel, the Torah, and the Psalms of David? This question remains to be addressed by Islamic scholarship.

### Qur'anic Conflicts with the Bible

The Qur'an is believed to be divine dictation from Allah to Mohammed. In contrast, the Bible is believed to be the inspired Word of God, messages relayed to humans, but through men who spoke or wrote them engaging their own language, thought patterns, and personalities (2 Timothy 3:16, 17).

Jeremiah spoke as a preacher inspired by God, and David as an inspired poet, etc.

Yet, while the Qur'an is believed to be a confirmation *of* the previous scriptures, there is actually a significant amount of contradiction *to* them. Many narratives from the Old and New Testament are hinted at in the Qur'an; however, significant differences in detail and purpose are present. A few examples follow.

**Sacrifice of Ishmael.** The Qur'an's version of Abraham's near sacrifice of his son is believed to involve Ishmael (surah 37:100-111), the father of the Arab people, rather than Isaac, as the Bible teaches (Genesis 22).

**Adoption of Moses.** Surah 28:9 insists that it was Pharoah's wife who adopted Moses, rather than Pharoah's daughter (Exodus 2:10). This change would make Moses heir to the royal throne of Egypt.

**Samaritans construct the golden calf.** According to surah 20:85-97 the calf worshiped by the Israelites in the desert at Mount Horeb was constructed by a Samaritan. However, Exodus 32:2-4 states that Aaron constructed the idol. Furthermore, the term *Samaritan* was not used until 722 B.C., several hundred years after this incident recorded in Exodus.[9]

**Trinity.** Islam's holy book relates the Trinity as three different gods, existing as Father God, Mother Mary, and Son Jesus (surah 5:116; 4:171), whereas the Bible teaches the Trinity as one God, but existing in three expressions, as the Father, Son, and Holy Spirit (John 17:21; Matthew 28:18-19).

**Jesus.** The Qur'an insists that Jesus was not the Son of God, and that He was never crucified, and therefore, never resurrected (surahs 4:157; 5:110; 5:75), emphatically rejecting this issue as stated in the Bible (John 1:1-3; John 20:31; 1 Corinthians 15:1-4). This denial of the gospel rejects God's plan of salvation through Jesus' sacrifice as well. Conversely, Muslims adhere to the teaching that one must save oneself by performing good works, rather than accepting God's free gift of salvation through faith in Christ.

### The Role of the Qur'an

Some assert that the Qur'an's place in Islam is not equivalent to the Bible's place in Christianity, but more precisely, to the role of Jesus Christ Himself. The Muslim writer Yusuf K. Ibish made the following interesting statement about the Qur'an:

> It is not a book in the ordinary sense, nor is it comparable to the Bible, either the Old or New Testaments…If you want to compare it with anything in Christianity, you must compare it with Christ Himself….Christ was the expression of the Divine among men, the revelation of the Divine Will. That is what the Qur'an is.[10]

The Word of God in Islam became the Qur'an, a tangible book, whereas in Christianity the Word of God is Jesus, who became flesh and dwelt among us. Kenneth Cragg offers another comparison between the Qur'an and Jesus:

> The revelation (Qur'an) communicated God's Law. It does not reveal God Himself…the genius of Islam is finally law and not theology. In the last analysis, the sense of God is a sense of Divine command. In the will of God there is none of the mystery that surrounds His being. His demands are known and the believers' task is not so much exploratory, still less fellowship, but rather obedience and allegiance.[11]

Christianity says that God discloses Himself through Jesus. By contrast, Islam emphasizes not an understanding of or a personal relationship with God, but rather, a book that reveals the commands of Allah.

### Authenticity of the Qur'an

Muslim scholarship presents several arguments to show why the Qur'an is the absolute Word of God:

- Its extraordinary literary style
- Its recitation by an illiterate prophet

- Its preservation

- Its unity

- Its fulfilled prophecies

- Its ability to change lives

### 1. Unique literary style of the Qur'an

When recited in Arabic, the Qur'an does present a melodious, eloquent rhythm. The Qur'an itself asserts its amazing qualities: "this Qur'an is not such as can be produced by other than Allah" (surah 10:37). Also, "If the whole of mankind and Jinns were to gather together to produce the like of this Qur'an, they could not produce the like thereof even if they backed up each other with help and support" (surah 17:88).

Nevertheless, it is not the sole work in Arabic or among other languages that possesses such poetic eloquence and strength. C.G. Pfander, the Islamic academician, stresses, "It is by no means the universal opinion of unprejudiced Arabic scholars that the literary style of the Qur'an is superior to that of all other books in the Arabic language."[12] Mohammed was obviously gifted in poetry, but other texts such as Shakespeare's work and Homer's *Odyssey* and *Iliad* display a similar brilliance in their own languages. Can beauty and elegance really prove a text's divine inspiration?

Although the Qur'an contains eloquently rhyming portions, many critics claim that it is not without error.[13] Ali Dashti, the Iranian Shiite scholar, attests to grammatical irregularities within the Qur'an:

> The Qur'an contains sentences which are incomplete and not fully intelligible without the aid of commentaries; foreign words, unfamiliar Arabic words, and words used with other than the normal meaning; adjectives and verbs inflected without observance of the concord of gender and number; illogical and ungrammatically applied pronouns which sometimes have no referent; and predicates which in rhymed passages are often remote from the subjects.[14]

Furthermore, not everyone who has read the Qur'an agrees upon its magnificence. Carlyle, speaking for many Westerners, says: "It is as toilsome reading as I ever undertook, a wearisome, confused jumble, crude, incondite. Nothing but a sense of duty could carry any European through the Koran."[15]

With the ambiguous grouping of text within surahs and the lack of chronological grouping of the surahs themselves, many Muslims rely heavily on the Hadith, written two to three hundred years after the prophet's death, to clarify and expand upon the Qur'an. While the Qur'an conveys the essence of the message of Mohammed, many question its "perfection" and whether it is divinely inspired at all. Dr. Tisdall says of the Qur'an:

> The Qur'an breathes the air of the desert, it enables us to hear the battle-cries of the Prophet's followers as they rushed to the onset, it reveals the working of Mohammed's own mind, and shows the gradual declension of his character as he passed from the earnest and sincere though visionary enthusiast into the conscious imposter and open sensualist.[16]

The Qur'an does display eloquent rhythm and rhyme—but as to its perfection and divine utterance, many have their doubts.

### 2. Was Mohammed really illiterate?

Muslims declare that the Qur'an is a miracle in itself, since the man who originally recited it was illiterate. By the same reasoning, they say Mohammed's recitation of the Qur'an affirms his claims to prophethood.

For several reasons, critics have questioned the claim of Mohammed's illiteracy.

First, the word used to describe Mohammed's illiteracy is *al ummi* in Arabic (see surah 7:157), meaning "the unlettered one." But this term is also used to describe "the Gentile Prophet," as Mohammed is called in other surahs (see 62:2).[17]

Second, tradition records two incidents in which Mohammed would have needed literacy skills. Mohammed signed the
Treaty of Hudaibah, striking out "Apostle of Allah" when the
Meccans refused to accept that title, and writing in its place,
"Son of Abdu'llah."[18] Also, on his deathbed, Mohammed is said
to have asked for pen and ink in order to appoint a successor,
but he died before he could write down the name.[19] The emi-
nent scholar of Islam, W. Montgomery Watt, asserts that "it is
known that many Meccans were able to read and write, and
there is therefore a presumption that an efficient merchant, as
Muhammad was, knew something of the art."[20]

Finally, Muslim scholars regard Mohammed as "perfect in
intellect."[21] Mohammed was known as a prolific poet, and an
intelligent man such as himself would not have been the first to
teach himself to read and write.

For all these reasons, significant doubts surround the claim
that Mohammed was illiterate.

### 3. Perfect preservation of the Qur'an

Has the Qur'an been perfectly preserved? And if so, would that
indicate divine inspiration?

Several critics deny the perfect preservation of the Qur'an.
The only extant version is the compilation by Uthman; all original copies by eyewitnesses were burned.

While the Qur'anic version that stands today is a faithful
copy of the revision by Uthman, this remaining copy does not
exactly reflect Mohammed's original.[22] Researchers assert that
several varying texts existed prior to Uthman's revision. In his
book, *Materials for the History of the Text of the Qur'an*, the distinguished European archaeologist Arthur Jeffrey addressed the
state of the Qur'an prior to Uthman's standardization of the
text.

> When we come to the accounts of 'Uthman's recension, it
> quickly becomes clear that his work was no mere matter of
> removing dialectical peculiarities in reading [as many Mus-

lims claim], but was a necessary stroke of policy to establish a standard text for the whole empire...there were wide divergences between the collections that had been digested into Codices in the great Metropolitan centres of Medina, Mecca, Basra, Kufa and Damascus....Uthman's solution was to canonize the Medinan Codex and order all others to be destroyed...there can be little doubt that the text canonized by 'Uthman was only one among several types of text in existence at the time.[23]

Another discrepancy regards the so-called "Satanic Verses" inserted into the text of the Qur'an. According to one version from an early revelation in Mecca, Allah allowed intercession with certain idols:

Did you consider al-hat and al-Uzza

And al-Manat, the third, the other?

Those are the swans exalted;

Their intercession is expected;

Their likes are not neglected. (surah 53:21-23)

Sometime later, Mohammed received another revelation that omitted the lines about interceding to pagan gods. Apparently both versions were recited publicly; Mohammed explained that Satan had tricked him by inserting the fallacious verses without his knowledge.[24]

Some Muslims have tried to discredit this story, but it seems implausible that later generations of Muslims would have invented such a tale about their own prophet. One contemporary Muslim, Rahman, viewed this incident as plainly logical because it would assert that Mohammed was still a human being, who can make mistakes. Montgomery Watt explains:

The first thing to be said about the story is that it cannot be a sheer invention. Muhammad must at some point have recited as part of the Qur'an the verses which were later rejected as satanic in origin. No Muslim could possibly have invented such a story about Muhammad, and no reputable

Muslim scholar would have accepted it from a non-Muslim unless fully convinced of its truth. The Muslims of today tend to reject the story since it contradicts their idealized picture of Muhammad; but, on the other hand it could be taken as evidence that Muhammad was "a human being like themselves" (41:6…).[25]

Another incident related in the Hadith raises a question as to the divine, direct preservation of the Qur'an. Abdollah b. Abi Sarh served as one of Mohammed's scribes in Medina. Dashti narrates the following story regarding this scribe:

On a number of occasions he had, with the Prophet's consent, changed the closing words of verses. For example, when the Prophet had said, "And God is mighty and wise" ('aziz, hakim), 'Abdollah b. Abi Sarh suggested writing down "knowing and wise" ('alim, hakim), and the Prophet answered that there was no objection. Having observed a succession of changes of this type, 'Abdollah renounced Islam on the ground that the revelations, if from God, could not be changed at the prompting of a scribe such as himself. After his apostasy he went to Mecca and joined the Qorayshites.[26]

From these accounts, it appears likely that discrepancies about the text's preservation exist, and that the extant text may have been compiled incompletely or differently than the original Qur'an recited by Mohammed.

### 4. Unity of the Qur'an

Many Muslims claim that the Qur'an's continuity and wholly consistent contents prove its divine inspiration. Yet several critics have noted apparent contradictions within this holy book.

Several abrogations (*mansukh*) were apparently necessary in light of the corrections made in later verses (*nasikh*). Yet an explanation for the "substitutions" is given in surah 2:106: "Such of our revelations as We abrogate or cause to be forgotten, we bring (in place) one better or the like thereof. Knowest thou not that Allah is able to do all things?"

As already noted, many examples of abrogations are in-cluded in the Qur'anic text. Near the beginning of Moham-med's ministry, the Muslims are instructed to exercise tolerance toward those of other faiths (surah 2:256); yet later Muslims are urged to "slay the idolators wherever ye may find them" (surah 9:5). Again, where Allah claims that humans have a free will, "Then whosoever will, let him believe, and whosoever will, let him disbelieve" (surah 18:29), later, Allah says He has already sealed their fate in advance: "Every man's fate We have fas-tened [o]n his own neck: On the Day of Judgment We shall bring out [f]or him a scroll, Which he will see [s]pread open" (surah 17:13). A contradiction also exists in the number of days it took for the creation of the world: six, according to surah 7:54, but eight, according to surah 41:9-12. In recounting the annunciation of Mary's coming virgin birth, surah 19:17-21 states that one angel came to deliver the message, while in surahs 3:42 and 45 several angels come to announce Jesus' con-ception. Confusion remains as to how all of these variations can be considered unified, when they so evidently contradict one another.

### 5. Were prophecies of the Qur'an fulfilled?

Does the Qur'an contain accurate, supernatural prophecies that have been fulfilled, thus signifying divine revelation? Few out-side of the Muslim faith find any unusual, substantive prophe-cies within the Qur'an. Yet supporters present the following as evidence.

First, Mohammed prophesied victory in battle. He is known as the valiant warrior of Islam and has even been called "the prophet of the sword." History has shown that Islam spread rapidly by this method of conversion, particularly dur-ing its early years. Is it surprising that Mohammed, or any other religious military leader, would motivate his troops with encouragements such as, "Fight courageously, the Lord will give us victory"? Troops felt particularly motivated to fight for

Mohammed with his promises of immediate entrance into Paradise if soldiers were to be killed in a holy war (see Qur'an surah 3:157, 195), and the threat of execution for not submitting to Islam (surah 5:33). With such advertised options, it is not surprising that Mohammed claimed victory in his many battles—but does this indicate a supernatural and prophetic prediction of victory?

Another more substantive example concerns Mohammed's prediction of a Roman defeat over the Persian army, which initially occurred at Issus. "The Roman Empire has been defeated In a land close by; but they (even) after (this) defeat of theirs will soon be victorious Within a few years" (surah 30:2-4). Well-known Muslim commentator Yusuf Ali explains that "within a few years" (*bidh'un*) indicates a time period from three to nine years.[27]

In reality, the conquest of Jerusalem by the Persians occurred from A.D. 614 to 615, and the first victory in Roman retaliation occurred in A.D. 622; but they did not win a complete victory over the Persians until A.D. 625. The date of the initial prophecy of Mohammed is not clear, but even so, the final defeat of the Persians occurred in a space of at least ten to eleven years, not the required three to nine years. Additionally, the dialect of this passage did not contain vowels in Uthman's edition, and ambiguity remains as to whether the prophecy was actually "they shall defeat" (*sayaghlibuna*), or "they shall be defeated" (*sayughlabuna*), a difference of only two vowels. Furthermore, the prediction is not long-range or atypical for the time; a perceptive observer of the contemporary political situation could have predicted a similar outcome.[28]

### 6. Has the Qur'an changed lives?

Finally, apologists of the Qur'an argue for its authenticity on the basis that its revelation has changed lives. But any book that provides rules for all aspects of life should be expected to change a person's life if that individual commits to following them. Ajijola asserts the comprehensive nature of the Qur'an:

> The Qur'an is a comprehensive code of life covering every aspect and phase of human life. This Book of God lays down the best rules relating to social life, commerce and economics, marriage and inheritance, penal laws and international conduct, etc.[29]

Without question, the Qur'an has affected the lives of countless Muslims, encouraging them to submit to Allah and to perform righteous acts. And how does it compel believers to devoutly follow their faith? Why submit to Allah's commands and His will? The threat of eternal damnation and the promise of eternal paradise.

The Qur'an continually reminds Muslims about the horrific place of hell, and lists the things they must do in order to earn the opportunity to spend eternity in paradise. Muslims in Mohammed's day had one sure way of assuring their eternal destiny: dying while fighting for the cause of Allah. Warriors were promised a paradise filled with beautiful women if they would fight for the cause of Islam. Tradition states the value Mohammed placed on the sword:

> The sword is the key of heaven and of hell; a drop of blood shed in the cause of God, a night spent in arms, is of more avail than two month's fasting and prayer. Whoever falls in battle, his sins are forgiven at the day of judgment.[30]

Another perk to joining the Muslim forces: soldiers were allowed to keep four-fifths of the booty gained from victories in battle.[31] To refuse, however, meant a gruesome death in this life and an eternity of hell in the next:

> The only reward of those who make war upon Allah and His messenger and strive after corruption in the land will be that they will be killed or crucified, or have their hands and feet on alternate sides cut off, or will be expelled out of the land. Such will be their degradation in the world, and in the Hereafter theirs will be an awful doom. (surah 5:33)

Some Christians and Jews had the option to convert or pay high taxes instead (surah 9:5, 29). With such unappealing options, it is no surprise that many converted to Islam, and that the religion spread swiftly! The spread of Islam does not necessarily indicate the divine inspiration of Allah, but surely does reflect the efficacy of using force.

While adopting clear statutes for living should affect how one lives, isn't it of greater importance what those guidelines command? The doctrine of Karl Marx definitely transformed the lives of millions, but does that mean that God inspired his message?

What remains to be answered is, "Does the message of the Qur'an promote the principles that can best benefit the individual and society as a whole?" Does it change people for the better, not only outwardly, but inwardly as well?

It would not be true to say that the principles of Islam taught in the Qur'an have not had a degree of positive impact on the lives of individuals. Many moral teachings found within its pages have attracted millions of righteousness–seeking people. Yet when one compares its teachings, leaders, and cultural effects to that of previous revelations, such as the Bible, they seem to come up short.

More than a century and a half ago, William Paley, the author of *Evidences of Christianity*, summarized the issue like this:

> For what are we comparing? A Galilean peasant accompanied by a few fisherman, with a conquerer at the head of his army. We compare Jesus, without force, without power, without support, without one external circumstance of attraction or influence, prevailing against the prejudices, the learning, the hierarchy, of his country, against the ancient religious opinions, the pompous religious rites, the philosophy, the wisdom, the authority, of the Roman empire, in the most polished and enlightened period of its existence,— with Mahomet (Mohammed) making his way amongst Arabs; collecting followers in the midst of conquests and triumphs, in the darkest ages and countries of the world, and when success in arms not only operated by that com-

mand of men's wills and persons which attend prosperous undertakings, but was considered as a sure testimony of Divine approbation. That multitudes, persuaded by this argument, should join the train of a victorious chief; that still greater multitudes should, without any argument, bow down before irresistible power—is a conduct in which we cannot see much to surprise us; in which we can see nothing that resembles the causes by which the establishment of Christianity was effected.[32]

### A Christian Evaluation of the Qur'an

Muslims revere the Qur'an as the divine dictation of Allah's exact words, and therefore give it great honor and respect. A Christian who wishes to enter into dialogue with a Muslim should therefore respect the Islamic value system and carefully and lovingly address issues of difference.

Christians can never accept the Qur'an, however, as a God-inspired text. Revelation 22:18-19 declares that no part of the Bible must be omitted, nor should a newer teaching ever be incorporated into it: "I warn everyone who hears the words of the prophecy of this book: If anyone adds anything to them, God will add to him the plagues described in this book. And if anyone takes words away from this book of prophecy, God will take away from him his share in the tree of life and in the holy city, which are described in this book."

The Qur'an, by its assertion that it supersedes the Bible as God's final revelation, disqualifies itself. It contains new information contrary to the contents of the Bible and omits vital teachings contained within the Bible, in violation of Revelation 22:18-19. It denies the crucifixion and resurrection of Jesus Christ, rejects the Trinity, and repudiates God's key attributes and His plan of salvation for humankind.

Rather than communicating the desire of almighty God to have a personal, loving relationship with each individual, the Qur'an pictures a distant, unknowable Allah, whom Muslims strive to please by completing good works. Islam through the Qur'an offers laws for life, but lacks the power of the Holy Spirit necessary to follow them.

### Summary

Of Islam's holy books, Muslims advocate that previous scriptures were revealed by Allah to mankind on earth, but some have been lost. Some such as the Torah (Tawrut), Psalms (Zabur), and Gospel (Injil) have been corrupted by Jews and Christians because they do not mention Mohammed or coincide with his teaching (although they were revealed hundreds of years before him). The only book that Muslims view as accurate and valid for today is the Qur'an.

Mohammed received his revelations through dreams, visions, and intense seizures, and faithful followers recorded his revelations bits at a time over a twenty-three-year period. Cited in the Qur'an is the compilation of these revelations completed shortly after Mohammed's death, a revision taken from some forty different versions circulating at the time.

The authenticity of the Qur'an was examined on the basis of its claims to be of extraordinary literary style, recited by an illiterate prophet, preserved, unified, to have fulfilled prophecies from its contents, and having changed lives. However, from further study doubts about these claims to divine inspiration have been expressed by several scholars of the Qur'an. Furthermore, the Qur'an is not acceptable as a God-inspired book for Christians because it contradicts many areas of the previous revelation in the Bible.

Muslims are taught never to question the Qur'an as it is the absolute Word of Allah, and by following its commands they hope to find favor on the terrifying Day of Judgment, which is the fifth fundamental belief of Islam.

## ○ 12 ○

# The Day of Judgment

The doctrine of the Day of Judgment provides a dominant and highly motivating element in the religion of Islam. It inspires devoted Muslims to try to fulfill all of their prescribed duties; it rallies warriors to fight for the cause of Islam; and it strikes fear and anxiety in Muslims lying on their deathbeds. Smith and Haddad's *The Islamic Understanding of Death and Resurrection* states:

> So intense is the Qur'anic concern for and insistence on the day to come when all will be held accountable for their faith and their actions, that the ethical teachings contained in the Book must be understood in the light of this reality. Faith in the day of resurrection for the Muslim is his specific affirmation of God's omnipotence, the recognition of human accountability as a commitment to the divine [unity].[1]

The Qur'an clearly teaches that each person will be judged for his or her actions on earth, and will be rewarded or punished in the afterlife according to his or her deeds:

> Every soul shall have a taste of death: and only on the Day of Judgment shall you be paid your full recompense. Only he who is saved far from the fire and admitted to the garden will have attained the object (of life): for the life of this world is but goods and chattels of deception. (surah 3:185)

Faithful Muslims hope for heaven, while all others can expect nothing but doom and the fires of hell.

### End Times According to Islam

Islam also predicts what will happen when history finishes in the "Last Hour." Surah 33:63 contends that no one but Allah will know the time of its coming: "Men ask thee concerning the Hour: say 'The knowledge thereof is with Allah (alone)': and what will make thee understand? Perchance the Hour is nigh!"

While the exact time cannot be known, several signs will occur on earth to warn humankind that the hour is near. One Hadith from Al-Muslim insists that the prophet Mohammed gave the following remark:

> Thereupon he [Muhammad] said: "It will not come until you see ten signs." And (in this connection) he made a mention of the smoke; the *Dajjal* [often called Anti-Christ]; the beast; the rising of the sun from the west; the descent of Jesus, son of Mary; the [Gog] and Magog; and land-slidings in three places, one in the east, one in the west, and one in Arabia at the end of which fire would burn forth from Yemen, and would drive people to place of their assembly.[2]

Many Muslim commentators insist that the most important sign is that of Christ's return to earth to defeat the Antichrist, when He will establish Islam as the best religion, then marry, die, and be buried next to Mohammed.

### Resurrection According to the Qur'an

When the final day has come, the Qur'an says that angel Israfil (the angel of death) will blow a trumpet loudly, and all living things on the earth will die (souls already dead will be waiting, either tormented or peaceful, in their graves, in heaven, or roaming about the earth). Then Israfil will blow the trumpet a second time and all things will be resurrected:

> The Trumpet will (just) be sounded when all that are in the heavens and on earth will swoon except such as it will

please Allah (to exempt). Then will a second one be sounded when behold they will be standing and looking on! (surah 39:68)

Orthodox Islam declares that Allah will recreate the body of each individual in its original form and will rejoin every soul to its body. Then, for a certain period of time—from 1,000 (surah 32:5) to 50,000 (surah 32:5) years—all will be given the command to "bow in adoration." While the believers will readily obey, unbelievers will be unable to do so (surah 68:42). Then will come the dreadful day of reckoning.

### Judgment Day According to Islam

All human beings and jinn will be gathered into the presence of Allah, where He will begin to judge them by their faith and deeds:

> When Allah assembles people in His presence, He will begin to judge them on a scale of absolute justice. Everything a person does...including intentions and desires, will be accounted for on this day. At that moment, nobody can help anyone else because a person's deeds and intention will speak for him.[3]

Contemporary Muslim author Muhammad Khouj continues to describe how the recording angels will assist in the process of documenting the good and bad deeds of each individual: "each individual has two angels—one on his right who records his good deeds and one on his left who records the bad deeds. By Allah's orders, these angels registered every single act and intention of every human being."[4]

These books are then weighed on a great scale (*mizan*), and if an individual's good deeds are heavy, that individual will attain salvation, but if his or her good deeds are too light, then into hell he or she will go (surah 23:102-103).

The final stage in this judgment process is the test of crossing a bridge over hell (*sirat*). The Qur'an mentions this bridge only obscurely, but the Hadith describes it in greater detail.

They picture it as narrow as a strand of hair, as sharp as a sword, and hotter than burning charcoal, with the searing flames of hell lapping down below. The more dedicated the individual had been during his or her lifetime, the easier it will be for him or her to cross over. Some will cross as swiftly and effortlessly as wind, others will crawl on their hands and knees — but if they make it across, they've made it to Paradise.

Those condemned at the judgment by their bad deeds, however, will be unable to cross, and will fall into the vast abyss of hell.[5]

### Islamic View of Hell

What will unbelievers encounter in hell? The Qur'an and the Hadith contain quite vivid descriptions.

Sinners will be thrown into a scorching lake of fire, where they will be fed with boiling, fetid water. Boiling water will be poured even over their heads, melting their skin and their inner organs. Sounds of wailing and wretched moaning will be heard as the scorched skins are constantly changed for new ones, so that the torment is both continual and intense.

People are chained together, with clothing of burning pitch and fire on their faces. Death lies all around them, but they are unable to die. If they try to escape, a giant iron hook will drag them back to the fiery pit.[6]

Christianity has a similar, but far less graphic understanding of hell. It pictures the place of the damned as a lake of fire, a place of eternal torment where there will be weeping and gnashing of teeth, a place devoid of the presence of almighty God.[7]

### Islamic View of Heaven

The Qur'an provides a quite different view of heaven. It describes "Gardens of Felicity" or "Paradise," a place where believers will be granted all their hearts' desires.

The faithful are promised the company of several beautiful, lustrous-eyed virgins, and the enjoyment of delicious wine without any of the intoxicating aftereffects (Muslims are not allowed to consume alcohol while on earth). True believers will be awarded with armlets of gold and pearls, along with embroidered silken garments, and will be waited on by men-servants. All manner of fruits and meats will be available to believers lounging about in the delightful Garden. Along with these physical pleasures will come great bliss and peaceful-ness.[8] (Muslims hold various opinions as to whether these descriptions should be taken literally or symbolically.[9])

In the Christian faith, heaven is described as a place of eternal bliss, where believers will worship God continually and where Jesus has gone to prepare a place for those who have put their faith and trust in Him. There will be no more crying or pain, and no need for light, for God Himself will be the light.[10] While Islam emphasizes many physical pleasures, Christianity highlights heaven's tremendous spiritual satisfaction.

### Salvation According to Islam

In Islam, man's primary problem is his weakness and forgetful-ness. Islam views human beings as being born into a state of perfection, which is tarnished whenever one sins. There is therefore no concept of the necessary redemption of one's soul. Herein lies a key difference between the Muslim and Christian understanding. Kateregga asserts:

> Islam does not identify with the Christian conviction that man needs to be redeemed. The Christian belief in the re-demptive, sacrificial death of Christ does not fit the Islamic view that man has always been fundamentally good, or that God loves and forgives those who obey his will.[11]

The Muslim writer Askar insists mankind's challenge is "...not so much to explore God as to remember that there is one."[12]

### How Does a Muslim Go to Heaven?

The Qur'an teaches that two things are required to achieve eternal bliss: faith (*iman*) and action (*amal*). Surah 5:9 explains, "To those who believe and do deeds of righteousness hath Allah promised forgiveness and a great reward."

But what exactly is meant by "having faith"? Abul Quasem, author of *Salvation of the Soul and Islamic Devotions*, contends that:

> It has three basic ingredients—so basic that the absence of any one of them negates the presence of faith as a whole....All three elements are needed for salvation... (including) belief in the oneness of God, belief in the prophecy of Muhammad, and belief in life after death.[13]

Traditionally, Muslim theologians have pointed out five (some six) tenets necessary to faith (iman):

> God and his attributes, the prophets and their virtues, the angels, the sacred books, the day of resurrection, and *Qadar*, namely that God decrees everything that happens in the world....Whosoever believes in these six parts of the Islamic faith is called *Mu'min*, i.e., believer; and whoever denies these parts or any of them is called *kafir*, i.e., unbeliever.[14]

Many Muslims do not acknowledge the last tenet, *Qadar*, and thus accept only the first five principles.

If this is what constitutes faith in Islam, then what constitutes "actions"? The next section of this book will explore what are commonly called "the five pillars of Islam." Beyond these, the mercy of Allah is also required in order for a Muslim to enter heaven. One tradition of the prophet Mohammed relates the following conversation:

> [Mohammed maintained that] "without the mercy of God no one can attain salvation by virtue of his action."
>
> His companions asked, "Not even you, O the messenger of God?"
>
> He replied, "Not even I. God will, however, cover me with mercy."[15]

Allah is believed to show his mercy to sinners by increasing the weight of their good deeds and lessening their bad deeds when they are weighed on the scale on Judgment Day. Additionally, it is believed that Allah will, after a particular amount of time, rescue many formerly condemned to hell, for no reason of personal merit, but just because he wants to demonstrate compassion on His creatures.[16]

### Will Only Muslims Go to Heaven?

This is a controversial area. Some Muslims suggest that anyone who is a "doer of good" will enter heaven. They often quote surah 2:111-112 in support of this claim:

> And they say: "None shall enter paradise unless he be a Jew or a Christian." Those are their (vain) desires. Say: "Produce your proof if ye are truthful." Nay whoever submits his whole self to Allah and is a doer of good he will get his reward with his Lord; on such shall be no fear nor shall they grieve.

This text seems to suggest that the other "required" tenets of faith are not actually necessary, after all.

Later in Mohammed's revelations, the exception of salvation outside of Islam is allowed only for Jews and Christians, as expressed in surah 2:62:

> Those who believe (in the Qur'an) and those who follow the Jewish (Scriptures) and the Christians and the Sabians and who believe in Allah and the last day and work righteousness shall have their reward with their Lord; on them shall be no fear nor shall they grieve.

The Qur'an also points out, however, an incident that could be considered an abrogation: "If anyone desires a religion other than Islam (submission to Allah) never will it be accepted of him; and in the Hereafter he will be in the ranks of those who have lost (all spiritual good)" (surah 3:85). Even more strongly, surah 98:6 states, "Those who reject (Truth) among the People of the Book (Jews and Christians) and among the Polytheists will be in hell-fire to dwell therein (for aye). They are the worst of creatures."

This text seems to make clear that only Muslims will enter heaven. Hence, Christians, Jews, Buddhists, Hindus, atheists — anyone who is not a Muslim — will be excluded from Paradise.

On the other hand, some Muslims consider Jews who died before Jesus' revelation as holding to the true faith (with their limited revelation); therefore, they will be allowed into heaven. Similarly, Christians until the time of Mohammed's revelation were doing the best they could with their corrupted Bible, so they too will be allowed into heaven. But since all of mankind now has the most complete and final revelation through Mohammed, no one else is excused from accepting his prophethood or the tenets of Islam; therefore, non-Muslims from Mohammed's time forward cannot attain Paradise.

Will only Muslims go to heaven? Yes — but no Muslim can be sure which among them will be chosen for heaven.

### Can Muslims Have Assurance of Salvation?

As we saw earlier, Islam provides no assurance of salvation. Fear over one's eternal destiny has brought deep insecurity even from the beginnings of the religion. Al-Ghazzali gives the following example:

> Yet all the fathers used to refrain from giving a definite reply concerning belief, and were extremely careful not to commit themselves….Once upon a time Hassan (al-Basri) was asked, "Art thou a believer (in Islam)?" To which he replied, "If it be the will of God." Thereupon he was told, "O Abu Said, why do you qualify your belief?" He answered and said, "I fear saying 'yes,' and then God will say, 'Thou hast lied, Hassan.' Then I shall rightly merit His punishment…." Alqamah was once asked, "Are you a believer?" To which he replied, "I do hope so. If it be the will of God."[17]

Hence, the believer must wonder if his or her belief is the will of Allah, since He creates some for heaven and some for hell (surah 7:178-179). One can't know for sure what Allah will choose.

Some Muslims see this lack of an assurance of salvation as a motivation to continue in obedience. "Religious justification is thus the Muslims' eternal hope, never their complacent certainty, [not] for even a fleeting moment."[18]

Because Allah can be capricious, Muslims cannot avoid a certain degree of uncertainty as to whether all of one's efforts in the end will really be good enough. At times, Allah feels compassionate; at other times, He feels angry. What will He feel on Judgment Day? How can you know if all your good deeds will ever be enough?

These are very real issues for each of the 1.2 billion Muslims in the world. It is not surprising, then, that some Muslims boldly fight for the cause of Islam, or jihad. Muslims believe that if they die in a "holy war," they will immediately be granted Paradise—which is one way to alleviate spiritual stress and hopelessness.

### From Beliefs to Practices

The Qur'an not only teaches Muslims what they are to believe, it also shows them how they are to live. Islam offers rules for every part of life.

The next section gives an overview of the five central pillars (or practices) of Islam, vital to a Muslim's attainment of Allah's approval and entrance into heaven.

### Summary

Muslims are motivated to believe and act appropriately as they consider the frightening Day of Judgment. Each individual Muslim will be judged according to the amount of good and bad deeds he or she has acquired over his or her lifetime. Fear of the terror of hell and hope for the bliss of heaven are very real incentives for the 1.2 billion Muslims of the world today. However, due to the capricious nature of Allah, Muslims are never quite certain if they will attain heaven or not, no matter how many good deeds they have accomplished. The Qur'an only assures entrance into heaven by death through jihad, or holy war. Sadly, millions of Muslims have never heard of the loving Savior who came to die in their place, to forgive their sins, and to offer them hope of eternal life in heaven.

With an understanding of what Islam teaches about how one should believe, what does it teach about how one should live? Islam offers rules for every part of life. The five central pillars (practices) of the faith, vital to a Muslim's attainment of Allah's approval and entrance into heaven, are included in the next section.

*Part IV*

# The Basic Practices of Islam

What motivates a devoted Muslim to halt five specific times each day and utter prescribed prayers, or to journey all the way to Mecca to perform a pilgrimage, or give a percentage of his wealth for the cause of Islam, or fast the entire month of Ramadan, or kill himself and others in a "holy war"? As a slave renders services to his owner, so a Muslim performs duties unto Allah.

Muslims carry the ever-present awareness that their good deeds must outweigh their bad deeds on the Day of Judgment. They hope that by completing these duties of Islam, Allah will favor them and grant them entrance into heaven. These sacred duties, or pillars, of Islam, were taught and practiced by the prophet Mohammed, continually and faithfully executed by subsequent Muslims around the globe, and still are practiced to this day. Islam provides a complete way of life.

The five pillars are stated in the following Hadith: "Islam is based on five things: declaring that there is no god but Allah and that Mohammed is the messenger of Allah, the establishment of *Salah*, the payment of *Zakah*, the *Hajj* and

*Sawm* in the month of Ramadan" (Ghulam Sarwar, *Islam: Beliefs and Teachings* [London: The Muslim Educational Trust, 1989], 40).

Some Muslims, such as many Shiites, add a sixth pillar, jihad, or holy war.

Figure 13.1 below delineates the five central pillars of Islam generally in their state of importance, with the shahada, or creed of Islam, being the foundational, axial pillar, followed by ritual prayer (salat or salah), fasting in the month of Ramadan (sawm), performing pilgrimage to Mecca (hajj), and then almsgiving (zakat or zakah).

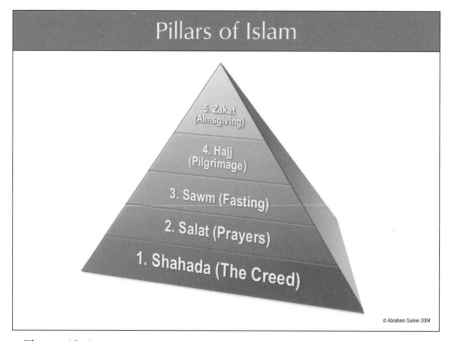

**Figure 13.1**

## ° 13 °

# The First Thing
# a Muslim Hears

Would you believe the very first sentence my Muslim parents whispered into my newborn ears as I entered the world—even before "I love you"—was, *La ilaha illa Allah, Mohammed rasul Allah* ("There is no god but Allah, and Mohammed is Allah's messenger")?

Faithful Muslim parents make it their duty to instill this creed of Islam firmly within their children. The first phrase a Muslim infant will hear at birth is this creed—the shahada. The shahada is uttered throughout the young Muslim's life, imbedding the religion of Islam within his heart and mind at the youngest age possible. And, if possible, this creed is also the last phrase a dying Muslim will hear before he passes into eternity.

### Short, but Powerful

One needs merely to speak these few words, the shortest creed of any major world religion, to accept Islam and become Muslim. This creed unites Muslims across the world, publicly stating the foundational beliefs of their community. The heart of Muslim theology and philosophy lies in this brief, yet often repeated statement, and it is always spoken in Arabic.

By speaking the shahada, one accepts not only the oneness of God, but also the teaching of Mohammed about Allah and all the tenets of the Islamic faith. When the prominent American Black Muslim Malcolm X wanted to become an orthodox Muslim, he too stated, "There is no god but Allah, and Mohammed is the Messenger of Allah."

Yet, as important as repeating the shahada is, by itself it is not enough. It represents only the first step toward reaching heaven. Islam teaches that both faith (iman) and practice (*din*) must blend together in the life of a believer to achieve Paradise.

The next pillar requires the most frequent activity on the part of a faithful Muslim. Five times a day, every Muslim is expected to practice a certain kind of prayer. Its regimented format contrasts interestingly with the Christian idea of prayer.

## ○ 14 ○

# Five Times
# Each Day

Unfurling his ornate prayer rug on the grass in the middle of a spacious, busy university campus one afternoon, a young Muslim began his ritual prayer to Allah. So intently did he focus on his sacred, methodical prayers, that he didn't notice as I watched from afar. He executed each motion in precise succession as he repeatedly bowed down, prostrate toward the prayer rug on the ground, ceremoniously uttering Qur'anic passages in Arabic from memory.

Prayer is the daily religious staple for the faithful Muslim. Surah 20:14 states the reason for such prayer: "Verily I am Allah: there is no god but I: so serve thou me (only) and establish regular prayer for celebrating My praise."

The Qur'an also stipulates prayer at five regular, specific intervals throughout the day: "set up regular prayers: for such prayers are enjoined on believers at stated times" (surah 4:103).

Before the Muslim community may enter into prayer, however, certain procedures must be followed. Five times a day, Muslims will hear the prayer call issuing from the local mosque. Then Muslims will perform a special cleansing ritual before they turn to face Mecca and perform the rite of prayer.

# Diagram of a Mosque

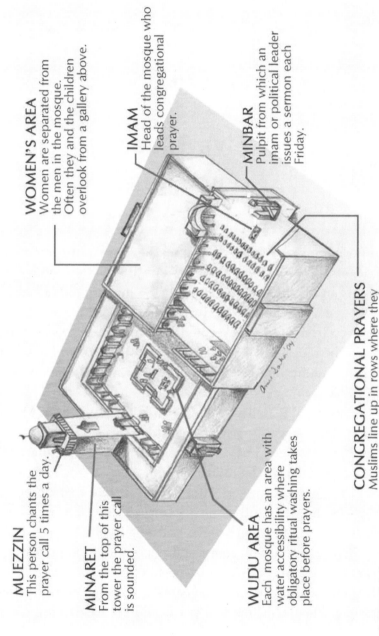

**MUEZZIN**
This person chants the prayer call 5 times a day.

**MINARET**
From the top of this tower the prayer call is sounded.

**WUDU AREA**
Each mosque has an area with water accessibility where obligatory ritual washing takes place before prayers.

**WOMEN'S AREA**
Women are separated from the men in the mosque. Often they and the children overlook from a gallery above.

**IMAM**
Head of the mosque who leads congregational prayer.

**MINBAR**
Pulpit from which an imam or political leader issues a sermon each Friday.

**CONGREGATIONAL PRAYERS**
Muslims line up in rows where they bow toward Mecca in prayer.

*Figure 14.1*

### The Call to Prayer

Every dawn in a Muslim country, one will awaken to the melodious prayer call booming loudly from the minaret of the local mosque, reminding Muslims of their duty to pray to Allah. (See figure 14.1 on facing page.) Always chanted in Arabic, the prayer caller (*Mu'adhdhin* or *Muezzin*) will summon Muslims to pray, either at the mosque in congregation with others (which is more meritorious), at home, at work, or wherever one finds oneself when the prescribed hour arrives.

If one offers his prayers in congregation, the reward is twenty-five times greater than at any other common place.[1] Special angelic note will be taken of prayers offered in the mosque; therefore more points will accrue for that individual, and on the Day of Judgment he may obtain a greater chance of going to heaven.

Regardless of the country, the call to prayer is always given in Arabic, broadcasting the following chant:

God is great! (*Allahu Akbar*)

God is great! (*Allahu Akbar*)

God is great! (*Allahu Akbar*)

God is great! (*Allahu Akbar*)

I bear witness that there is no god but Allah (*Ashhadu an la ilaha illallah*)

I bear witness that there is no god but Allah (*Ashhadu an la ilaha illallah*)

I bear witness that Mohammed is Allah's messenger (*Ashhadu anna auhammadar rasulullah*)

I bear witness that Mohammed is Allah's messenger (*Ashhadu anna auhammadar rasulullah*)

Rush to prayer (*Hayya 'alal salah*)

Rush to prayer (*Hayya 'alal salah*)

Rush to success (*Hayya 'alal falah*)

Rush to success (*Hayya 'alal falah*)

God is great! (*Allahu Akbar*)

God is great! (*Allahu Akbar*)

There is no god but Allah (*La ilaha illal lah*)

Five times each day this prayer call is heard: at dawn (*Fajr*); just after noon (*Zuhr*); in late afternoon (*'Asr*); just after sunset (*Maghrib*); and at night before retiring (*'Isha*). The morning prayer call adds an extra incentive: "Prayer is better than sleep (*Assalatu khairum minan naum*)."

### Why Do Muslims Perform Ablution?

Before a Muslim may offer prayers, he or she must perform ablution (*wudu*), an outer cleansing of the body, or else Allah will not accept the prayer. Cleanliness is of high priority, "for Allah loves those who turn to Him constantly and He loves those who keep themselves pure and clean" (surah 2:222). Allah will acknowledge only the prayers of one who is clean physically. Surah 5:6 specifies rules about washing:

> O ye who believe! when ye prepare for prayer wash your faces and your hands (and arms) to the elbows; rub your heads (with water); and (wash) your feet to the ankles. If ye are in a state of ceremonial impurity bathe your whole body.

A mosque will usually have separate areas for men and women to perform this cleansing ritual before they enter the main sanctuary.

Just as ancient Judaism laid out laws for proper ablution, so Islam has a particular method for performing this cleansing. Growing up as a Muslim, I too performed the following prescribed procedures for proper ablution:

> Declare one's intention (*Niyyah*) by stating in Arabic, "In the name of Allah, the most Merciful, the most Kind (*Bismillahir rahmanir rahim*)."
>
> Next, wash both hands to the wrists three times.
>
> Rinse out the mouth three times.
>
> Clean out nostrils by sniffing water three times.
>
> Wash the face, from right to left ear, three times.

Wash arms from wrist to elbow three times, right then left.

Run wet hands over head from forehead to back of head three times.

Using wet fingers, clean the ears inside and out.

Wet the nape of the neck with the backs of one's wet hands.

Wash both feet to the ankles, right then left.

Certain acts will invalidate the cleansing ritual, and ablution will have to be repeated. These unacceptable acts include:

1. Natural discharges, such as urination, flatulation, or defecation.
2. The flow of blood or pus.
3. Vomiting.
4. Falling asleep.[2]
5. Touching one's genitalia.[3]
6. Engaging in sexual intercourse.

What if prayer time comes and you can find no water? Many Muslim countries have miles of dry desert, which can make cleansing with water difficult, particularly when traveling. In cases where no suitable water can be found, clean sand or dirt may be used in the place of water:

> But if ye are ill or on a journey or one of you cometh from offices of nature or ye have been in contact with women and ye find no water, then take for yourselves clean sand or earth and rub therewith your faces and hands. Allah doth not wish to place you in a difficulty but to make you clean and to complete His favor to you that ye may be grateful. (surah 5:6)

### How Do Muslims Pray?

Once properly cleansed, the Muslim worshiper performs the regimented process of *rak'ahs*. What is a rak'ah? Each rak'ah involves first standing, then bowing to the ground twice, prostrating the body by touching the forehead to the ground. The worshiper first faces toward the Ka'ba in Mecca, utters "Allah is great" (*Allahu Akbar*), then recites the first chapter of the Qur'an (*Fatiheh*) in Arabic, as well as other Qur'anic verses.

Throughout the five daily appointed prayer times, each Muslim must complete at least seventeen rak'ahs (thirty four total times touching the forehead to the ground). Obligatory prayers must be spoken in Arabic, regardless of whether the worshiper understands their meaning. After the compulsory bows are completed, one may pray in his or her own language, if desired.

The physical act of prostration demonstrates the duty of believers to submit to Allah. The Islamic community center of worship, or mosque (*masjid*), literally means "a place of prostration."[4]

Just as Christians gather for congregational worship on Sunday, so a special prayer (*Salatul Jumu'ah*) is offered in the mosque for Muslims just after noon on Friday. All male adults are required to participate; women can choose whether to physically go to the mosque, depending upon household duties.

Men and women are always separated during worship times at the mosque. Often the women stay in an area where they cannot be seen or heard by the men, but where they can see and hear what the men are doing in the main sanctuary. The mosque is a very serious and quiet place; the only time noise should be heard is when prayers are being offered, or when a sermon (*khutbah*) is being given, such as on Fridays. When prayers are offered in a congregation, one person leads, while the congregation follows. There is no singing or use of instruments in a mosque, as there is in many Christian church services. Rather, only the human voice is utilized for worship.

While for some Muslims prayer may be a spiritual exercise, for most it is merely a required, mechanical act, without great spiritual or moral value. Prayer is a repetitive performance done for Allah. It does not emphasize communication with Allah or a pure state of heart, but rather stresses outward actions.

### How Is Christian Prayer Different?

How does a Muslim's prayer differ from that of a Christian? They both offer praise to God, involve repentance, and present supplication—but there are some key differences.

The Bible teaches that God is most concerned with the state of our heart. "Man looks at the outward appearance, but the Lord looks at the heart" (1 Samuel 16:7). Jesus taught that prayer is not a means of boasting before men, but rather a private communion with God. Consider His words in Matthew 6:5-6:

> And when you pray, do not be like the hypocrites, for they love to pray standing in the synagogues and on the street corners to be seen by men. I tell you the truth, they have received their reward in full. But when you pray, go into your room, close the door and pray to your Father, who is unseen. Then your Father, who sees what is done in secret, will reward you.

Jesus also taught that God is not pleased with meaningless repetitions, but rather with sincere, heart-felt communication. God already knows our needs before we even ask: "And when you pray, do not keep on babbling like pagans, for they think they will be heard because of their many words. Do not be like them, for your Father knows what you need before you ask him" (Matthew 6:7-8).

In Matthew 6:9-13, Jesus gave us an example of what a Christian prayer should be like. It is often called "The Lord's Prayer":

> Our Father in heaven,
> Hallowed be your name,
> Your kingdom come, your will be done
> On earth as it is in heaven.

Give us today our daily bread.
Forgive us our debts,
As we also have forgiven our debtors.
And lead us not into temptation,
But deliver us from the evil one.

While Christians may read verses of Scripture as a part of worship—similar to Muslims quoting the Qur'an—the Bible does not have to be quoted in the original Hebrew or Greek, languages, which most Christians do not understand. Rather, when one reads and recites the Bible, it should be done in a translation that he or she can understand; otherwise, it will merely be a futile exercise of speaking meaningless words. While Scripture quotation may be a part of prayer, prayer is really about personal communication with God.

Christians may also pray in their own native language; it is not necessary to pray in Hebrew or Greek. Muslims, on the other hand, must say the obligatory prayers in Arabic. Why the difference? Yahweh does not desire idle words spoken out of obligation to a set of rules and regulations, but rather heart-felt communication to which He gladly and lovingly responds. In the biblical book of Isaiah, God makes this clear: "These people come near to me with their mouth and honor me with their lips, but their hearts are far from me. Their worship of me is made up only of rules taught by men" (Isaiah 29:13).

While in Islam the outward cleanliness makes prayer acceptable to Allah, in Christianity inward cleanliness supersedes outer cleanliness. God desires a pure heart, because He knows it will prompt righteous actions. While Muslims perform ablution, a Christian cleanses spiritually in prayer through confessing sins and humbling oneself before God. Jesus admonished the Pharisees on the importance of inward cleanliness:

> Woe to you, teachers of the law and Pharisees, you hypocrites! You clean the outside of the cup and dish, but inside they are full of greed and self-indulgence. Blind Pharisee! First clean the inside of the cup and dish, and then the outside will also be clean. (Matthew 23:25-26)

Yahweh of the Bible desires a personal relationship with His creation, not mere actions performed robotically. God commands believers to "love the Lord your God with all your heart and with all your soul and with all your mind" (Matthew 22:37). Loving God by performing certain outward duties alone does not bring Him pleasure; rather, He requires us to offer all that we are: "Therefore, I urge you, brothers, in view of God's mercy, to offer your bodies as living sacrifices, holy and pleasing to God—this is your spiritual act of worship" (Romans 12:1). God desires that we willingly and joyfully submit ourselves to Him in all areas of life, whether in our actions, thoughts, or desires (James 4:7).

The dedication of devout Muslims to pray faithfully five times a day is admirable, but sadly, they never experience the personal presence of God through Jesus Christ. Jesus promises not only that God will answer the believers' prayers, but that His very presence will be with them when they pray. "Again, I tell you that if two of you on earth agree about anything you ask for, it will be done for you by my Father in heaven. For where two or three come together in my name, there am I with them" (Matthew 18:19-20).

When I was a Muslim, I never knew if Allah really heard my prayer. I did not feel His presence or receive answers when I prayed, as I do today, now that I know God personally through Jesus Christ. As a Muslim, I prayed five specific times each day, but now as a Christian, I can pray anytime and continually, since I have an ongoing relationship with God throughout the day and night: "Be joyful always; pray continually; give thanks in all circumstances, for this is God's will for you in Christ Jesus" (1 Thessalonians 5:16-18, see also Psalm 63:6).

As a young Muslim I never missed a prayer, for I was told that each missed prayer would result in years of punishment in hell. My motive for prayer was usually out of guilt and obligation; it was my duty as a Muslim. As a Christian, however, I enjoy the sweet presence of God's Holy Spirit in prayer, and I have personally experienced His answers to my prayers. The primary difference in prayer between a Muslim and a Christian has to do with a personal connection with God instead of the fulfilling of ritual actions and prescribed speech.

In addition to prayer, both Islam and Christianity also practice fasting as a part of worship. But again, significant differences in purpose and process quickly become apparent.

# ○ 15 ○

# A Grueling Month

During Ramadan, the month of the Islamic fast (*sawm*), my Muslim family's grocery bill actually soared much higher than during all other months of the year. Why?

Although Muslims are required to fast from all food, drink, smoking, and conjugal relations during the daylight hours (sunrise to sunset), the feasting begins after the sun goes down! Muslims may then eat and drink as much as they desire, and my family usually ate more during a Ramadan night than on entire regular days during the other months of the year.

### Why Do Muslims Fast?

Islam teaches that Allah first revealed the Qur'an to Mohammed during the month of Ramadan. Ramadan is the ninth month on the Muslim lunar calendar, so Ramadan comes about ten days earlier each year, according to the solar calendar. This entire month is set aside for fasting, a practice designed to produce self-discipline: "O ye who believe! fasting is prescribed to you as it was prescribed to those before you that ye may (learn) self-restraint" (surah 2:183).

Fasting is required of all Muslim adults and adolescents. Some zealous Muslim families, such as my own, require anyone over the age of seven to participate in the fast. During this time, even the swallowing of one's own saliva, according to some extreme fundamentalists, would invalidate the fast.

As this month sometimes falls in the summer and at times in the winter, it can be especially difficult for those who must labor outside in harsh weather conditions. The fast is easier for the wealthy, as they can relax indoors; but for the proletarian population, the fast can be especially grueling. Only a few circumstances permit a Muslim to postpone or be excused from fasting: women who are pregnant or menstruating, travelers, and the elderly or ill who cannot safely endure the fast.

A great religious fervor sweeps the Muslim community during the month of Ramadan. Muslims read more of the Qur'an, offer more prayers than usual, show more kindness to fellow Muslims and heap more persecution on non-Muslims.

One night is considered particularly auspicious during Ramadan: the "Night of Power" (*Lailatul Qadr*). Muslims believe that during this night hundreds of years ago Mohammed received his first revelation from Allah. Faithful believers are taught to pray as much as possible on this night, for it is extremely meritorious. The Qur'an asserts that "The Night of Power is better than a thousand months" (surah 97:3).

Muslims hold a great celebration, called "Breaking the Fast" (*Idul Fitr*), on the day the fast ends. On this day, special prayers are performed in congregation, Muslims visit friends and family to eat specially prepared sweets in one another's homes, and don new clothes purchased just for this special event.

Some fervent Muslims also fast during other times of the year for additional merit or for a specific purpose, yet these other fasts are not mandatory or as meritorious.

### How Does a Muslim Fast Differ from a Christian Fast?

Muslims perform the Islamic pillar of fasting as a duty to be fulfilled. It is commanded of them as part of their obedience and submission to Allah: "(Allah desireth) that ye should complete the period, and that ye should magnify Allah for having guided you (by giving the Qur'an), and that [perchance] ye may be thankful" (surah 2:185). A Muslim is to learn self-restraint and thankfulness for the pleasures and comforts he or she forgoes during the fast.

In Islam, fasting is intended to please Allah by following His command; this earns a reward in heaven. As one Muslim author describes it, "the duty of fasting is only for Allah's sake and there is a very pleasing and attractive reward for this in the life after death." Ramadan is also "a month of...a means of avoiding the punishment of Hell."[1]

A Muslim fasts during Ramadan to make his or her body suffer, not necessarily to seek after God for an answer or solution, as in the Christian fast. Christians may fast from various things that bring them comfort or feel dear to them, such as food or certain activities. They may ask, "what should I give up so I can better focus on God," or "what is distracting me from or interfering with my relationship with God?" A Christian does not fast merely to follow a rule or command, but to seek after God. While a season of Lent prior to Easter has been observed by Christians for centuries as a time of reflection and refocusing, one's salvation is not contingent upon the completion of such a fast.

Prayer and fasting go together for the Christian. Fasting is also to be a private thing between oneself and God, as Jesus instructed the believers:

> When you fast, do not look somber as the hypocrites do, for they disfigure their faces to show men they are fasting. I tell you the truth, they have received their reward in full. But when you fast, put oil on your head and wash your face, so that it will not be obvious to men that you are fasting, but only to your Father, who is unseen; and your Father, who sees what is done in secret, will reward you. (Matthew 6:16-18)

The difference in motivation between Muslim and Christian fasting comes down to *duty* to God versus *desire* for God, and *performance* of obedience versus a *petition* from the heart. Without a personal relationship with God through Jesus Christ, Muslims cannot experience the same closeness with God during fasting that Christians can; fasting for them essentially means abstaining from comfort.

To follow the third pillar of Islam, dutiful Muslims give up their daytime comforts during the month of Ramadan. Muslims are also required to give of their wealth in almsgiving. This leads to the fourth pillar, *zakat*.

## ○ 16 ○

# The 2½ Percent Duty

Having been an orphan himself, it is said that Mohammed had special concern for the poor and needy. From the very beginning, almsgiving (zakat) had a place in the Islamic faith.

At first, almsgiving was optional for Muslims. Only later did it become a required pillar of the faith. Surah 2:227 identifies almsgiving as a necessary means for salvation: "Lo! those who believe and do good works and establish worship and pay the poor due, their reward is with their Lord and there shall no fear come upon them neither shall they grieve." The wealthy who do not give of their abundance receive a vivid warning:

> Allah's Apostle said, "Whoever is made wealthy by Allah and does not pay the Zakat of his wealth, then on the Day of Resurrection his wealth will be made like a bald-headed poisonous male snake with two black spots over the eyes. The snake will encircle his neck and bite his cheeks and say, 'I am your wealth, I am your treasure.'" (Hadith 2.468)[1]

Although no one can gain heaven without giving, this Hadith indicates that the wealthy have a special duty to perform this important pillar.

The Hadith also outlines specific dues for various classifications of people (some may give in livestock or gold, etc., according to the bounty of their trade), but generally Muslims are required to give 2½ percent of their income after paying household expenses, taxes, etc. Muslims are encouraged to give additional charity if possible; the merit for further giving is highly regarded. Surah 2:110 assures Muslims that their giving, along with their good deeds, will go before them and aid them in their attainment of heaven on the Day of Judgment: "Establish worship, and pay the poor due; and whatever of good ye send before (you) for your souls, ye will find it with Allah."

Consequently, Muslims faithfully give 2½ percent of their income. I have even seen beggars on the street in my native country share what they have received with another beggar— even beggars must give this same percentage of their possessions.

### What Happens to the Money?

How do Islamic organizations use all the funds given to them by faithful Muslims?

Money given for zakat may go to help the poor and needy. A beggar is not expected to show appreciation for a gift, however, because the giver contributes the funds primarily to receive a reward in heaven. Dr. William Miller, a prominent former missionary to Muslims, asserts, "Beggars do not express appreciation for what they receive, lest they by doing so deprive the giver of the reward which God will give him." These beggars "perform an important service by receiving the alms of the believers."2

The money received from zakat may also be used for the cause of Islam: evangelization programs or building mosques; to pay those who collect the money; or to help travelers, debtors, and new converts to Islam. Surah 9:60 outlines ways the zakat may be used:

> Alms are for the poor and the needy and those employed to administer the (funds); for those whose hearts have been (recently) reconciled (to truth); for those in bondage and in

debt; in the cause of Allah; and for the wayfarer: (thus is it) ordained by Allah and Allah is full of knowledge and wisdom.

While Muslims give faithfully of their income to be used for these purposes, they do so usually out of sheer duty, to fulfill what Allah has commanded. How does this compare with Christian giving?

### How Does the Zakat Compare to the Christian Tithe?

The Old Testament directs believers to give ten percent of their earnings—their "firstfruits," or the first and best of their income—back to God (see Exodus 22:29; Deuteronomy 17:1). The New Testament adds that one should give cheerfully and generously of what one has, but not out of compulsion.

> Remember this: Whoever sows sparingly will also reap sparingly, and whoever sows generously will also reap generously. Each man should give what he has decided in his heart to give, not reluctantly or under compulsion, for God loves a cheerful giver. (2 Corinthians 9:6-7)

Christian charity has gone to help the poor and needy; to support those in ministry; for evangelization and the establishment of churches, hospitals, and schools; as well as for many other ways of supporting and blessing the community.

While Muslims are also generally a very hospitable people (a characteristic that many foreigners have pleasantly experienced in Muslim countries), I have seen a difference in the priority of how Islam and Christianity tend to spend their funds. In Islam, building a several million dollar mosque gets higher priority than providing clean drinking water or adequate food and shelter for indigent Muslims. Yet in many Muslim countries, Christians have established fine hospitals, schools, and orphanages for the benefit of the people.

Why this difference? Perhaps because Muslim leaders believe that establishing Islam in the world has greater significance than anything else. The fatalistic Muslim view of Allah's will may also play a part. Islam holds that everything that happens is the will of Allah; therefore building a hospital to cure someone whom Allah has stricken may be out of His will. Sadly, many Islamic nations around the world suffer from third-world conditions perhaps partly because of this mind-set. Consequently, Islamic organizations have not established nearly as many hospitals and schools as has the Christian community. This fatalistic view is not shared by all Muslims, of course, especially not the more modern among them, many of whom practice medicine in the United States and elsewhere.

The Christian is taught to give the first and best of what God has given him or her, gratefully giving with a joyful heart as His steward. While the Christian learns to give out of love, the Muslim is bound by duty. Muslims fear what will happen to them on the Day of Judgment if they do not faithfully give 2½ percent of their earnings.

The next pillar after zakat requires a Muslim to give not only money, but also time and energy. This duty is very closely tied to one's salvation. Mohammed grafted the pillar of pilgrimage to Mecca into the religion of Islam as a continuance of ancient Arab customs. All Muslims are expected to engage in this life-changing activity, unless financial or physical constraints make it impossible.

° **17** °

# Following in the Footsteps of Mohammed

The city of Mecca is the very center of Muslim worship throughout the world, and the Ka'ba structure in particular. Toward this site Muslims bow every day in their ritual prayers. Mohammed was born here, and the city is considered so holy that non-Muslims are not allowed to enter it during the special time of hajj, the ritual pilgrimage that forms the fifth pillar of Islam.

### How Do Muslims Perform Pilgrimage?

In the twelfth month of the Islamic calendar, two to three million Muslims of different races, nationalities, and languages, all clad in white robes join together to circumambulate the Ka'ba seven times, and if possible kiss the black stone. They do this as part of the rituals involved in the pilgrimage, a series of practices Mohammed performed in his own day.

A map of the pilgrimage route is included in figure 17.1 on the following page. An explanation of the important rituals occurring at each location are indicated below:

1. Before entering the holy city of Mecca, pilgrims perform certain cleansing rituals at designated areas outside the

# The Pilgrimage (Hajj) Route

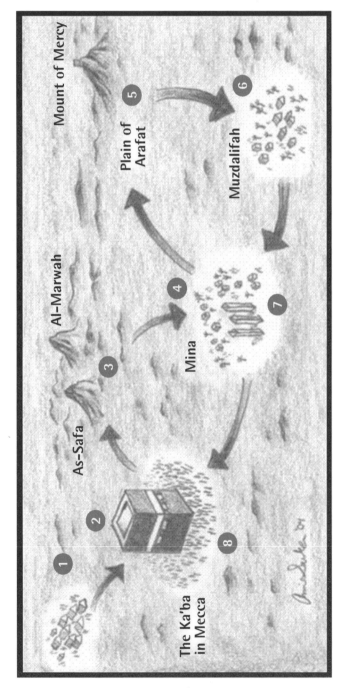

*Figure 17.1*

city. These rituals of Ihram, the intention of performing hajj, include men shaving their heads, cutting their nails, and trimming their beards. Both men and women wear white garments to strip away their differences in culture and class, symbolizing the equality of each person in the eyes of Allah.

2. Pilgrims journey to the Ka'ba, which is a small black cubed shrine near the center of the Great Mosque of Mecca, Al Haraam. Here they perform their first tawaf, or counter-clockwise circumambulation of the Ka'ba, seven times, while they chant, "Labbayka Allahumma Labbayk," which translates, "Here I am at your service, O Allah, here I am!"

3. Then, pilgrims perform the Sa'i, by running seven times between two small hills (As-Safa and Al-Marwah) reenacting the plight of Hagar when she went searching for water for her son Ishmael. Finally, pilgrims quench their thirst at the well of Zamzam, where it is believed that God provided a spring of water for Hagar and her son.

4. Next, pilgrims travel three miles to Mina where they camp for the night.

5. After that, a several mile journey is made to the plain of Arafat where Mohammed preached his final sermon. Here pilgrims stand from afternoon to sunset in honor of this event.

6. That same evening, pilgrims travel to Muzdalifah where they camp overnight.

7. On the third day of the pilgrimage, the pilgrims arrive again in Mina where it is believed that Allah tested Abraham's faith by commanding him to sacrifice his son Ishmael. There are three large stones set up that represent Satan, who tried to dissuade Abraham from following Allah's will; pilgrims pelt pebbles at these stones to symbolize how Abraham resisted the temptations of the Devil.

This event received international news attention when a stampede of pilgrims killed 244 people on February 1,

2004. However, it was not the most deadly hajj-related trampling incident. In 1990, a stampede killed 1,426 people.[1]

An animal is then sacrificed commemorating the ram that was provided in the place of Ishmael. This celebration is called 'Idu'l-Adha and is celebrated throughout the Muslim world. Muslims may also have their hair cut again to indicate that they have officially completed the rite of pilgrimage.

8. Pilgrims journey back to Mecca to complete a second tawaf, making seven circles around the Ka'ba, and then the Sa'i, running between the two hills, before returning to Mina. At Mina pilgrims will complete three additional days of prayer. Finally, the pilgrims return to Mecca a third time to make their final tawaf, circling the Ka'ba seven times as before, completing the hajj.

Many Muslims also journey to Medina to visit the tomb of Mohammed, although this is contrary to Mohammed's personal wishes. The prophet wanted none to venerate him.

Muslims believe that this act of pilgrimage will bring them closer to attaining heaven, and if some cannot go physically, they may pay for someone to go in their place. The hajj may be completed at other times during the year, but it is most meritorious if completed during this specific season.

When pilgrims return home, they are awarded the esteemed title of "Hajji" (one who has completed the hajj). Many Muslims who return describe the great amount of Muslim unity they felt during the hajj. Whether a king or a servant, all are dressed in the same manner and feel a sense of equality, as each is a servant of Allah.

As mentioned earlier, such was the experience of the famous African-American Muslim, Malcolm X. After performing the pilgrimage, he rejected the prejudiced slant of the Nation of Islam and said he wanted to follow true Islam, which embraces people of all ethnicities.

## Why Is the Ka'ba So Important in Islam?

It might be helpful to review what makes the Ka'ba so important that it would become the focus of the fifth pillar of Islam.

The prominent city of Mecca, located on the central western coast of Saudi Arabia, was a very holy site to the Arab people of Mohammed's day. The people believed a black meteorite had fallen there centuries before. This black stone became an object of veneration, and by the time of Mohammed, pilgrims had constructed an enclosure around it, called the Ka'ba.

This shrine at Mecca and the ritual practice accompanying it became precious to the Arabs as an integral part of their cultural heritage. Over time the Ka'ba became an abode for various idols, relics, and paintings. The Arabs eventually set aside a certain several month period each year for warring tribes to declare a truce in order to allow pilgrims safe travel to Mecca. During this annual pilgrimage to Mecca, pilgrims visited the Ka'ba to worship the idols, circle around it seven times, and touch or kiss the sacred black stone.[2]

Mohammed and his followers performed this very pilgrimage in A.D. 629. He performed each of the ancient customs associated with the Ka'ba, thus incorporating them into Islam and setting the example for all future Muslim pilgrims. At the end of the pilgrimage, Mohammed stated, "this day I have perfected your religion for you" (surah 5:5).[3]

When Mohammed and his army returned to Mecca and conquered the city in 630, he cleansed the Ka'ba of the idols and is believed to have installed the worship of one God, Allah; yet he retained the rituals associated with the pilgrimage to the Ka'ba.

Islam claims that the sacred black stone inside the modern wall of the Ka'ba fell from heaven during Adam and Eve's day and that Abraham and Ishmael built a house of worship there, but that later pagan people began collecting idols inside of the Ka'ba until Mohammed came to cleanse the building in A.D.

630.[4] Muslims consider the Ka'ba the first house of worship dedicated to the one true God.

### Does Christianity Have a Similar Pilgrimage?

Christianity has no ritual pilgrimage equivalent to the regimented hajj of Islam. In the Christian idea of pilgrimage, such as a visit to Israel, one may visit the empty tomb where tradition says the body of Jesus rested until His resurrection, or be encouraged and moved by the experience of walking where the Savior walked—but such activities do not aid one in attaining salvation. Salvation comes by grace through faith, "not by works"—such as pilgrimage—"lest any man should boast" (Ephesians 2:9).

No one has to travel to the tomb of Jesus or to the Temple Mount in Jerusalem or anywhere else to feel God's presence, because the Bible says our very bodies have become the temple of the Holy Spirit. When one accepts Jesus Christ as Savior, his or her heart feels set on a pilgrimage, not just at one specific time in a year or once in a lifetime, but that person seeks after and fellowships with God continually.

### A Sure Way to Paradise?

The pillar of hajj demonstrates the importance of traditions and rituals in the religion of Islam. It exemplifies the continual struggle of Muslims to gain entrance to heaven: hard work to perhaps complete enough good deeds, yet never knowing if one's upright conduct will be enough.

There is one practice, however, that many Muslims believe will absolutely assure their entrance into heaven—the act of holy war, or jihad. The next chapter will address this controversial issue highlighted in current events as well as several other significant Islamic practices.

## ° 18 °

# Jihad and Other
# Muslim Practices

The words "holy war" and jihad have become more familiar to the Western world after the atrocities of September 11, 2001. Many Americans are asking, "Why do Muslim terrorists hate us so much?" "What does the Qur'an teach about holy war?" and "Do all Muslims really believe in and practice jihad?"

### The Meaning of Jihad

While holy war for the cause of Islam (jihad) was common in the formative years of Islam, not all Muslims today interpret jihad as an aggressive, violent act in the name of Allah. Rather, as one Muslim author defines it, "Jihad is the use of all our energies and resources to establish the Islamic system of life, in order to gain Allah's favour."[1]

In Arabic, *jihad* literally means "struggle" or "to try one's utmost." Jihad has two primary emphases: (1) one should apply effort to control personal motives and actions; (2) one should establish right (*ma'ruf*) and remove evil (*munkar*) from society, which may include fighting (see surah 2:216, 244).[2]

Adherence to the first five pillars of Islam helps one to engage in jihad and inspires him or her to live and die for the cause of Islam. Jihad involves perfecting oneself as well as one's society.

Muslims believe that the way of Islam is the right way, and that it is their duty to urge others to carry out Allah's commands. Surah 3:110 affirms that the Islamic way of life is superior to all others and provides the model for all mankind: "Ye are the best of peoples evolved for mankind enjoining what is right forbidding what is wrong and believing in Allah."

The Shiite branch of Islam accepts jihad as the sixth pillar of the faith. The Sunni branch of Islam, which comprises nearly ninety percent of all Muslims, believes jihad to be merely another Islamic practice.

Modern Muslims vary in their interpretation of jihad. As a Sunni Muslim, I was never taught to engage in such violent actions as the terrorists committed on September 11. Killing innocent people and oneself was never supported or encouraged. If Islam was being attacked by those of another faith, however — such as missionary work or the destruction of mosques — it was my duty to defend Islam with my very life.

Some Muslim extremists interpret jihad as ridding the earth of all evil. This includes exterminating anyone who does not follow the way of Islam. This is not a new idea, but found enthusiastic support in Islam's founder, Mohammed.

### Does the Qur'an Support Aggressive Violence?

At first Mohammed tried to peacefully spread the religion of Islam, but with little success. After thirteen years he began using the sword, a strategy that allowed him to conquer all of Arabia. The same tradition enabled his followers to achieve the rapid spread of Islam after his death. But what motivated others to fight for Mohammed and the cause of Islam?

Mohammed admonished his followers that Allah looks with less favor upon those believers who stay home and refrain from fighting. (See surah 4:95-96.) He convinced his soldiers that Allah would reward them for their bravery with bountiful plunder, and that "martyrs" who died in battle would be granted eternity in Paradise. This doctrine is clearly expressed in the Qur'an: "And if ye are slain or die in the way of Allah, forgiveness and mercy from Allah are far better than all they could amass" (surah 3:157). Surah 3:195 promises:

> So those who fled and were driven forth from their homes and suffered damage for My cause, and fought and were slain, verily I (Allah) shall remit their evil deeds from them and verily I shall bring them into Gardens underneath which rivers flow. A reward from Allah. And with Allah is the fairest of rewards. (surah 3:195)

Many questioned Mohammed when he insisted that his followers fight during the sacred months of pilgrimage in Arabia, a time when all warring Arabian tribes held a temporary truce. Mohammed assured them that the injustice done to the Muslims by the Meccans (not allowing Muslims to perform pilgrimage) amounted to grave persecution, and that "persecution is worse than killing" (surah 2:17). Thus, Mohammed deemed fighting appropriate and necessary, even during the so called "forbidden" months.

The early history of Islam shows how violent assault was utilized not only for defense, but also for aggressive dominance of other peoples. Mohammed and his followers felt sure that they were carrying out the wishes of Allah in killing those who did not accept Islam.

In surah 9:73 it reads, "O Prophet (Mohammed), contend against the infidels and be rigorous with them." Another command to kill unbelievers states, "kill those who join other gods with God wherever ye shall find them, and seize them, and lay wait for them with every kind of ambush; but if they shall convert and observe prayer and pay the obligatory alms let them go on their way" (surah 9:5).

Islam's history and Holy Scripture clearly supply support for violent aggression against non-Muslims in order to establish Allah's right way on the earth. Several groups of modern radical Muslims attest to this practice today. Most modern Muslims, however, believe that the season of fierce, hostile invasion of other lands and peoples pertained only to the initial spread of Islam, and should not be practiced today. They believe that Islam should spread through peaceful methods. According to this group, the only appropriate occasion for violent jihad is the necessary defense of Islam against assailants.

### Jesus' Approach to Enemies

Jesus provides an interesting contrast to the aggressiveness of Islam as practiced by Mohammed and his early successors. Jesus taught His followers not only to tolerate their enemies, but to "love your enemies and pray for them who persecute you" (Matthew 5:44).

Jesus did not advocate that his followers repay persecution with slaughter, as Mohammed did—and apparently, his earliest followers understood and practiced his instructions. While the early church suffered intense persecution, it did not retaliate with aggression, but with love. And what happened? Their godly (and often costly) response resulted in the rapid growth and expansion of the faith.

### Rules for Family and State: Shari'ah

The basic practices of reciting the creed of Islam (shahada), praying ritual prayer (salat), fasting in the month of Ramadan (sawm), performing pilgrimage to Mecca (hajj), almsgiving (zakat), and holy war (jihad) provide the general outline for the Islamic way of life. But what about detailed guidelines for family and society? These rules appear in the Islamic law, or shari'ah, which dictates all aspects of Islamic life and society.[3]

The shari'ah, literally "the clear path," is "both a personal rule of life and a system of law that confirms the rights and duties given by God."[4] It is based on four main sources: the Qur'an; the sunna (practice of the Prophet, the Hadith), the *ijma* (consensus of Muslim scholars), and the *qiyas* (analogical deductions from the three sources just mentioned).[5]

This Islamic law, dating back to seventh-century Arabian culture, includes rules about what Allah has commanded, recommended, deprecated, forbidden, and feels neutral about.[6] Prominent Islamic scholar Montgomery Watt notes that during the Umayyad period, when Islamic civilization flourished, great effort went into developing and elaborating Islamic law. This study of law became the core of Islamic higher education.[7]

Islamic nations vary a great deal in the extent to which they implement shari'ah. Some nations have adopted a more secular system of government, while others have blended Islamic law with Western legal systems. The most fundamental Islamic nations have retained shari'ah in its entirety and rely upon it completely for their system of government. When shari'ah absolutely rules an Islamic nation, only the judiciary truly holds power.

Consequences of breaking laws outlined in the shari'ah can be as severe as public stoning, amputation, or beheading. The shari'ah is viewed as Allah's absolute statutes, and therefore, breaking those decrees is considered disobedience to Allah Himself. The Islamic courts hear cases, pronounce judgment, and enforce punishments.[8]

The interpretation of shari'ah differs markedly from country to country. In Afghanistan under the leadership of the Taliban, shari'ah was implemented and interpreted in the strictest sense; women, for example, were not allowed to work outside of the home or even leave their homes without being fully covered and accompanied by a male relative. Images of subordinated Afghan women conjure a view of life for Islamic women very different from what the Western world experiences. The Qur'an and many teachings in the Hadith also permit husbands to beat disobedient wives and to stone adulterers. Surah 4:34 reads, "Men are in charge of women because Allah hath made the one to excel the other....As for those from whom ye fear rebellion, admonish them and banish them to beds apart, and scourge them."

Yet, it must be understood that the whole Islamic world does not put such laws into practice. Women have served as head of state in several large Islamic nations, such as Indonesia, Bangladesh, and Pakistan. As this book is written, the prime minister of the third largest Islamic country in the world, Bangladesh, is a woman. In fact, the last three prime ministers of this Islamic nation have been women, elected by the people of their country.

When Islam ventured into new lands outside Arabia, it took on a form amenable to the culture of the people it encountered. Therefore, most Muslim women in my native Bangladesh do not wear the complete covering, or *burqa*, as in other countries, such as Afghanistan or Saudi Arabia. Rather, they continue to wear saris, because ethnically they are Bengali Indian, and they have retained that part of their culture while blending or replacing other practices with Islamic ones. According to Nicholas Birch in his October 31, 2003, article in *The Christian Science Monitor*, Turkey, with a more secularized government, even passed a law forbidding women to wear head scarves in public offices. Implementation of Islamic law differs significantly depending on how it is interpreted.

Growing up in a devout Muslim home, I don't remember ever hearing my father even yell at my mother, and I certainly never saw him beat her. Abuse toward women was unthinkable in my upbringing, although it is allowed under some interpretations of Islamic law.

To say that mistreatment of women does not occur in some Muslim homes and communities would be inaccurate; but is this injustice against women restricted to the Muslim world?

The difference between a democracy, such as the United States, and other nations governed by Islamic law, is that the law of the Western democracy generally allows for greater protection against physical abuse. Sadly, under Islamic law women are commonly left unprotected by the law and are therefore subject to the treatment of their families and the norms of their societies, be they noble or unjust.

### Family Laws: Marriage and Children

Many in the Western world harbor great curiosity about the status of women and family relations in an Islamic setting.

Islam considers marriage a civil contract between a man and his wife. Traditionally, marriages are arranged by the families of the man and woman; but modern Muslims often make their own choice in a mate, and then the two parties negotiate. A dowry is customarily an important part of the marriage process.

Islam is known for its authorization of polygamy (more specifically, polygyny, or having multiple wives, not just multiple marriages). Although Mohammed married eleven women (and acquired two concubines), Allah permitted his abundance of wives as the exception and instructed Mohammed to teach that a man could marry up to four wives, and more than one only if he treated the women fairly.[9]

According to seventh-century Arab custom, Mohammed insisted that women cover themselves modestly with a veil, so as to not display their beauty (surah 24:31). Today, the extent of covering varies considerably in Muslim countries. Some allow women to appear in public without even a head covering (such as Turkey), while some countries forbid women to leave their homes without first covering their entire body except for the hands (such as Saudi Arabia).

Islam allows, but does not encourage, divorce. Yet Islamic law permits only the husband to divorce the wife, not vice-a-versa, unless the husband goes missing or the woman converts to Islam and has a non-Muslim husband.[10] To divorce his wife, the husband merely needs to say, "I divorce you" three times, and the marriage has ended. In the event of a divorce, the husband is granted custody of the children.

Raising children is an important part of family life, and the children must always be raised Muslim, regardless of the wife's religion. Muslim men are allowed to marry women of other faiths, but Muslim women are excommunicated if they marry a non-Muslim.

Although the Qur'an does not command it, the circumcision of males is widely practiced, and occurs either in infancy or early childhood.

### Rules about Money

The Qur'an clearly prohibits the charging of interest (*riba*). Consider surah 2:278: "O ye who believe! Observe your duty to Allah and give up what remaineth (due to you) from usury, if you are (in truth) believers."[11] Studies by Bawden and by Taylor and Evans suggest that the basis for the Islamic prohibition against riba is linked to the core Islamic belief that one should not gain a profit where one has not taken risk.[12] For the same reason, Islam prohibits gambling.

Conventional banks do not generally offer a no-interest option to their clientele, so a special Islamic banking system has developed in many predominantly Muslim countries. The recent studies of Aggarwal and Yousef report Islamic banks operating in more than sixty countries, mostly in the Middle East and Asia, as well as the three countries of Iran, Pakistan, and Sudan, which have totally converted to the Islamic banking system.[13]

Islamic banks are governed by a board of Muslim scholars, as well as by "fatwas," complex legal rulings based on the Qur'an.[14] Each Islamic bank employs a shari'ah board. This group of religious experts ensures that the bank's products conform to Islamic law.[15] Ariff's studies suggest that Islamic banks have three distinguishing factors: (1) interest-free banking; (2) multi-purposed (as opposed to purely commercial) capabilities; and (3) strongly equity-oriented elements.[16] What constitutes the main difference between Western and Islamic style banking? Abdel-Hakim suggests that the Islamic banking system concentrates more on the people and their businesses, whereas the Western style focuses more on the accounts. Islamic banking is therefore considered more "grass roots."[17]

Bawden notes the need for Islamic banking in Western countries, and reports that restrictions on Islamic banks in the United Kingdom created a real area of difficulty in 1999. He reports that two to three million Muslims in the United Kingdom preferred to keep their money at home, rather than willingly ignore Islamic principles by setting up a conventional banking account.[18]

The strict codes associated with Islamic banking have not stopped Western bankers from beginning a dialogue with Islamic clientele, and an Islamic-style system is starting to develop in the Western world. Western Muslims have begun to seek financial services that reflect their religious beliefs.[19]

### Islam's Dietary Laws

Islamic law also closely follows the Mosaic law in the area of dietary regulation. It forbids eating pork and other specific types of meat, although Islamic law permits the consumption of camel meat. In Islam, meat of permitted animals may be consumed only if the name of Allah is pronounced over the animal during its slaughter. Only then does the meat become lawful (*halal*).

Muslims also are forbidden to consume alcohol, although other types of drugs and smoking are permitted. Outside of Muslim countries, such as the United States, stores selling halal foods are becoming more prevalent.

## Muslim Holy Days

Because the Islamic calendar is based on lunar months—a lunar year is about ten days shorter than a solar year—Islamic festivals are celebrated at different times each year, according to the Western calendar.

At the end of Ramadan, the month of fasting, Muslims celebrate the breaking of the fast with the festival *Idul Fitr* (on the new moon starting the next month *Shawwal*). The festive, anticipated day of Idul Fitr is joyously celebrated through donning new clothes, attending a special community prayer service, giving gifts to children and the poor, eating special foods, and visiting friends and relatives. A common greeting heard during this season is *"Eid mubarak,"* or *"A blessed 'Eid.'"*

The other major Islamic festival (holy day) of the year besides Idul Fitr is one that celebrates the willingness of Abraham to sacrifice his son at God's command. *Idul Adha*, as the holiday is called, is celebrated on the tenth day of the last month of the Islamic year, *Dhu-l-Hijja*, and it coincides with the end of the appointed time for performing the pilgrimage to Mecca.

This holiday is also known as the feast of sacrifice. After congregational prayer, each family traditionally sacrifices a flawless cow, with the meat divided into three parts: one third is distributed to the poor; one third to friends and relatives; and the final third is cooked and eaten at home. If a family cannot afford a cow, a smaller animal, such as a goat or lamb, may be sacrificed in its place.

Other minor holy days celebrated in the Muslim world include the birthday of the prophet Mohammed (*Maulid al Nabi*) in the third Islamic month of *Rabi' I*; and the festival of *Ashura*, on the tenth day of the month of *Muharram*. Muharram is the first month of the Islamic year, and originally Ashura was celebrated as the Jewish festival of Passover. Now it commemorates the story of Noah's ark touching dry land again. Shiite Muslims also celebrate the martyrdom of Husain ibn 'Ali, Mohammed's grandson, during this holiday.[20]

*How Do Muslim Holy Days Compare with Christian Ones?*

Just as the Qur'an shares many similarities with the Bible, but has the heart of the gospel taken out, so also Muslim holidays carry a shadow of the divine, yet lack the meaning of personal connection with almighty God that could make the holidays spiritually significant.

Caner and Caner assert that Ramadan provides a direct contrast to the Christian celebration of Christmas. "Ramadan is the antithesis to Christmas. It pits the revelation of the Holy Bible against the revelation of (the) Qur'an."[21] Furthermore,

> Christian holidays remember divine interventions, while Islamic celebrations are based upon human accomplishment. In Christianity, we celebrate Easter as the resurrection of our Lord Jesus and His completion of the sacrifice for our sins. In Islam, 'Eid-ul-Adha celebrates Abraham's willingness to sacrifice Ishmael, not Allah's substitution of the ram in the thicket. In Christianity we celebrate the birth of the Savior, Jesus Christ, for our redemption. Islam celebrates Mawlid al-Nabi, the birth date of Muhammad, their warrior. Christianity and Judaism recognize Passover as the work of God sparing the firstborn children of the Israelites. Muslims mark the end of their own personal sacrifice in Ramadan with 'Eid-ul-Fitr. The complete inversion of the purpose of holy days cannot be overstated.[22]

Muslims continue to sacrifice animals in remembrance of Abraham's willingness to sacrifice his son, unaware that God already has made the ultimate sacrifice for the sins of humankind through His Son, Jesus Christ.

God desires our hearts, not just our ritual. God states in Hosea 6:6, "For I desire mercy, not sacrifice, and acknowledgment of God rather than burnt offerings." The observance of rituals is meaningless to God without a personal relationship with Him.

Sadly, Islam fails to benefit from the celebration of interaction with a personal, loving God, and is left to observe the efforts of mankind in striving to know God. How should

Christians respond? Part V presents a Christian response to Islam, including how to effectively share one's faith with a Muslim.

### Summary

Part IV presented the five foundational pillars of Islam that should be practiced by all Muslims: the shahada, or creed of Islam, ritual prayer (salat or salah), fasting in the month of Ramadan (sawm), performing pilgrimage to Mecca (hajj), and almsgiving (zakat or zakah). These sacred duties, or pillars, of Islam were taught and practiced by the prophet Mohammed, and were continually and faithfully executed by subsequent Muslims around the globe, and still are to this day. Muslims carry the ever-present awareness that their good deeds must outweigh their bad deeds on the Day of Judgment. They hope that if they complete these duties Allah will favor them and grant them entrance into heaven.

Beyond the five central pillars, other distinctive Islamic practices such as jihad (holy war), and key practices regarding family, money, diet, and holy days were discussed. Jihad is added as the sixth pillar by the Shiite sect of Islam. While Muslims are instructed to defend Islam with their life if necessary, not all Muslims consider it appropriate to spread their religion by violent methods as was practiced during the inception of Islam. Islam's detailed guidelines for a complete way of life are indicated in Islamic law (shari'ah), which is interpreted differently from country to country.

While the religion of Islam emphasizes the outward manifestation of righteous deeds, it misses the root of the problem — the heart. Jesus taught that the inside of one's thoughts and motives must be pure, then good deeds will automatically flow out as well. Isaiah 29:13 emphasizes how God is not pleased with merely following rules set up by man, but by a whole heart committed to Him: "The Lord says: 'These people come near to me with their mouth and honor me with their lips, but their hearts are far from me. Their worship of me is made up only of rules taught by men.'" Islam as a works-based religion follows a set of rules, but misses the relationship with God that makes living a righteous life possible and worthwhile.

How can Christians help Muslims to experience the life-changing power of the gospel of Jesus Christ? Part V addresses a Christian response to Islam.

*Part V*

# A Christian Response to Islam

Muslims are motivated by their eternal fate in heaven or hell, which is decided by Allah's will. Many Muslims strive fervently to gain passage to heaven by their good deeds, yet Islam provides no assurance of salvation. How can these Muslims know the hope of salvation found through Jesus Christ? This section will discuss the needs of Muslims, from the perspective of someone who used to be one. It will also suggest a Christian response to Islam and how to respectfully share God's love and message of hope with a Muslim.

## ◦ **19** ◦

# Is Islam an
# Anti-Christ Religion?

Should Islam be considered an anti-Christ religion? Is the religion of Islam pitted against the person of Jesus Christ?

Mohammed, the founder of Islam, taught that the God who revealed the Qur'an is the same God who revealed the Torah to Moses and the Gospel to Jesus. He further considered Jesus a respected prophet and expected Him to return to earth before the end of history.

So how can Islam be considered an anti-Christ religion?

To answer that question, one must examine the person and purpose of Jesus Christ as recorded in the Bible, and then determine whether Islam's concept of Jesus concurs with the truth. If not, Islam must be considered an anti-Christ religion.

### Islam Denies the Gospel

Bassam Madany, radio missionary to the Arab world for more than two decades, insists that, "Of all the major religions of the world, Islam is the only one which is definitely anti-Christian at its core."[1]

Islam categorically denies the gospel of Jesus Christ. While it claims Jesus as a real prophet, it yet denies that He is Son of God, that He died on the cross (and that He therefore rose from the dead), or that He offered Himself to God as a perfect sacrifice to win salvation for all who would place their trust in Him.

Since Islam denies the very heart of who Jesus is and why He came to earth, the religion must be seen as opposing the message and purpose of Jesus Christ, and therefore has been considered an anti-Christ religion. But what exactly is this Christian gospel that Islam rejects?

### Definition of the Gospel

Islam asserts that the original Gospel (Injil) was a book of laws similar to the Torah of Moses, sent as a revelation to the Prophet Jesus. Muslims teach that this message was lost and that Christians today possess only a corrupt version of the original (although Muslims themselves cannot produce their "original" to compare with the Christian version). Therefore, Allah revealed the message of the Qur'an to Mohammed in order to perfect and supersede this lost Gospel of Jesus.

However, Madany attests that:

> The gospel is not primarily a book, and it is not a law that El Massih (Jesus the Messiah, according to the Qur'an) received from heaven as if he were a mere prophet like David and Moses. The gospel is the power of God unto salvation... the gospel is a dynamic message of God...Matthew, Mark, Luke, John, Romans and every part of the written Word of God are the gospel...If the gospel were a book of law, as [Muslims] think it is, then it would be a dry book, incapable of communicating the way of salvation.[2]

The genuine gospel proclaims that Jesus Christ, the Son of God, died on the cross as a sacrifice for the sins of mankind, was buried and rose again so that as many as receive Him might have eternal life.

Paul, an apostle of Jesus Christ, gives a definition of the gospel in 1 Corinthians 15:1-4:

> Now, brothers, I want to remind you of the gospel I preached to you, which you received and on which you

have taken your stand. By this gospel you are saved, if you hold firmly to the word I preached to you. Otherwise, you have believed in vain. For what I received I passed on to you as of first importance: that Christ died for our sins according to the Scriptures, that he was buried, that he was raised on the third day according to the Scriptures.

For good reason, Paul warned believers in Jesus Christ of false teachers and prophets who would come and try to persuade them to accept a different gospel. Listen to his warning:

I am astonished that you are so quickly deserting the one who called you by the grace of Christ and are turning to a different gospel—which is really no gospel at all. Evidently some people are throwing you into confusion and are trying to pervert the gospel of Christ. But even if we or an angel from heaven should preach a gospel other than the one we preached to you, let him be eternally condemned! (Galatians 1:6-8)

Amazingly, nearly two millennia ago Paul warned Christians of those who sought to distort the gospel of Jesus in ways that are evident even today. Paul forewarned that these false teachers may claim they received a new revelation through an angel, but yet their new revelation will change or deny the truth of the gospel.

Does Islam fit into this category? Mohammed claimed that an angel gave him the message of Islam, a message that contradicts the Bible at several crucial points. Most significantly, Islam denies the gospel of Jesus Christ as recorded in the Bible, and so it indeed proclaims a "different gospel."

### Jesus Is the Savior

I well remember the strong sense of uncertainty I felt as a Muslim. I knew that I had to complete a sufficient amount of good deeds before I died, yet I never knew if Allah would ultimately feel pleased with my life. I never knew if I had done enough good deeds for Allah to grant me Paradise. Millions of Muslims toil under the same anxiety today. I felt inexpressibly glad to find hope and assurance of my salvation when through faith I began a personal relationship with Jesus Christ.

The heart of Yahweh's message for humankind in the Bible is that of redemption through His amazing love. He promises salvation to all who will accept the risen Jesus as Savior and Lord, *not* to those who work hard enough to earn the divine admission price to heaven. As the apostle Paul writes, "to the man who does not work but trusts God who justifies the wicked, his faith is credited as righteousness" (Romans 4:5).

### Tackling a Spiritual Force

Islam accepts many positive things about Jesus, such as His status as a sinless prophet and a performer of great miracles. Yet Islam denies the heart of the gospel and in its place substitutes a religion based on good works. For this reason, many have felt compelled to classify Islam as an anti-Christ religion.

Reza Safa, a former radical Muslim, asserts that Islam is not merely a peaceful religion existing alongside Christianity, but rather, that it is an "antichrist force":

> With the fall of communism, the world was ready to embrace another antichrist force, a spiritual principality that would resist and oppose freedom and truth. This force, however, would be covered with a religious outfit and would possess a greater authority over the lives and minds of its followers than communism ever did. This power that would soon become a threat to world peace was a spiritual force called Islam.[3]

How should Christians perceive and confront this "spiritual force"? How can they best interact with the challenge of Islam? The next three chapters suggest how Christians can reach out to Muslims with the love and truth of the genuine gospel of Jesus Christ.

## ◦ 20 ◦

# Anticipating Muslim Arguments

When Christians think "evangelism," they tend to think of winsome efforts and strategies designed to encourage people to find eternal life through faith in Jesus Christ. This is natural and good—and yet, believers in Christ should realize that they aren't the only ones out to present their faith in as attractive a package as possible.

Muslims have their own evangelistic programs.

Would it surprise you to learn that Muslims, like many Christians, are instructed on the beliefs of other faiths (although sometimes with inaccurate information, as with the Christian Trinity)? Many receive effective training on how to argue the supremacy of their own religion. In fact, Muslims are so convinced their religion is supreme, they also feel it is their duty to bring the whole world into the fold of Islam. To understand Muslim arguments it is important to consider the Muslim mind-set, especially how a Muslim views his or her own faith in relation to the other religions of the world.

In this chapter I hope to communicate the mind-set of Muslims, spoken from someone who used to be one. Only when we understand the perspective of the Muslim people can we truly

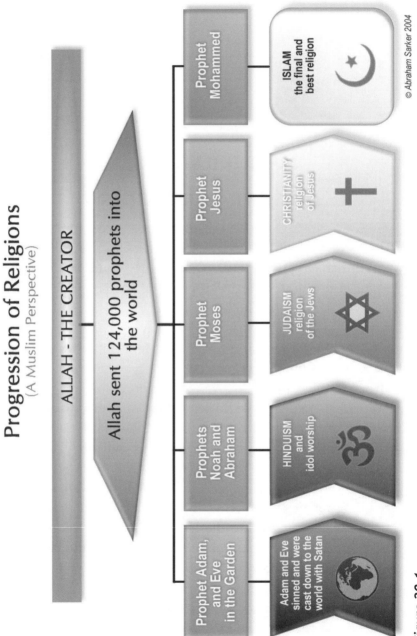

Figure 20.1

reach out to them with the love of Christ and the message of the gospel.

### How Do Muslims View Islam?

Believers in Islam consider their religion the final and best for all of mankind. Prophet Mohammed is considered the "seal of the prophets." No other prophets were necessary after him because the Qur'an, which was revealed to him in the seventh century, is the ultimate Word of God, superseding all previous revelations and religions. Consider the information presented in figure 20.1 on the facing page as the way a Muslim mind sees the progression of religions over history.

*Allah sent 124,000 prophets.* According to the Muslim mindset as illustrated in the chart, Allah (the God of Islam) sent 124,000 prophets into the world to guide human beings on the right path. The six major prophets of Islam include Adam, Noah (Nuh), Abraham (Ibrahim), Moses (Musa), Jesus ('Isa), and Mohammed. Although Allah is believed to have sent books (revelations) to many of these prophets, most of these holy books are currently lost. However, it is important to note that Islamic teaching contends Allah only tried to communicate his law to mankind through prophets, never by sending his Son, Jesus Christ.

*Adam and Eve in the Garden.* According to Islam, when Allah created the first human beings, Adam and Eve, He placed them in the Garden of Eden, which was in heaven. The story of the first humans is similar to the one in the Bible, yet the Bible describes the location of the Garden of Eden as an area in modern-day Iraq, rather than a place in heaven. The Qur'an describes how Satan (Iblis) beguiled Adam and Eve into eating the forbidden fruit in the Garden, thus disobeying Allah. Then, according to Islam, Adam, Eve, and Satan were cast down to the world Allah had created, because of their disobedience. Since this point Allah and Satan have been in a tug-of-war trying to persuade humans to follow their ways.

*Prophets Adam, Noah, and Abraham.* During this first period of time, including the prophetic periods of Adam, Noah (Nuh), and Abraham (Ibrahim), the people of the world practiced the worship of many gods. Muslims consider this polytheism, including worship of idols, like unto Hinduism. During Noah's time the people were so distorted by pagan worship that Allah destroyed the earth by a flood, and started again with Noah's family. Abraham is the prophet that Muslims consider their forefather, the one who introduced the concept of one God, transcendent over all creation. This concept of monotheism was the next step in the progression of religion.

*Prophet Moses.* The next major prophet to come was Moses (Musa) who introduced Judaism and brought the laws of Allah (Torah) to the people of Israel. Those who followed him became Jews. Judaism was the next major progression in religion. However, Moses prophesied that the revelation was not complete, and that the Messiah would be coming next.

*Prophet Jesus.* Subsequently, Islam teaches that Jesus ('Isa) (merely a prophet in Islam) came as the Messiah for the Jewish people, bringing the revelation of Allah called the Injil (Gospel), which contained laws similar to the Torah of Moses. Those who followed Jesus became Christians. With this phase of Christianity, Islam deems the progression of religion almost complete. Yet, here is where Christianity draws a line; the Bible teaches that Jesus is the Alpha and the Omega, His life fulfilled thousands of years of prophecy for the redemption of mankind. Jesus is the way, the truth, and the life; there is no other way to the Father except through Him (John 14:6).

However, Islam insists that Mohammed's existence as the next prophet was necessary because Jesus could not bring the full revelation from Allah, as his life was shortened due to the conflict with the Jews. Muslims believe that Jesus actually foretold Mohammed's coming, and that this prophecy is mentioned in the Christian Bible. In John 14:16-17 Jesus says, "I will ask the Father, and he will give you another Counselor to be with you forever—the Spirit of truth. The world cannot accept him, because it neither sees him nor knows him. But you know him, for he lives with you and will be in you." Muslims insist that this verse refers to Mohammed, while Christians understand its reference to the Holy Spirit.

*Prophet Mohammed.* Finally, Muslims assert that Allah sent Mohammed, the best and final prophet, to reveal the Qur'an, the most perfect book, which supersedes and completes all others. Furthermore, Muslims believe that anyone who was born after Mohammed's time errs if they do not follow the religion of Islam. Those who came before Mohammed did the best they could following the religion of Judaism, until Jesus; then the faithful believers were found within the teachings of Christianity, until Mohammed. Therefore, Muslims believe that all of these previous prophets, including Jesus, were Muslims, and that everyone who followed the prophets before Mohammed was also Muslim. Now the best religion to follow is neither of these two previous faiths of Judaism and Christianity, but, of course, Islam.

Donald Tingle relates a story often told by Muslims to illustrate this same concept. A group of travelers journeyed in a hot, barren desert and came to an oasis where they refreshed themselves. Some remained there to enjoy the relief from the arid heat while others moved along on their journey. After traveling for some time the group found a second oasis that was more beautiful than the first. They refreshed themselves with the clean water and felt relief under the shade of the palm trees. Afterward, some from the group decided to stay at this second oasis, while the rest of the group traveled on. Those who continued on the journey found a third oasis that was even more lush and beautiful than the first two. This oasis offered a flowing spring leading to a cool pool of water surrounded by multiple green shade trees and perfumed flowers. They found refreshment there, and realized they had finally made it to the finest resting place of all.[1]

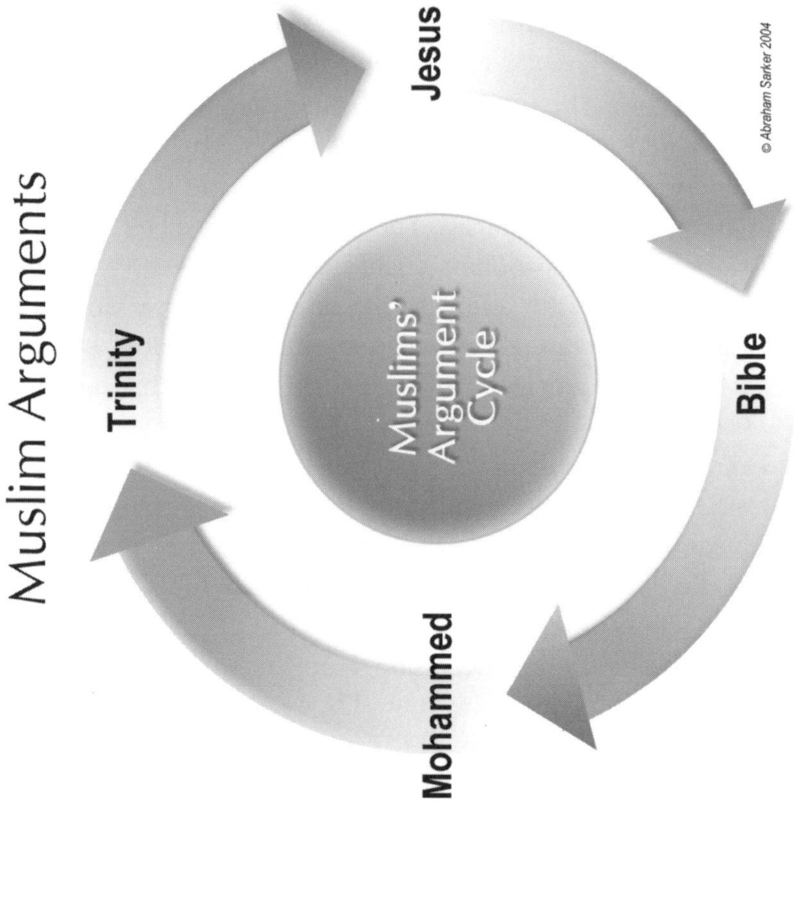

Muslim Arguments

Jesus

Bible

Mohammed

Trinity

Muslims' Argument Cycle

© Abraham Sarker 2004

*Figure 20.2*

Muslims would assert that the first oasis was Judaism, the best religion at its time. However, then came Christianity, the second oasis, which was a better religion than Judaism. Finally, Muslims believe they have reached the third oasis, Islam, which is the best religion of all.

To a Muslim, his or her own religion is the best and final religion, so why should he or she take a step backward and accept Christianity, or two steps backward to accept Judaism, or worst of all, become Hindu? Mohammed abhorred idol worship and taught adamantly against it as one of his fundamental teachings, thus the emphasis of monotheism in Islam.

This brings us to the point of Muslim arguments about the Christian beliefs in God as a Trinity, the person of Jesus Christ, the inerrancy of the Bible, and the role of Mohammed.

Consider the diagram in figure 20.2 on the facing page that highlights the circle of arguments a Christian will often encounter in dialogue with a Muslim.

### Arguments about the Trinity

Most Muslims will begin their arguments against Christianity with a few objections to the Trinity. They often attack the fact that the word *Trinity* does not appear in the Christian Bible. And so they wonder — why do Christians believe in such an unimaginable doctrine?

First, they are correct that the word *Trinity* appears nowhere in Scripture (although it does appear in the Qur'an, as noted previously). Yet the absence of the word does not mean the absence of the doctrine.

Christians believe in only one God, as do Muslims, but see God expressed in the Bible as existing in three Persons: Father God, Son Jesus, and the Holy Spirit (see Matthew 28:18-19; John 14:7; 17:21). Most Muslims automatically assume that the term "Son of God" implies a biological relationship between father and son, but Christians understand this relationship as a unique spiritual communion.

Second, many good examples about how to explain the Trinity have been offered, such as the three states of water or the three parts of an egg. Consider the first example. Water exists in three forms, including ice, liquid water, and water vapor. Each of these states is different in form and purpose, but each is still 100 percent $H_2O$. Or ponder the image of the egg. Eggs contain a yolk, egg white, and shell, each of which serves an important purpose, but together they make one complete egg. These examples each feature one whole item with three distinctive parts or states, with each part serving a different purpose, yet together acting as one. In a roughly similar way, God exists as one God, but in three forms of Father, Son, and Holy Spirit. Consider the diagram in figure 20.3 as another explanation of the Trinity.

To be honest, these sorts of examples failed to help me much as a Muslim in my struggle to understand the true nature of God. It did not make logical sense to me how one God could

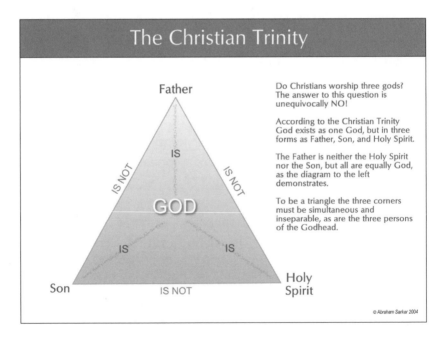

Figure 20.3

exist in three parts. The core problem, of course, was that my eyes had not yet been opened to the truth. Before I could see, God had to change my heart and open my eyes. By His grace, God granted me faith to accept what I could not fully understand.

A better response to Muslims who inquire about the Trinity might be to mention that we humans cannot understand everything about God. If I were to place a miniscule ant on the palm of my hand and ask him, "Little ant, can you tell me how the human brain works?" the ant would obviously be unable to comprehend my words, let alone the human brain, which humans themselves are still seeking to understand. In a similar way, we humans are like tiny ants in our finite understanding. We cannot comprehend everything about God, only that which He reveals to us. We must pray for Muslims, that their eyes and hearts will also be opened to the truth.

Accepting the Trinity, as well as many other issues in life, requires faith. When Muslims challenge me about believing in the Trinity, I ask them if there is anything in Islam that requires faith to believe. Muslims believe, for example, that from the Dome of the Rock in Jerusalem (where a mosque currently stands) Mohammed was taken to the seventh heaven in the blink of an eye, where he talked with Allah, negotiating how many times believers should have to pray each day. Within moments he returned to earth and communicated the events of this "night journey" to his followers. Muslims accept this event unquestioningly — yet believing in this miraculous story also requires faith.

Even though the concept of the Trinity is difficult for most Christians to grasp, and even more so for Muslims, this is a fundamental teaching of Christianity and the Bible gives ample support for it. When you find yourself ministering to Muslims concerning the Trinity, I suggest that you first accept God's truth about His triune nature yourself, and then earnestly pray that your Muslim friend will also have faith to believe.

## Arguments about Jesus

The next issue likely to be raised by a Muslim concerns the person and purpose of Jesus. The issue of Jesus is critical to effectively sharing the gospel with Muslims.

As we have seen, while Muslims acknowledge many wonderful characteristics about Jesus, such as His sinless life, performing of miracles, and even His role as a Messiah, they deny the heart of His person and mission. Islam denies that He was the Son of God and flatly rejects the idea that He was ever crucified or raised from the dead.

Muslims accept the word of the Qur'an, which declares that Jesus was no more than a prophet and that Allah never intended for him to die on the cross. They believe that since Allah would never allow one of His prophets to be harmed so brutally, He caused Judas to die on the cross in Jesus' place. So if Jesus did not die, then He could not be raised to life again, and therefore never provided a sacrifice for the sins of the world — nor was such a sacrifice ever necessary.

This sacrificial aspect of Jesus' life simply does not fit with Muslim theology. Muslims refuse to accept that God would come personally to earth in human form to provide a way of salvation through His Son. Islam has no concept of grace through faith, as in Christianity. Islam contends that the only way one can, perhaps, enter Paradise, is by submitting to Allah through obeying His law.

To effectively minister to Muslims about the person of Jesus, I suggest that you first recognize that while Muslims do believe in Jesus (known to them as 'Isa), they misunderstand His attributes and the significant events of His life. Muslims do not know the same Jesus that you and I know.

Consequently, we need to help Muslims realize that Jesus came more than five hundred years before Mohammed and that His life was well documented by contemporary sources. The four biblical accounts of Jesus' life (Matthew, Mark, Luke, and John) concur on the main events and teachings of Jesus' life. Strong evidence for Jesus' death and resurrection is found in the authentic and well-documented text of the Bible. The circumstances of Jesus' crucifixion are also documented through the writings of other non-Christian sources from the first two centuries, including Jewish historian Josephus, Roman historian Cornelius Tacitus, and historians Julius Africanus and Thallus.[2] The vast evidence we still have today existed before the time of Mohammed. Overwhelming evidence exists to indicate that the events of Jesus' life as recorded in the Bible actually happened.

Even though more evidence documents the reliability of the New Testament Scriptures than any other text from the ancient world, most Muslims refuse to accept it as legitimate.[3] Consequently, the authority of the Bible is the next Muslim argument that often surfaces.

### Arguments about the Bible

Muslims believe that Allah gave a revelation to Moses in the Torah and to Jesus in the Gospel, as well as books to other prophets. Muslims contend, however, that the Bible in existence today has been corrupted, that it differs from the original versions Allah gave to His prophets of old.

Muslims further assert that Christians have misinterpreted portions of the Bible (particularly those that should foretell Mohammed's coming), and have left out whole sections of their Scripture (see surah 5:13-15). If you ask a Muslim, "where, then, are these books that Allah has sent to mankind?" Muslims will answer that they no longer exist, except in heaven.

This answer does not intellectually satisfy most Christians, because the Bible is the most documented text of the ancient world.[4] In fact, of the thousands of ancient copies of the Bible still extant, hundreds existed before Mohammed was born and therefore before the Qur'an came into existence.

The Muslim claim that the Bible contains serious error seems particularly incredible because Mohammed himself advised fellow Muslims to consult with "People of the Book" — Jews and Christians — about their copy of God's Word in order to understand the Qur'an! (See surah 10:94.) Why would Mohammed entreat Muslims to consult the Bible if it was so badly corrupted? This issue creates bewilderment in and of itself.

When a Muslim challenges me about the validity of my Bible, I often respond with a similar challenge for them: "How do you know the Qur'an is the word of God?" And then, "How would you argue for the validity of the Qur'an, when out of several variant copies in circulation during Uthman's leadership of the early Muslim community, only one copy was chosen and the others burned, leaving no others to verify its authenticity?"[5] A Muslim must *believe* that the copy he or she possesses today is the version Mohammed originally received and intended to pass on to future Muslims.

A word should be said here about various Bible translations, since the abundance of Bible versions can cause problems for a seeking Muslim. Historically, Muslims have felt hesitant to translate the Qur'an into other languages, out of fear that its text would be misinterpreted; thus their belief in the importance of it remaining in its original language. Therefore, it can be confusing to Muslim seekers when they encounter different versions of the Bible. This was true of my own experience.

I remember my first Sunday visit to a church after I became a Christian. As the preacher read a few verses from the Bible, I followed along in my own copy of the text, but to my surprise and concern, I realized that my Bible verses did not match his. After the service I visited the pastor and declared that I must have a corrupted version of the Bible. He gave me a new Bible in the King James Version, but not until later did someone explain to me that both the New International Version (NIV) that I had been reading, and the King James Bible, were equally correct versions of the Bible.

Christians need to gently explain to their Muslim brothers and sisters, as someone did to me, that these translations of the

Bible express the same meaning; only the wording has been modified. The biblical message remains as intact and true in these translations as in the original languages.

Although Muslims will customarily refuse to recognize the validity of the Christian Bible, amazingly, they attempt to find evidence for the validity of their revered prophet within the Bible's pages. That brings up the next subject of concern for Muslims: the role of the prophet Mohammed.

### Arguments about Mohammed

Muslims resolutely believe that Mohammed is the last and best prophet ever sent by Allah. Consequently, they ask in frustration, "Why can't Christians accept Mohammed? We accept your prophet, Jesus; why can't you accept our prophet, Mohammed?"

Muslims contend that Christians should accept Mohammed as the final prophet of God because the Bible prophesied his coming. They believe that John 14:16-17 — where Jesus states that a Counselor would come after Him — indicated Mohammed's impending arrival.

While the word translated "Counselor" is similar to the Arabic name "Ahmad," a nickname for Mohammed, other descriptions in the Bible of this "Counselor" are totally inconsistent with the character and events of Mohammed's life.[6] In fact, this passage clearly refers to the coming of the person of the Holy Spirit, the third person of the Trinity.

You might quote John 14:16-17 to your Muslim friend, where Jesus states, "I will ask the Father, and he will give you another Counselor to be with you forever — the Spirit of truth. The world cannot accept him, because it neither sees him nor knows him. But you know him, for he lives with you and will be in you." And then you could ask, "How could it be possible for this 'Spirit of Truth' to be Mohammed? Not only was Mohammed not living with Jesus' disciples at the time Jesus gave this prophecy, but he would not even be born for another five hundred years! Jesus also explained that this Counselor would be *in* his disciples, another impossibility for Mohammed."

Clearly, this Muslim assertion that the Bible prophesied the coming of Mohammed (as the "Counselor" to come) is impossible.

Why can't Christians accept Mohammed's message or his role as a prophet of God? Although he was a strong leader in seventh-century Arabia and his influence as the founder of Islam has reached many parts of the globe, the answer to this question is simple: his message contradicts the message of the Bible.

I suggest that you respect the Muslims' revered prophet by acknowledging that Mohammed was a very religious man who abhorred idols and had the ability to win the allegiance of many in the midst of difficult circumstances. Yet when we compare his life to that of Jesus Christ, he falls short. The Qur'an itself admits that Mohammed had to ask forgiveness for his sins, yet the Qur'an never mentions that Jesus ever committed even a single sin. That fact alone begs for a closer examination of the true identity and mission of Jesus Christ.

### It's Not Impossible

Muslims will present many arguments against Christianity and in favor of Islam when you engage in dialogue with them about matters of faith. The discussion will not likely be easy. But never forget the power of the gospel or the work of the Holy Spirit.

A Muslim really can see the truth and accept Christ as Savior—it's not impossible. My life is proof of the power of the gospel to change lives!

What is it that will cause the eyes of a Muslim to be opened so that he or she can see Christ as Savior and Lord? How can we best share the good news with a Muslim in a way that makes sense and meets a real need? Let's look at that next.

## ° 21 °

# How to Share the Gospel
# with a Muslim

When was the last time you heard someone really long for the salvation of a friend or countryman? Do you remember what that yearning sounded like? I wonder—did it sound anything like the following?

> Brothers, my heart's desire and prayer to God for the Israelites is that they may be saved. For I can testify about them that they are zealous for God, but their zeal is not based on knowledge.

In this way, the apostle Paul expressed his breaking heart for the lost sheep of Israel (Romans 10:1-2). But couldn't this yearning also be felt for Muslims?

Many Muslims are equally zealous for Allah, the god of Islam, but their zeal goes for naught because they do not know God through a personal relationship with Jesus Christ.

How can Christians help Muslims find the true God, so that they too may have the hope of eternal salvation through Jesus? How can we sensitively and effectively communicate the gospel of Jesus Christ to our Muslim friends and acquaintances?

### What Causes Muslims to Turn to Christ?

I believe that the grace of God made possible my conversion from Islam to the truth of Christianity, but I am convinced that God chooses to engage followers of Jesus Christ in the process of planting, tending, and reaping the harvest of souls. I believe that God led me, as a Muslim, to the cross of Jesus Christ through the following four areas, four areas critical to the salvation of other Muslims, as well.

### 1. Your Prayer

Never underestimate the fervent, effectual prayer of the righteous. It really does "avail much" (James 5:16)! I genuinely believe that a Christian like you prayed that God would save a Muslim in Bangladesh, even possibly prayed that God would give a Muslim in Bangladesh a dream that would lead him to the truth. As a result, I am here today professing faith in Jesus Christ.

Prayer is an essential tool in leading a Muslim to Christ, for it is not we who draw them, but the Holy Spirit Himself who draws them to the truth. The importance and power of prayer cannot be overstated.

There is great power in prayer. God's promise in His Word is steadfast, as Jesus assured us: "Again, I tell you that if two of you on earth agree about anything you ask for, it will be done for you by my Father in heaven. For where two or three come together in my name, there am I with them" (Matthew 18:19-20).

After I became a Christian, I faithfully prayed that my family would believe on Christ too; now, several years later, three of my family members in Bangladesh have trusted Christ. I continue to pray for the rest of them, that they all may come to know our Lord and Savior.

How earnestly does God want to save Muslims? We know that our prayers for the salvation of Muslims agree with God's will for them because His Word says, "He is patient with you, not wanting anyone to perish, but everyone to come to repentance" (2 Peter 3:9). God loves Muslims, just as He loves all of humankind, all the men and women He created in His image. He longs for them to open their hearts to receive His love and accept His plan for their lives.

How then should we pray for Muslims? Jesus said, "the harvest is plentiful, but the workers are few. Ask the Lord of the harvest, therefore, to send out workers into his harvest field" (Luke 10:2). Many Muslims are seeking and ready to receive the gospel, but they have never had the opportunity to hear it. We should pray for workers to go and bring these seeking Muslims into the family of God.

We must also realize, however, that prayer for Muslims involves spiritual warfare. Ephesians 6:12 tells us "our struggle is not against flesh and blood, but against the rulers, against the authorities, against the powers of this dark world and against the spiritual forces of evil in the heavenly realms." The enemy comes to steal, kill, and destroy, and is already doing so through the vehicle of Islam, but Jesus has overcome and He wants Muslims to know eternal life through Him.

God already has used dreams and visions to prepare the hearts of many Muslims to hear the gospel of Jesus. Luis Palau, the well-known international evangelist, says that he has heard countless stories about Muslims who report having dreams in which Jesus appears to direct them to a book or a person or a video that can lead them to eternal life. Pray that dreams like these would continue and that they would be a catalyst to salvation for many. Pray that God would bring opportunities in your path to share the love and truth of Christ with a Muslim friend.

I feel led to pray for Muslims as Paul prayed for those in Ephesus, that "the eyes of your heart may be enlightened in order that you may know the hope to which he has called you, the riches of his glorious inheritance in the saints" (Ephesians 1:18). Men and women caught in the mind-set of Islam are steeped in darkness and hopelessness, but thankfully, Jesus is the light of the world! His light brings bright sunshine to those lost in the darkness of fear and despair. We have the privilege to shine His light so that others may see, as a city set on a hill.

### 2. Your Example

"Let your light shine before men, that they may see your good deeds and praise your Father in heaven" (Matthew 5:16). Jesus emboldens us to follow this command, for our ultimate aim in life is to glorify God.

I cannot express how powerful to a Muslim is the example of a Christian committed to serving God. Simply seeing the morality and joy of one called a follower of Jesus speaks volumes to Muslims.

Muslims often have a skewed perception of what a Christian is; they often associate Christianity with the ungodly things done by those claiming to be "Christian," or they mistakenly assume someone is a Christian by default. In Islamic countries, there is no "separation of church and state" as commonly understood in the United States. Actions allowed and promoted by the government are consistent with Islamic law. Hence, many Muslims, especially those living outside of the Western world, assume that the same is true elsewhere, and that therefore the United States must be a Christian country that promotes Christian beliefs and practices, and that most of the people living here are "Christian." In other words, many Muslims equate American with Christian; therefore everything American must also be Christian, including its films, music, media, etc.

Even before talking about Jesus with a Muslim, living a godly life in front of your Muslim friend will impact him or her in an amazing way. As one Christian song states, "You're the only Jesus some will ever see." Seeing a godly marriage and family in which loving and serving God and others remains the central concern will spark interest and curiosity in the mind of a Muslim. Deep down, they long for the personal relationship with God that makes living a godly life possible.

The religion of Islam is very much a works-based religion. Many Muslims feel driven by their fear of not acquiring enough good works to enable them to enter heaven. Consequently, they feel anxious and pressured.

Once, while my wife and I engaged in after-dinner conversation with some Muslim friends, they lit up cigarettes and offered us some as well, but we declined. "No thanks, we don't smoke," we replied. They also offered us alcohol and expressed real surprise when we said, "We appreciate your offer, but we do not drink." The couple glanced at each other in wonder and ironically told us, "You are better Muslims than we are!" — even though they knew we professed Christianity.

This seemed a puzzling statement at first, but it left an impression on my wife and me. We finally realized that while they knew they were supposed to live a righteous life (Islamic law forbids the consumption of alcohol), they were expressing their inability to do so. And they felt impacted by the evidence of the Holy Spirit's life-changing power in our lives.

The word *Muslim* literally means "one who submits to God." Shouldn't we as believers in Christ also be "submitted to God" through Jesus Christ? We should let our light shine so before men that they will see the working power of the Holy Spirit in us who believe.

While it is true that a godly life will speak loudly to Muslims, it is also true that a lifestyle not fully submitted to the lordship of Jesus Christ will leave Muslims disinterested and disenchanted. If we are going to witness for Christ, it is imperative that our lifestyle match our words, for too often Muslims get turned off by the hypocrisy of Christians who say one thing and do another. Many Muslims are generally moral people, with values similar to our own. So if they do not see at least the same level of morality in us as in them, what will attract them to Christ? We would be doing a disservice to the message of Christ by our sloppy spiritual lives.

While we will still make mistakes—becoming a Christian does not mean that we stop being humans—Muslims must see the power of God working through lives fully submitted to the lordship of Jesus Christ. Furthermore, not only will a godly example impact Muslims, but so will a genuine, Christlike love.

### 3. Your Love

Jesus gave us two central commands: to love God, and to love our neighbors as ourselves (see Matthew 22:37-40). It is amazing how abundantly this love can flow from God to us to others—when we allow it to.

God's love for mankind is equally extended to Muslims. We must pray that God will give us the same heart for them that He has, that we will want to develop friendships with Muslims and eventually to share with them the hope and joy found in a relationship with Jesus Christ. Muslims must see that our love is genuine and that it will continue to flow whether or not they choose to accept our faith. We must love unconditionally, as the Father loves us.

May we express by our lives the same attitude described by the apostle Paul: "We loved you so much that we were delighted to share with you not only the gospel of God, but our lives as well, because you had become so dear to us" (1 Thessalonians 2:8).

Dr. William Miller, missionary to Muslims in the Middle East, related a moving story of the effectiveness of Christian love. "It was Mr. Wilson's tears that led me to become a Christian," stated Abbas, a Muslim cleric in Iran.

Abbas went to visit Mr. Wilson, a missionary in his area, several times to discuss Christian doctrine, not with the intent of becoming a Christian, but to humiliate the missionary by arguing the superiority of Islam. While Mr. Wilson patiently tried to explain the common misunderstandings Muslims have about Christianity and to respond to the arguments Abbas presented, the Muslim cleric proudly objected, feeling triumphant in defeating the missionary until, to his surprise, he saw the missionary begin to weep.

Years later, Abbas would explain that, "Mr. Wilson came here, he talked with me and argued with me, but I felt I had overcome him, and I was feeling very proud of myself. Then that man of God felt so sorry for me in my unbelief and pride that he began to weep. His tears did for me what his arguments did not do. They melted my heart, and I believed and became a Christian. Later I was baptized."[1]

God used the power of the gospel and the missionary's heartfelt love to draw this Muslim and his entire family to faith in Christ.

I can also relate to the effectiveness of Christian love in my own life. Not only did believers share the message of the gospel with me, but they shared their lives as well. Where my natural family disowned me when I came to faith in Christ, my Christian friends quickly became my family, caring for me personally and helping me to grow spiritually.

It is through this God-given love that we should share the good news of the gospel.

### 4. Your Witness

While God alone can grant eternal salvation, I believe that God gives followers of Jesus Christ the privilege to witness for Him on this earth. As Saint Francis of Assisi stated, "Preach the gospel at all times. When necessary, use words."

Our lifestyle must present the message of the gospel before our words speak it aloud. After you address the areas of your prayer, example, and love, then is the time to verbally offer your witness.

Share with your Muslim friend not only the message of the gospel and how he or she can find assurance of salvation in Christ, but report what God has done personally in your own life. While Muslims can try to discount what the Bible says, they cannot refute your own experience; and all people, deep down, hunger for the kind of hope, joy, and peace you have through a personal relationship with God in Christ.

Beyond these four general suggestions about how to share the gospel with a Muslim friend, consider a few practical "do's" and "don'ts" about the most effective strategy to use in discussing your Christian faith with a Muslim.

## A Few Do's

### 1. Develop Friendships
Muslims are hospitable people. They want to see the same extension of friendship from you, so show Muslims your true friendship.

How? You can show your Christian love by reaching out in many ways. Invite them to social activities and to your church fellowship, and if you feel comfortable, invite them into your home. Develop genuine relationships with your Muslim friends.

Followers of Islam live all around us, in our places of work, in our neighborhoods, on our university campuses, and just about everywhere else. Many Muslims, especially new immigrants to America, long to build friendships with Americans. When bonds of trust are established, Muslims are much more willing to listen and respect what you have to say.

After you have developed a friendship, listen for and be sensitive to the spiritual and physical needs of your Muslim friend. These needs often reveal an opportunity to show Christian love and to witness for Christ.

### 2. Respect Your Muslim Friend
Respect Muslims as people and respect their religion. Try to see them as God sees them, as people He loves, but who remain lost without the truth of Jesus Christ.

Consider Paul's tactics with the unbelievers in Acts 17. Paul respected the Greeks in Athens by concurring that they were very religious, that they even had an altar "TO AN UN-KNOWN GOD." Paul took this opportunity to explain who this "unknown God" really was. Instead of initially attacking their misunderstanding of worshiping many gods, Paul gently took them from their current understanding and proclaimed the truth about the Creator, the Lord of heaven and earth, and His plan of salvation through Jesus Christ.

Additionally, with the current tragedy of Islamic extremist terrorism, it is important that we do not stereotype all Muslims as terrorists. Not all Muslims are terrorists, and not all terrorists are Muslim. Instead, respect the beliefs of your Muslim friends, get to know them individually, and value them as people. You will see a much better response from Muslims if they see that you genuinely respect them.

### 3. Share Your Personal Testimony

Be prepared to describe what God has done in your own life. Most Muslims long for a personal connection with God, but they do not think it is possible. Be a witness for Christ by giving your testimony about what Jesus has done in and for you. "Always be prepared to give an answer to everyone who asks you to give the reason for the hope that you have. But do this with gentleness and respect" (1 Peter 3:15).

Although Muslims often argue when issues of faith are discussed, I have found that sharing a personal testimony leaves an impact that arguments cannot. Muslims may try to attack Christian doctrine, but they cannot counter personal experience. Just as the blind man Jesus healed gave testimony: "One thing I do know. I was blind but now I see!" (John 9:25), so also we can relate to Muslims areas of God's faithfulness in our own lives.

Usually Muslims will argue with me about doctrinal issues, but they are speechless in response to my personal testimony. Once when I was sharing my testimony with a successful Muslim businessman from Pakistan, "Ali," he intensively listened to my testimony, but made no argument. Just a year later, he gave his life to Christ. Don't underestimate the significance of your testimony.

### 4. Be Knowledgeable about Islam

Christians must emphasize the unique elements of the gospel message. But in order to claim that Christianity offers the truth and the "best deal," one must become familiar with other faiths, otherwise no effectual comparison can be made. Believers in Jesus Christ must have at least a general understanding of the teaching of Islam and the Muslim mind-set if they are going to effectively witness to Muslims.

I vividly remember how Peter, the man who led me to Jesus, was familiar with Islam and my spiritual struggles as a Muslim. Therefore, he was effective in communicating the gospel to me. My hope is that this book will be a tool for you to understand Islam and the Muslim mind-set as you seek to reach out to Muslims with the truth.

### A Few Don'ts

### 1. Don't Argue about Allah, the Trinity, or Jesus as the Son of God

While debates between the Muslim and Christian positions have spurred discussion and interest, there is also a danger in such activities. William Miller, missionary to Muslims, offers a worthy caution for Christians who fervently desire to communicate the truth of the Christian faith, but who forget to speak the truth in love.[2] Miller reminds us that we must beware of the temptation to "put more importance on the triumph of truth than on the salvation of sinners."[3]

Remember, Jesus loved those who murdered Him! It is essential that we too love and pray for those who oppose the gospel, rather than respond to them with contempt. Consider a few suggestions regarding how to sensitively tailor your methods of conversation in order to most effectively meet your Muslim friend's needs.

First, don't refer to Allah as a false or pagan god. This will immediately bring a barrier in your witness. In the mind of a Muslim, the term "Allah" does not refer to an idol, but to the Creator of heaven and earth. Instead of arguing about this term, acknowledge the truth that there is only one God (as Muslims would readily agree). Explain to your Muslim friend the nature of God as you understand Him. Communicate what God means to you.

Second, don't waste time arguing about the Trinity, as your argument will rarely cause a Muslim to believe. The Trinity is a doctrine that requires faith to accept. Instead, pray for your Muslim friend to have the faith to believe, and focus your conversation on the person and purpose of Jesus.

Third, don't initially refer to Jesus as the Son of God. This terminology brings a barrier and confusion for many Muslims and can be explained later.

### 2. Don't Attack Mohammed or Islam

Don't attack your Muslim friend's belief in the prophet Mohammed or Islam. Muslims are taught to believe that their religion is the final and best religion. Hence, their religion and revered prophet are very dear to most Muslims. While you may not agree, respect their beliefs yet without compromising your own convictions.

### 3. Don't Presume You Know Their Beliefs

Don't presume that you know what your Muslim friend believes. Not all Muslims follow orthodox Islam, and your Muslim friend may have a different understanding of his or her own religion. Ask your friend thought-provoking questions. Muslims are usually more than happy to talk about Allah, and this brings an opportunity for discussion about your beliefs, as well.

Don't even presume that you know who the Muslims are. Contrary to the stereotype often communicated in the American media, not all Muslims are Arab, nor are they all terrorists. Actually, less than 20 percent of all Muslims come from the Middle East, and the four largest Islamic nations by population—Indonesia (141 million), Pakistan (94 million), Bangladesh (84 million), and India (82 million; 11 percent of the nearly 1 billion population are Muslim)—are not even in this region of the world.[4]

In America, many of these Muslims hold professional jobs, strive to raise God-fearing families, and love their home country, the United States. While a percentage of the Muslim world carries hostilities against America for its governmental policies and pro-Israeli stance, not all Muslims practice jihad or holy war against non-Muslims. Most view jihad as a struggle to better oneself and one's society, and do not view aggression as a necessary part of their faith unless it comes in their own defense.

### 4. Don't Forget to Pray

As one godly educator and witness for Christ at Cambridge University stated, "To influence you must love, and to love, you must pray."[5] If we want to be effective in our witness to the Islamic world, we must first love Muslims. And that God may plant His love for them in our hearts, we must pray.

It is crucial when ministering to a Muslim that you remain sensitive to the leading of the Holy Spirit. Allow Him to guide you into every word and action (or to refrain therefrom).

And don't be afraid to pray in front of your Muslim friend! Many Muslims don't think Christians pray. I know that might sound ludicrous, but honestly, as a Muslim, I doubted whether they did. As a Muslim, I prayed faithfully five times a day, yet nothing in the information I had acquired about Christians led me to believe that Christians prayed as well, or that their faith in God impacted their life in the least. So I felt amazed one day when I saw a Christian praying over his food. I thought he must be very righteous to pray even over his meal!

While Muslims are required to pray at least five times a day, their prayers differ tremendously from a Christian's prayer, mainly because they pray out of obligation, and they may not feel a closeness to God or receive answers to prayer.

Prayer is the key to preparing both yourself and the hearts of Muslims, whether here in the United States or abroad, many of whom live in societies that seldom have opportunity to even hear the good news of the gospel.

### What Do They Need?

We all know we should witness to our Muslim friends about the gospel of Jesus Christ—but what is it that Muslims most need? What are they missing in Islam that Christ has to offer?

Let's take a look.

## ° 22 °

# What Does Christ Have to Offer to Muslims?

Although I didn't know it at the time, as a Muslim I longed for what Christ had to offer. Eventually I came to see that the Christian faith doesn't offer Muslims a good deal; in fact, it offers a GREAT deal!

Consider the following four areas, key to the gospel of Jesus Christ, that met the deep void in my life I felt as a Muslim.

### A Personal God

When I was a Muslim, I saw God as a distant, capricious judge who sent every individual either to heaven or to hell. His will was unknowable and I had no personal connection with Him. Although I prayed faithfully five times each day, I never knew if Allah was really listening, because my prayers weren't being answered.

My relationship to Allah was like a slave to his master. I performed my good deeds, hoping Allah would be pleased; yet I never knew if my good deeds would be enough. Allah of Islam seemed remote and inaccessible. Consequently, the concept of a *personal* relationship with God felt as foreign to me as it does to most Muslims. Yet, deep within me I longed for a personal God.

As Peter shared the gospel with me (see chapter 2), I saw that I could have such a personal relationship with God through Jesus Christ. I could actually call God my Father! (See Romans 8:15 and 1 John 3:1.) I learned that Jesus came personally to earth and lived among humankind, ultimately giving His life for us. Jesus declared that His disciples no longer had to relate to Him as a slave would to a master, but as friends: "I no longer call you servants, because a servant does not know his master's business. Instead, I have called you friends, for everything that I learned from my Father I have made known to you" (John 15:15).

I had been yearning for just such an opportunity to speak with and know a God who wanted a personal relationship with me—and vast numbers of Muslims still do.

### A Loving God

The next great deal Christianity offers Muslims is the knowledge and experience that God loves us each unconditionally. In Islam, Allah may love those who follow all the rules, but He doesn't love sinners.

I learned from the Bible that God loved me even when I was a sinner. Before I was born, even though He knew all of the wrong things I would do, God still chose to love me and to provide Jesus as a sacrifice for my sins. God loved us so much that He sent His own Son to die in our place, so that we could spend eternity in heaven with Him.

Romans 8:38-39 brings me great comfort, for it assures me of God's steadfast love: "For I am convinced that neither death nor life, neither angels nor demons, neither the present nor the future, nor any powers, neither height nor depth, nor anything else in all creation, will be able to separate us from the love of God that is in Christ Jesus our Lord."

What good news it is to know that we are loved by our Creator unconditionally, and that nothing can separate us from His amazing love!

## A Savior

As a Muslim I struggled to live a righteous life. I prayed five times a day. I fasted during Ramadan. I fulfilled all of my Islamic duties — and yet I, along with all other Muslims, could not say whether Allah would send me to heaven or hell when I died.

Quite simply, there is no assurance of salvation in Islam. As a Muslim, I lived in fear of never completing enough good works. Even if I amassed many more good deeds than bad ones, Allah might still change His mind at the last moment and condemn me to hell.

But Jesus died on the cross to pay for our sins and we can have assurance of salvation through faith in Christ. The famous Scripture verse of John 3:16 emphasizes this wonderful truth about God's love for us: "For God so loved the world, that he gave his one and only Son, that whoever believes in him shall not perish but have eternal life." What good news this is!

Sometimes when I witness to Muslims, I ask them, "Would you consider yourself a good Muslim?" Usually the answer is, "yes." Then I ask, "Do you pray five times a day, fast during Ramadan, and fulfill all of the prescribed duties a good Muslim should complete?" A few devout Muslims can answer this question in the affirmative, but the majority — and particularly most of those in the United States — live as nominal Muslims. When presented with this challenge, many Muslims realize that their lack of fervor for their faith could place them in hell for quite some time (at least, this is what the Qur'an teaches). This reflection on the teachings of their own faith often makes them uneasy with their current spiritual status and sometimes opens discussion for salvation in Christ.

I sometimes use a powerful biblical illustration in my own witness to Muslims. I tell them about the two thieves hanging on their own crosses next to Jesus. One thief ridiculed Jesus. The other realized his own sin and his fast approaching death and turned to Jesus, saying, "Jesus, remember me when you come into your kingdom." Jesus answered him, "I tell you the truth, today you will be with me in paradise" (Luke 23:42-43). The second thief knew that he was dying and that he had only a few moments before his last breath. He did not have the time to fulfill any Muslim duties, such as pray five times a day, fast in the month of Ramadan, or make a pilgrimage to Mecca. Yet, Jesus, with His amazing grace, offered this repentant sinner eternal life.

What good news it is to know that Jesus has already paid for our sins and that we can have assurance of our salvation right here, before we die. The assurance of salvation is a great deal that Christ offers to Muslims!

### The Holy Spirit

The Holy Spirit is a treasure and a gift too wonderful for words. There is no equivalent in Islam.

When Jesus ascended into heaven, He left the Holy Spirit to guide and comfort the believers He left behind. When Mohammed died, however, he left behind only the Qur'an, which pictures Allah as distant and unknowable. The only guide Islam has today is the Qur'an, and it offers little spiritual guidance or comfort, especially when compared to the guidance and comfort of the Holy Spirit. The Holy Spirit speaks to us through the Bible and remains with us and in us, supernaturally guiding and empowering us in every good work (see John 16:13; Acts 1:8; 1 John 3:24; 2 Timothy 1:14).

Islam does not offer the comforting presence of the Holy Spirit, as believers in Jesus Christ experience. Nor does Islam offer the empowering of the Holy Spirit to live a righteous life, an element so crucial to the Christian's daily life.

These four needs—for a personal God, a loving God, a Savior, and the Holy Spirit—were all extremely important to me. Millions of Muslims today are looking for this same hope, expressed in the gospel. Will you share this message, so the 1.2 billion Muslims of the world may live and die with hope?

## A Final Challenge

Can Muslims accept Christ? My life is living proof that this is possible.

God has called us to reach out to our world with the message of His gospel, to let others know of the hope, joy, and peace to be found in a personal relationship with Jesus Christ.

How can you be a part of God's plan for Muslims? It is imperative that you pray, be a godly example, share Christlike love, and witness for Christ.

And what does Christ have to offer Muslims? Christ offers a GREAT deal! Where Allah of Islam is distant, the God of Christianity is a personal Father. Where Allah shows conditional love, our God shows love unconditional and everlasting. Where Islam offers hopelessness, Jesus is the living Savior. Where Islam has a book without a guide, Christianity has a living, Holy Spirit, guiding, comforting, and empowering every believer.

God loves Muslims, and just as He saved me from the bonds of Islam, I know that His arm is not too short to extend His saving grace to Muslims across the globe and right here in America. In fact, millions of Muslims right now are longing for what Christ has to offer through a vital, personal relationship with God.

Will you share this message of hope?

## Appendix A
# Mohammed's Life at a Glance

| Year | Age of Prophet | Event |
|------|----------------|-------|
| 570 A.D. | Birth | Mohammed born in Mecca, Saudi Arabia; his father died while Mohammed was still in the womb |
| 576 | 6 years | Death of Mohammed's mother, 'Amina |
| 582 | 12 | Mohammed's first business trip to Syria |
| 595 | 25 | Mohammed's marriage to Khadija |
| 610 | 40 | Mohammed's first revelation; beginning of prophethood |
| 615 | 45 | Migration of Muslims to Abyssinia (Ethiopia) |
| 619 | 49 | Death of Khadija, Mohammed's first wife, and Abu Talib, Mohammed's uncle |
| 620-621 | 50-51 | Men from Yathrib visit Mohammed in Mecca, accept Islam, and later invite Mohammed to govern Yathrib (Medina) |
| 622 | 52 | *Hijra* — Mohammed escapes from Mecca and flees to Yathrib (Medina) |
| 623 | 53 | Mohammed marries 'Ayisha (age 9) |
| 624 | 54 | Muslim victory at Battle of Badr |
| 625 | 55 | Muslim defeat by Meccans at Battle of Uhud |
| 627 | 57 | Meccans unsuccessfully attack Muslims at Medina |
| 628 | 58 | Muslims attempt to perform pilgrimage in Mecca, but are stopped by Meccans; treaty between Muslims and Meccans |
| 629 | 59 | Muslims enter Mecca for pilgrimage; Meccans vacate the city |
| 630 | 60 | Muslim conquest of Mecca; Mohammed destroys all idols in the Ka'ba |
| 632 | 62 | Mohammed's last sermon. Death of Prophet Mohammed on June 8, A.D. 632 |

# What's the Difference Between Islam and Christianity?

Many have asked, "What's the difference between Islam and Christianity? They both believe in one God, Jesus, the Day of Judgment, and living a righteous life—right? So, aren't they basically the same?"

While Islam accepts many truths from the Bible, it denies the heart of the gospel, the very purpose for Jesus' coming. It is imperative for a Christian to understand the uniqueness of the gospel in the Bible as it compares to the teachings of Islam, in order to respectfully and effectively witness for Christ to a Muslim.

The following gives a brief comparison of the belief systems of these two faiths.

| Belief | Islam | Christianity |
|---|---|---|
| ORIGIN | Mecca, Saudi Arabia, with the life of the prophet Mohammed (A.D. 570-632) | Israel, with Jesus Christ (approx. A.D. 30) |
| NATURE OF GOD | Monotheistic, the Creator, Distant, the Judge, Capricious, Conditionally Loving, Impersonal, Unknowable, Vague | Monotheistic, the Creator, Personal, Father, Unconditionally Loving, Unchangeable, a Trinity, Merciful, sent His Son Jesus to save the world |

| ***Monotheistic*** | ***Monotheistic*** |
|---|---|
| *"Say: He is Allah the One and Only; Allah the Eternal Absolute He begetteth not nor is He begotten; And there is none like unto Him."* (surah 112) | *"Hear, O Israel, the Lord our God, the Lord is one."* (Mark 12:29) |

| ***Master-Slave Relationship*** | ***Father-Child Relationship*** |
|---|---|
| A human's duty is to submit to the will of Allah in everything as an obedient slave. The purpose for the creation of mankind is given in Qur'an surah 51:56, which reads: | While the human response is to serve and worship God, God's love is so great that He grants humans the opportunity to be a part of the family of God. |

252

| Belief | Islam | Christianity |
|--------|-------|--------------|

**NATURE OF GOD** *(continued)*

*Islam:* *"I have created...men that they may serve me."*

*Christianity:* *"Yet to all who received him [Jesus], to those who believed in his name, he gave the right to become children of God—children born not of natural descent, nor of human decision or a husband's will, but born of God."* (John 1:12-13)

*"Ye have received the Spirit of adoption, whereby we cry, Abba, Father."* (Romans 8:15 KSV)

### Conditionally Loving / Unconditionally Loving

*Islam:* Love from Allah is conditional, based on how well an individual submits to Allah's will. Allah loves those who love and obey him, yet not those who don't believe.

*"Say, (O Muhammad, to mankind): If ye love Allah, follow me; Allah will love you and forgive you your sins. Allah is Forgiving, Merciful. Say: Obey Allah and the messenger. But if they turn away, Lo! Allah loveth not the disbelievers (in His guidance)."* (surah 3:31-32)

*"...for Allah loveth not transgressors."* (surah 2:190)

*Christianity:* Jehovah of the Bible loves unconditionally. His nature is loving.

*"God is love."* (1 John 4:16)

Therefore, His actions that result from His nature are also loving. The difference in Jehovah's love is that He loves all of mankind, even those who sin and are still in unbelief.

*"But God demonstrates his own love for us in this: While we were still sinners, Christ [Jesus] died for us."* (Romans 5:8)

### Capricious / Unchangeable

*Islam:* The Qur'an asserts that no change can be made to the Word of Allah.

*"no change can there be in the Words of Allah."* (surah 10:64)

Yet, many examples of abrogations are included in the Qur'anic text. Near the beginning of Mohammed's ministry the Muslims are instructed to exercise tolerance toward those of other faiths (surah 2:256), yet later Muslims are urged to

*"slay the idolators wherever ye may find them."* (surah 9:5)

*Christianity:* Jehovah of the Bible does not change, and neither do His words which He revealed to mankind. His nature is consistently loving and just.

*"I the Lord do not change."* (Malachi 3:6)

*"Heaven and earth will pass away, but my words will never pass away."* (Mark 13:31)

*"I tell you the truth, until heaven and earth disappear, not the smallest letter, not the least stroke of a pen, will by any means disappear from the Law until*

| Belief | Islam | Christianity |
|---|---|---|
| **NATURE OF GOD** *(continued)* | Again where Allah claims that humans have a free will in surah 18:29 | *everything is accomplished."* (Matthew 5:18) |

*"Then whosoever will, let him believe, and whosoever will, let him disbelieve."*

Later, Allah says He has already sealed their fate in advance:

*"Every man's fate We have fastened [o]n his own neck:*

*On the Day of Judgment We shall bring out [f]or him a scroll, Which he will see [s]pread open."* (surah 17:13)

It seems that Allah changes in His instructions to the Muslims as recorded in the Qur'an. He has power to change His laws and previous revelations, and is not consistent in nature.

*"None of Our revelations do We abrogate or cause to be forgotten but We substitute something better or similar; knowest thou not that Allah hath power over all things?"* (surah 2:106)

*"Every good gift and every perfect gift is from above, and cometh down from the Father of lights, with whom is no variableness, neither shadow of turning."* (James 1:17 KJV)

### Distant, Unknowable

There is no concept of a personal relationship with almighty God (Allah) in Islam.

Rather, believers offer up prayers and other duties to please God, who resides in heaven. In order for Allah to hear one's prayer, the believer must be ceremonially clean (having performed the ritual ablution) and must pray certain words in Arabic (even if one does not understand what they mean). These prayers must also be offered at five specific times each day.

### Personal

God takes delight in having a close, personal relationship with the human beings He created.

*"Now this is eternal life; that they may know you, the only true God, and Jesus Christ, whom you have sent."* (John 17:3)

*"Don't you know that you yourselves are God's temple and that God's Spirit lives in you?"* (1 Corinthians 3:16)

*"If ye had known me, ye should have known my Father also: and from henceforth ye know him, and have seen him."* (John 14:7)

| Belief | Islam | Christianity |
|---|---|---|
| **NATURE OF GOD** *(continued)* | Allah only communicated His revelations to a few special prophets. In Islam, God never sent His Son to reveal Himself to mankind, and there is no Holy Spirit to dwell in and with believers.<br><br>*"It is not fitting for a man that Allah should speak to him except by inspiration or from behind a veil or by the sending of a Messenger to reveal with Allah's permission what Allah wills: for He is Most High Most Wise."* (surah 42:51)<br><br>The will of Allah is unpredictable, and Allah Himself cannot really be known or discerned, yet submission to Him is required of all mankind. | *"Abide in me, and I in you. As the branch cannot bear fruit of itself, except it abide in the vine; no more can ye, except ye abide in me."* (John 15:4 KJV)<br><br>*"Behold, I stand at the door, and knock: if any man hear my voice, and open the door, I will come in to him, and will sup with him, and he with me."* (Revelation 3:20 KJV)<br><br>Believers in Jesus Christ can have an ongoing relationship with God, praying to God continually (in their own language), and their prayers are answered.<br><br>*"Pray continually."* (1 Thessalonians 5:17)<br><br>*"Again, I tell you that if two of you on earth agree about anything you ask for, it will be done for you by my Father in heaven. For where two or three come together in my name, there am I with them."* (Matthew 18:19-20) |
| **WILL OF GOD** | Allah is sovereign and all-powerful, He created all that is, and He wills all that happens. Qur'an surah 9:51 states,<br><br>*"Say: 'Nothing will happen to us except what Allah has decreed for us: He is our protector': and on Allah let the believers put their trust."*<br><br>Everything that occurs is by the will of Allah, and He guides some rightly, and leads others astray.<br><br>*"Whom Allah doth guide he is on the right path: whom He rejects from His guidance such are the persons who perish. Many are the Jinns and men We have made for Hell...."* (surah 7:178-179) | God desires that all the people He has created will choose to love Him and walk in His ways. Clearly, in 2 Peter 3:9 Jehovah of the Bible is<br><br>*"patient with you, not wanting anyone to perish, but everyone to come to repentance."*<br><br>Jehovah (God) knows the future, but does not create some individuals intending for them to perish in Hell. Any individual's eternity is spent in Hell because of his or her own choices and the natural consequences thereof, not because God desired that end for them when He created them. |

| *Belief* | *Islam* | *Christianity* |
|---|---|---|
| **NATURE OF MAN** | All people are born as true Muslims, pure and innocent. Islamic theology considers the event of the "fall" as a minor single slip by Adam and Eve, which was entirely forgiven after they repented. No further effect on man occurred from their disobedience. Man sins out of weakness and forgetfulness. | The event of Adam and Eve's disobedience, "the fall," is considered an important turning point in mankind's relationship to God, resulting in mankind thereafter being born with a sinful nature, separated from God by sin. Romans 5:12 explains, <br><br>*"...sin entered the world through one man, and death through sin, and in this way death came to all men, because all sinned...."* <br><br>Therefore, mankind is in need of a Savior, and God provided a plan of salvation through the person of Jesus Christ. |
| **HOLY SCRIPTURES** | The Qur'an, the revelation received by Mohammed from the angel Gabriel, is the final and best revelation for mankind. It supersedes the previous revelations given by Allah's earlier prophets (including the Torah of Moses and the Gospel of Jesus). <br><br>*"He hath revealed unto thee (Mohammed) the Scripture with truth, confirming that which was (revealed) before it, even as He revealed the Torah and the Gospel."* (surah 3:3) | The Bible (Old and New Testaments) <br><br>*"All scripture is given by inspiration of God, and is profitable for doctrine, for reproof, for correction, for instruction in righteousness."* (2 Timothy 3:16 KJV) |

### Authority of the Bible

Muslims are admonished to learn from the People of the Book (Jews and Christians).

*"...ask those who have been reading the Book from before thee."* (surah 10:94)

Yet the Qur'an states that the People of the Book misinterpret and withhold parts of the scriptures (especially the parts that foretell Mohammed's coming), so the version Christians

### Authority of the Qur'an

Although Mohammed claimed he was continuing the revelation from the Torah, Psalms, and Gospel, the very heart of Jesus' gospel (good news) is missing in Mohammed's revelation. Mohammed accepted Jesus as merely another prophet. He rejected Jesus' death and resurrection, and the plan of salvation through Christ alone.

In Galatians 1:6-8, several centuries before Mohammed was born, the apostle Paul warned believers in Jesus

| Belief | Islam | Christianity |
|--------|-------|--------------|
| HOLY SCRIPTURES (continued) | and Jews have today is corrupted and unacceptable to Muslims. | Christ of those who would come and try to dissuade them to accept another gospel. |

*"But because of their breach of their Covenant We cursed them and made their hearts grow hard: they change the words from their (right) places and forget a good part of the Message that was sent them nor wilt thou cease to find them barring a few ever bent on (new) deceits: ...From those too who call themselves Christians We did take a Covenant but they forgot a good part of the Message that was sent them so We estranged them with enmity and hatred between the one and the other to the Day of Judgment. And soon will Allah show them what it is they have done: O People of the Book! there hath come to you Our Apostle revealing to you much that ye used to hide in the Book and passing over much (that is now unnecessary): There hath come to you from Allah a (new) Light and a perspicuous Book."* (surah 5: 13-15)

*"I marvel that you are turning away so soon from Him who called you in the grace of Christ, to a different gospel, which is not another; but there are some who trouble you and want to pervert the gospel of Christ. But even if we, or an angel from heaven, preach any other gospel to you than what we have preached to you, let him be accursed."* (NKJV)

Mohammed's message took many truths from the Bible, yet changed them in significant ways, even distorting the understanding of who the person of Jesus Christ is, and the purpose for which He was sent.

Therefore, in light of the scriptures already given in the Old and New Testaments, the message that Mohammed received from the angel and consequently taught (the Qur'an), must be considered as a "different gospel," and is not acceptable as God-inspired.

| | | |
|--------|-------|--------------|
| TRINITY | Islam adheres to strict monotheism and denies that God could exist as one, but in three persons. The Trinity is also often misunderstood to be the Father, Mother Mary, and Son Jesus. | The Bible teaches that God exists as three persons in complete unity of will, purpose, and action, yet functioning in three different ways as a "Trinity." The Old and New Testaments support the Christian belief in a Triune God consisting of the Father God, Son Jesus, and Holy Spirit, the three in one. |

*"And when Allah saith: O Jesus, son of Mary! Didst thou say unto mankind: Take me and my mother for two gods beside Allah? he saith: Be glorified! It was not mine to utter that to which I had no right."* (surah 5:116)

*"O people of the Book! commit no excesses in your religion: nor say of Allah aught but truth. Christ Jesus the son of Mary was (no more than) an Apostle of Allah and His Word which*

*"That all of them may be one, Father, just as you are in me and I in you."* (John 17:21)

*"All authority in heaven and on earth has been given to me. Therefore go and make disciples of all nations, baptizing them in the name of the Father and of the Son and of the Holy Spirit."* (Matthew 28:18-19)

| Belief | Islam | Christianity |
|---|---|---|
| TRINITY (continued) | *He bestowed on Mary and a Spirit proceeding from Him: so believe in Allah and His Apostles. Say not "Trinity": desist: it will be better for you: for Allah is One Allah: glory be to him: (for Exalted is He) above having a son."* (surah 4:171, see also surah 19:35) | |

JESUS

Jesus is an esteemed prophet in Islam. He is recorded to have performed miracles, and is the only prophet to be absolutely sinless. The name of Jesus ('*Isa* in Arabic) is mentioned ninety-seven times in the Qur'an, and he is given such honorary titles as "the Messiah" (surah 4:171; 5:72), "the Spirit of God," and "the Word of God" (surah 4:169-171). He is considered a "Sign unto Men" and "Mercy from (God)" (surah 19:21), as well as "the Speech of Truth" (surah 19:34).

However, these same terms have different meanings from the Muslim and Christian perspectives.

Jesus is the Son of God and the Savior for mankind. He is called the Son of God because of His unique covenant fellowship with God. He is the only Redeemer of God's elect (1 Tim. 2:5, 6); who, being the eternal Son of God, became man (John 1:14; Gal. 4:4), to die as a sacrifice for the sins of the world.

### Crucifixion / Resurrection

Muslims believe that Jesus was not crucified, but that he was taken up to heaven and someone was crucified in his place.

*"That they said (in boast) 'We killed Christ Jesus the son of Mary the Apostle of Allah'; but they killed him not nor crucified him but so it was made to appear to them."* (surah 4:157)

In the Qur'an surah 5:110 Allah is telling Jesus how He (Allah) withheld the Jews from killing Him (Jesus):

*"And behold! I did restrain the Children of Israel from (violence to) thee when thou didst show them the*

### Crucifixion / Resurrection

The Bible provides strong historical evidence for the crucifixion and resurrection of Jesus, verified by many witnesses, confirmed by the abundance of manuscripts, over 5,000 New Testament copies, dating back to within 100 to 225 years of the actual first-century writers.

Paul asserts a definition of the gospel in 1 Corinthians 15:1-4:

*"Now, brothers, I want to remind you of the gospel I preached to you, which you received and on which you have taken your stand. By this gospel you are saved, if you hold firmly to the word I preached to you. Otherwise, you have believed in vain. For what I received I*

| Belief | Islam | Christianity |
|---|---|---|

**JESUS**
**(continued)**

*Clear Signs and the unbelievers among them said: 'This is nothing but evident magic.'"*

*passed on to you as of first importance: that Christ died for our sins according to the Scriptures, that he was buried, that he was raised on the third day according to the Scriptures."*

### Messiah

Nowhere in the Qur'an does it explain exactly who or what the Messiah is. In some Islamic teaching Messiah means "the anointed one," and therefore this title is applied to Mohammed as well. The distinction Muslims make for Jesus is that He was the Messiah for the Jewish people only, His ministry was limited to this people group.

### Messiah

The Old Testament contains several detailed prophecies of a specific Messiah. This coming Messiah was prophesied to be born in Bethlehem (Micah 5:2) of King David's lineage (Isaiah 11:1-5), yet was the "son of man" that existed from the ancient of days (before time), and that all people would worship Him in His everlasting dominion (Daniel 7:13-14).

This Messiah would have His hands and feet pierced, and have people casting lots for His clothing, thus indicating circumstances of Christ's coming crucifixion (Psalm 22). Jesus fulfilled these and many other prophecies spoken about Him, leading Christians to conclude that He was the Messiah spoken of by so many prophets of old.

Furthermore, Jesus' role as the Messiah would benefit all of humanity, not just the Jewish nation.

*"For I am not ashamed of the gospel of Christ: for it is the power of God unto salvation to every one that believeth; to the Jew first, and also to the Greek."* (Romans 1:16 KJV)

Jesus confirmed this when he spoke of the Gentile centurion who asked Jesus to heal his servant,

*"I tell you the truth, I have not found anyone in Israel with such great faith. I say to you that many will come from the east and the west, and will take their places at the feast with Abraham, Isaac, and Jacob in the kingdom of heaven."* (Matthew 8:10-11)

| Belief | Islam | Christianity |
|---|---|---|

**JESUS**
*(continued)*

### Return to Earth

According to Islam, Jesus will return to earth just before the end times in order to accomplish several specific objectives. He will: (1) kill the Antichrist (*al-Dajjal*), (2) kill all the pigs, (3) destroy all the synagogues and churches, (4) break the cross, (5) establish the religion of Islam, (6) live for forty years, (7) marry, (8) die, and be buried beside Mohammed in the prophet mosque of Medina.

### Return to Earth

Jesus will come back suddenly, at a time that no one except God knows. He will return the way He ascended, in the clouds, visibly, with a loud command and a trumpet sound. Jesus will usher in the resurrection, the dead in Christ shall rise first, and the righteous that are living will be caught up with Him in the clouds. The biblical account does not include a time of earthly marriage and the building of a physical human family for Jesus. Conversely, His coming will be a time of sorting out the righteous from the unrighteous (Matthew 24–25; 1 Thessalonians 4:13-18).

### Son of God

Jesus (Isa) is not the Son of God, but merely a human prophet, bringing the "Gospel" revelation from Allah.

*"Christ the son of Mary was no more than an Apostle; many were the Apostles that passed away before him."* (surah 5:75)

### Son of God

Jesus is the Son of God because of His unique covenant (not biological) relationship with God.

Consider John 1:1-3 where Jesus' role is developed further:

*"In the beginning was the Word, and the Word was with God, and the Word was God. He was with God in the beginning. Through him all things were made; without him nothing was made that has been made."*

*"But these are written that you may believe that Jesus is the Christ, the Son of God, and that by believing you may have life in his name."* (John 20:31)

### Virgin Birth

Islam accepts the virgin birth of Jesus. The Islamic account asserts that Angel Gabriel delivered the message of the miraculous birth to Mary:

*"He (Angel Gabriel) said: I am only a messenger of thy Lord, that I may bestow on thee a faultless son.*

### Virgin Birth

The record of Jesus' birth through the Virgin Mary is recorded in the Gospels.

*"This is how the birth of Jesus Christ came about: His mother Mary was pledged to be married to Joseph, but before they came together, she was found to be with child through the Holy Spirit."* (Matthew 1:18)

| Belief | Islam | Christianity |
|---|---|---|
| JESUS (continued) | *She (Mary) said: How can I have a son when no mortal hath touched me, neither have I been unchaste!*<br><br>*He (Angel Gabriel) said: So (it will be). Thy Lord saith: It is easy for Me. And (it will be) that We may make of him a revelation for mankind and a mercy from Us, and it is a thing ordained.*" (surah 19:19-21) | This confirmed the prophecy of Isaiah about the coming Savior:<br><br>*"Therefore the Lord himself will give you a sign: The virgin will be with child and will give birth to a son, and will call him Immanuel [God with us].*" (Isaiah 7:14) |
| MOHAMMED | Islam teaches that Mohammed is the last and best prophet sent by Allah to mankind. Through him was revealed the final and best revelation.<br><br>*"[Mohammed] is the messenger of Allah and the Seal of the Prophets."* (surah 33:40)<br><br>Orthodox Islam does not claim Mohammed to be divine, but his example is emulated throughout the Muslim world as the perfect model for mankind. | Mohammed was a very religious man who abhorred idol worship and passionately believed in one god, Allah. However, although he appears to have begun his mission as a sincere proclaimer of truth as he saw it, somewhere along the way it seems he was swayed by personal and political gain to proclaim a "different gospel."<br><br>The revelations of a prophet of God, according to the Bible, must agree with revelations given before. Mohammed's message contradicted the Word of God revealed by previous apostles and prophets, and he cannot therefore be considered as God's prophet. Rather, he is one of the false prophets foretold by Christ in Matthew 24:24-25, who would lead many astray. |
| BASIC TENETS | The five mandatory beliefs:<br>• Allah (monotheism)<br>• Angels<br>• Prophets<br>• Holy Scriptures<br>• Day of Judgment<br><br>The five pillars (practices) of Islam include the<br>• *Shahada*, or creed of Islam<br>• Ritual prayer (*salat* or *salah*)<br>• Fasting in the month of Ramadan (*sawm*)<br>• Performing pilgrimage to Mecca (*hajj*)<br>• Almsgiving (*zakat* or *zakah*). | Jesus said that all of the other laws given by God fall under two great commandments:<br><br>*"Jesus said unto him, Thou shalt love the Lord thy God with all thy heart, and with all thy soul, and with all thy mind. This is the first and great commandment. And the second is like unto it, Thou shalt love thy neighbour as thyself. On these two commandments hang all the law and the prophets."* (Matthew 22:37-40 KJV) |

| Belief | Islam | Christianity |
|--------|-------|--------------|
| BASIC TENETS *(continued)* | Some Muslims add holy war (*jihad*) as the sixth pillar in this set. | |
| SALVATION | There is no Savior in Islam. Muslims must save themselves by performing good deeds. | Salvation is not earned through good works, but rather is a gift from God. |

Islam column (continued):

The Qur'an teaches that two things are required as means to salvation: faith (*iman*) and action (*amal*). Surah 5:9 explains *"To those who believe and do deeds of righteousness hath Allah promised forgiveness and a great reward."*

Islamic teaching asserts that God (Allah) will weigh one's good and bad deeds on a scale on the Day of Judgment. If an individual has acquired more good than bad deeds he may go to heaven, but there is no assurance of one's salvation because Allah may change His mind at the last minute.

*"He punishes whom He pleases and He grants mercy to whom He pleases and towards Him are ye turned."* (surah 29:21)

However, Mohammed taught that if one dies in a holy war for the cause of Islam he or she will be granted Paradise (heaven).

Christianity column (continued):

*"For by grace are ye saved through faith; and that not of yourselves: it is the gift of God: Not of works, lest any man should boast."* (Ephesians 2:8-9 KJV)

One must repent of one's sins and believe in the Lord Jesus Christ as Savior to receive this salvation.

*"For God so loved the world that he gave his one and only Son, that whoever believes in him shall not perish but have eternal life. For God did not send his Son into the world to condemn the world, but to save the world through him."* (John 3:16-17)

Those who receive the gift of Jesus Christ have assurance of salvation and eternal life in heaven.

*"I write these things to you who believe in the name of the Son of God so that you may know that you have eternal life."* (1 John 5:13)

Salvation comes through nothing and no one except Jesus Christ.

*(Jesus said) "No one comes to the Father, except through me."* (John 14:6)

Humans must be born not only of the flesh but also of the Spirit, or "born again."

*"Jesus answered... Verily, verily, I say unto thee, Except a man be born again, he cannot see the kingdom of God."* (John 3:3 KJV)

Dr. Miller, long-term missionary to Muslims, highlighted the differences between these two faiths with the following elucidating statement:

> It is the difference between faith in a loving Father in heaven, who like the good shepherd seeks for the one who is lost till he finds it, and submission to the unpredictable will of an all powerful God who is unlike anything that one can imagine, and is therefore unknowable; between putting one's trust for salvation and forgiveness in God's Son who died as a sacrifice for sinners, and attempting to save oneself by doing works of merit, which will never be enough to cancel one's sins; between following a living Lord who conquered death by rising from the tomb on the third day and is with his disciples always, and making a pilgrimage to the grave of a man who died more than 1,300 years ago and whose tomb is not empty; between the possibility of living a pure and holy life in the power of the Holy Spirit, and struggling in one's own strength to overcome sin and Satan and live a life pleasing to a holy God; between having as one's example and guide the sinless Son of God, and the "Prophet" from Mecca who, according to the Koran, was only a man like other men, and was commanded by God to repent of his sins; between facing death with the assurance of immediate entrance into the Father's House to be forever in the holy presence of Christ, and undergoing the terrifying questioning of the two angels, and the possibility of final entrance into the fires of hell.

Clearly, a significant difference exists between Islam and Christianity. Although the two faiths appear to share many common beliefs, further study reveals undeniable and critical variances.

May it soon be said for the many Muslims who, like myself before I met Christ, have not yet seen the light of the truth: "the people walking in darkness have seen a great light; on those living in the land of the shadow of death, a light has dawned" (Isaiah 9:2).

# Glossary of Islamic Terms

**'Abdu'llah:** Mohammed's father, literal meaning — "servant of Allah"

**'Abdu'l-Muttalib:** Mohammed's grandfather

**Abu Bakr:** a wealthy and respected merchant of Mecca who was Mohammed's close friend and the first man to accept Islam outside of the prophet's family; according to Sunni Muslims he was the first Muslim caliph. He gave his daughter, 'Ayisha, in marriage to Mohammed after Khadija's death.

**Abu Talib:** Mohammed's uncle who looked after Mohammed as an orphan

**AH:** "After Hijrah" (anno hegirae) – an abbreviation for the years of the Muslim calendar, which begins after the flight of Mohammed (in A.D. 622)

**'Ali ibn Aby Talib:** Mohammed's cousin and second convert to Islam. 'Ali later married Mohammed's only daughter, Fatima, and succeeded Mohammed as the fourth caliph of Islam.

**Allah:** Arabic word for God

**'Amina:** the mother of Mohammed

**'Ayisha:** Mohammed's youngest and favorite wife

**caliph:** literally, the "successor" in Arabic, but came to refer to the role of the religious and political leader who would govern the Muslim community

**Dawud:** prophet David

**Fatima:** Mohammed's daughter and only surviving child through his first wife, Khadija

**fatwa:** legal/religious sentence pronounced by a Muslim religious leader through the use of Islamic law

**five pillars:** principal religious duties of Islam including recitation of the creed (shahada), prayers (salat), fasting (sawm), almsgiving (zakat), pilgrimage to Mecca (hajj)

**Hadith:** the oral traditions of Mohammed's words and actions, which were later written down

**hafiz:** one who has memorized the entire Qur'an, a professional reciter

**hajj:** pilgrimage to Mecca, one of the pillars of Islam

**halal:** food that has been prepared according to Islamic law

**hijra:** "migration" of Mohammed from Mecca to Medina (Yathrib) in A.D. 622. This signifies an important turning point in the religion of Islam and is the beginning of the Muslim calendar.

**Iblis:** the name for Satan in the Qur'an

**Ibrahim**: prophet Abraham

**ifter**: the breaking of the fast in the month of Ramadan

**iman**: Muslim beliefs (such as in God, angels, prophets, holy scriptures, and the Day of Judgment). Distinguished from them are the Muslim practices, or *deen*.

**infidels**: non-Muslims

**Injil**: According to Islam this Holy Scripture "Gospel" was revealed to the Prophet Jesus ('Isa), but the original has been lost, and only the corrupted Christian version remains.

**'Isa**: the Arabic name for Jesus

**Islam**: a religion founded by the prophet Mohammed. *Islam* literally translated means "submission" or "surrender" (to the will of Allah).

**jihad**: a holy war, a struggle for the cause of Allah (physical and/or with words)

**Ka'ba**: a cubicle stone structure in the city of Mecca that is believed to be the first house of worship dedicated to one God (built by Abraham and Ishmael). Muslims bow down toward this structure in their ritual prayers. The black stone housed inside of the structure supposedly fell from heaven and has been kissed by Mohammed and Muslims since his time. Millions of Muslims circle around this structure during the rite of pilgrimage (hajj).

**Khadija**: a wealthy widow of Mecca who married Mohammed after he worked for her caravan. She was Mohammed's first wife, fifteen years his elder, and the first convert to Islam.

**"La ilaha illa Allah, Mohammed rasul Allah"**: see shahada

**Mecca**: the birthplace of Mohammed, located in Saudi Arabia, it is the holiest city in Islam and must be visited for pilgrimage by all Muslims who are physically and financially able.

**Medina**: (formerly Yathrib) the second most holy city in Islam (after Mecca) where Mohammed fled in A.D. 622 during the hijra

**minaret**: a tower at a mosque from which prayer calls are given

**mi'raj**: night journey of Mohammed in which he dreamed he was taken from the Ka'ba in Mecca to Jerusalem's holy temple from which he went for a brief visit with Allah in heaven

**Mohammed**: (A.D. 570-632) the founder of Islam, he is considered Islam's "seal of the prophets" as he brought the final and complete revelation of the Qur'an from Allah.

**mosque**: building where Muslims gather for prayers and other congregational meetings

**Mount Hira**: a mountain near Mecca where it is believed Mohammed received his revelations from the angel Gabriel

**Musa**: prophet Moses

**Muslim**: literally, "one who submits" to Allah, a follower of Islam (and Mohammed)

**Nuh**: prophet Noah

**Quraish**: the prominent Arab tribe that controlled the Ka'ba during Mohammed's time and from which Mohammed traced his lineage

**Qur'an**: the revelation received by the prophet Mohammed from the angel Gabriel over a twenty-three-year period. Literally "Recitation," as that is how the revelation was originally received and transmitted on to others.

**rak'ah**: regimented obligatory prayer of Muslims

**Ramadan**: ninth month of the lunar year commemorating the giving of the Qur'an to Mohammed. During this month Muslims fast from sunrise to sunset as one of the pillars of Islam.

**rasul**: Allah's apostle or messenger, who brings a revelation from Allah. A distinction is made in Islam, however, between those individuals who simply carry information and proclaim God's news, traditionally "prophets," al nabbi in Arabic, and those who are also sent with divine Scripture to reform and lead mankind, called "messenger," or rasul.

**salaam**: Arabic word for peace. "Salaam Alekum" or "Peace be upon you" is a common greeting among Muslims.

**shahada(h)**: the fundamental creed of Islam, "La ilaha illa Allah, Mohammed rasul Allah" (There is no god but Allah, and Mohammed is Allah's messenger.)

**Shiite**: the major Islamic sect (besides Sunnis). Shiites believe that Ali, Mohammed's son-in-law, was the true successor to Mohammed.

**shirk**: the associating of anything (or anyone) with Allah, the only unpardonable sin

**Sunni**: the main sect of Islam who believes the true line of succession after Mohammed was the four caliphs: Abu Bakr, Omar, Uthman, and Ali

**surah**: (surat) a chapter in the Qur'an; there are a total of 114 altogether.

**tawhid**: the oneness of Allah

**Tawrut**: Original Holy Scripture of the Torah or Pentateuch of Moses (Musa), which Muslims believe has been lost

**Umar ibn al Khattab**: the second caliph of the Muslim community

**umma**: Muslim politico-religious community

**'Uthman**: an early convert to Islam and the third Muslim Caliph to succeed Mohammed

**Yathrib**: later renamed Medina, the second holiest city in Islam

**Zabur**: original Holy Scripture of the Psalms of the Prophet David, which Muslims believe has been lost

# Notes

## Introduction

1. Sharif Shuja, "Islam and the West: From Discord to Understanding," *Contemporary Review, vol. 278, no. 1624 (May 2001)*, 257-63.
2. Ibid.; "Varieties of Worship: American Mosques, U.S. Department of State International Information Programs," http://usinfo.state.gov/products/pubs/muslimlife/mosques.htm (February 19, 2004); "Varieties of Worship: Demographic Facts, U.S. Department of State International Information Programs," http://usinfo.state.gov/products/pubs/muslimlife/demograp.htm (February 19, 2004). The calculated number of Muslims in the United States varies depending on the source. However, a survey released in April 2001 by Hartford Seminary's Hartford Institute for Religious Research in Connecticut titled "Mosque in America: A National Portrait," part of a larger study conducted on American congregations called "Faith Communities Today," asserts that two million Muslims are actually involved with a mosque in some capacity. Some disagreements as to the numbers include factors of Muslims who don't participate in mosque activities or Muslims who have abandoned their faith since their arrival in the United States.
3. Manijeh Daneshpour, "Muslim Families and Family Therapy," *Journal of Marital and Family Therapy*, vol. 24, no. 3 (July 1998), 355-368.

## 4. The Early Life of Mohammed

1. Alhaj A. D. Ajijola, *The Essence of Faith in Islam* (Lahore, Pakistan: Islamic Publications, Ltd., 1978), 217.
2. Annemarie Schimmel, *And Muhammad Is His Messenger: The Veneration of the Prophet in Islamic Piety* (Chapel Hill: The University of North Carolina Press, 1985), 239, 256.
3. Joseph Gudel, *To Every Muslim an Answer* (Thesis, Simon Greenleaf School of Law, 1982), 72.
4. Lewis Hopfe, (ed.) Mark Woodward, *Religions of the World,* 7th ed. (Upper Saddle River, N.J.: Prentice Hall, 1998), 356.
5. Montgomery Watt, "The Way of the Prophet" in *Eerdman's Handbook to the World's Religions* (Grand Rapids, MI: William B. Eerdmans Publishing Company, 1982), 307.
6. Hopfe, 358.
7. Hopfe, 358; William A. Miller, *A Christian's Response to Islam* (Phillipsburg, N.J.: Presbyterian and Reformed Publishing Co., 1976), 45.
8. Ibid.
9. Miller, 15.

10. "Ingrid Mattson: What Is Islam?" http://www.cnn.com/2001 COMMUNITY10/18/mattson.cnna/ (October 18, 2001).

11. Martin Lings, *Muhammad* (London: George Allen and Unwin Ltd., 1983), 22.

12. Chart adapted from "Origin of the Arab People," *Understanding Islam: An Interfaith Evangelism Associate Manual* (Alpharetta, GA: North American Mission Board, SBC, 1995). Mohammed is believed to have descended from the tribe of Kedar, son of Ishmael. Several scriptural references indicate the region Bedouin people settled in. See Isaiah 42:11; 21:16-17; Jeremiah 49:28-29.

13. W. Montgomery Watt, *Muhammad's Mecca* (Edinburgh: Edinburgh University Press, 1988), 44-45.

14. Ibn Ishaq, *Sirat Rasul Allah [The Life of Muhammad]*, trans. A. Guillaume (New York: Oxford University Press, 1980), 81.

15. Robert Payne, *The Holy Sword, The Story of Islam from Muhammad to the Present* (New York: Harper and Brothers, 1959), 13-14.

16. J. Murdoch, *Arabia and Its Prophet* (Madras, India: The Christian Literature Society for India, 1992), 15.

17. Anis Shorrosh, *Islam Revealed: A Christian Arab's View of Islam* (Nashville, TN: Thomas Nelson, Inc., 1988), 50.

18. Payne, 13-14.

19. Ergun Mehmet Caner and Emir Fethi Caner, *Unveiling Islam: An Insider's Look at Muslim Life and Beliefs* (Grand Rapids, MI: Kregel Publications, 2002), 40-41.

20. Miller, 15.

21. Muhammad Husayn Haykal, *The Life of Muhammad* (North American Trust Publications, 1976), 70.

22. Ibn Ishaq, 106.

23. Haykal, 74.

24. Ibn Ishaq, 106-107.

25. See Hopfe, 360; Miller, 19-20; Norman Geisler and Abdul Saleeb, *Answering Islam: The Crescent in the Light of the Cross* (Grand Rapids, MI: Baker Books, 1993), 71.

26. Haykal, 231, 496.

## 5. The Ministry of Mohammed

1. Ibrahimkhan O. Deshmukh, *The Gospel and Islam* (Bombay, India: Gospel Literature Service, 1995) 12-13.

2. Ergun Mehmet Caner and Emir Fethi Caner, *Unveiling Islam: An Insider's Look at Muslim Life and Beliefs* (Grand Rapids, MI: Kregel Publications, 2002), 56; Anis Shorrosh, *Islam Revealed: A Christian Arab's View of Islam* (Nashville, TN: Thomas Nelson, Inc., 1988), 52, 58.

3. Deshmukh, 14-15.

4. Norman Geisler and Abdul Saleeb, *Answering Islam: The Crescent in the Light of the Cross* (Grand Rapids, MI: Baker Books, 1993), 73.

5. Deshmukh, 15-16; Lewis Hopfe, (ed.) Mark Woodward, *Religions of the World*, 7th ed. (Upper Saddle River, N.J.: Prentice Hall, 1998), 361.

6. Andrew Rippin and Jan Knappert, ed. and trans., *Textual Sources for the Study of Islam* (Manchester: University Press, 1986), 68-72; Arthur Jeffery, ed., *Islam, Muhammad and His Religion* (New York: The Bobbs-Merrill Company, Inc., 1958), 35-46; and John Alden Williams, *Islam* (New York: George Braziller, 1962), 66-69.

7. Deshmukh, 16; William A. Miller, *A Christian's Response to Islam* (Phillipsburg, N.J.: Presbyterian and Reformed Publishing Co., 1976), 24.

8. Muhammad Husayn Haykal, *The Life of Muhammad* (North American Trust Publications, 1976), 139-47.

9. *Shorter Encyclopedia of Islam*, ed. H.A.R. Gibb and J. H. Kramers (Ithaca: Cornell University Press, 1953), 397.

10. Geisler and Saleeb, 75.

11. Deshmukh, 18.

12. Ibid.; Hopfe, 363.

13. Caner and Caner, 56.

14. Shorrosh, 62-63.

15. Geisler and Saleeb, 77; Miller, 29.

16. *The New Encyclopedia Britannica*, 15th ed., 22:4.

17. Geisler and Saleeb, 78-79.

18. Tor Andrae, *Mohammed, the Man and His Faith*, trans. Theophil Menzel (New York: Harper & Row, 1955), 155-156.

19. Martin Lings, *Muhammad* (London: George Allen and Unwin Ltd., 1983), 267-268; Hopfe, 362.

20. Geisler and Saleeb, 79; Hopfe, 362; Miller, 32-33.

21. Miller, 33.

22. Geisler and Saleeb, 79; Hopfe, 362.

23. Miller, 35.

24. Ibid., 36-37; Shorrosh, 69-70.

25. "Prophet Muhammad's Last Sermon," *Alim: The World's Most Useful Islamic Software*, Multi-Media edition CD-ROM (ISL Software Corporation, 1996).

26. Caner and Caner, 59.

27. Miller, 37.

28. Caner and Caner, 61; Miller, 37; Shorrosh, 71.

29. W. Montgomery Watt, *Muhammad: Prophet and Statesman* (New York: Oxford University Galaxy Press, 1961), 228.

### 6. The World's Fastest-Growing Faith

1. "Ingrid Mattson: What Is Islam?" http://wwwcnn.com2001 COMMUNITY/10/18mattson.cnna/ (October 18, 2001).

2. Gayle Young, "Fast-growing Islam winning converts in Western World," http://www.cnn.com/WORLD/9704/14/egypt.islam/ (April 14, 1997).

3. Sharif Shuja, "Islam and the West: From Discord to Understanding," *Contemporary Review*, vol. 278, no. 1624 (May 2001), 257-63.

4. Ergun Mehmet Caner and Emir Fethi Caner, *Unveiling Islam: An Insider's Look at Muslim Life and Beliefs* (Grand Rapids, MI: Kregel Publications, 2002), 68-71; Anis Shorrosh, *Islam Revealed: A Christian Arab's View of Islam* (Nashville, TN: Thomas Nelson , Inc., 1988), 72-74.

5. Ibid.; Lewis Hopfe, (ed.) Mark Woodward, *Religions of the World,* 7th ed. (Upper Saddle River, N.J.: Prentice Hall, 1998), 377-379; David Kerr, "The Unity and Variety in Islam" in *Eerdman's Handbook to the World's Religions* (Grand Rapids, MI: William B. Eerdmans Publishing Company, 1982), 330-332.

6. Chart adapted from Elizabeth Breuilly, Joanne O'Brien, and Martin Palmer, *Religions of the World: The Illustrated Guide to Origins, Beliefs, Traditions & Festivals* (New York: Transedition Limited and Fernleigh Books, 1997), 69.

7. Caner and Caner, 71; Hopfe, 375-376; William A. Miller, *A Christian's Response to Islam* (Phillipsburg, N.J.: Presbyterian and Reformed Publishing Co., 1976), 38; Montgomery Watt, "The Way of the Prophet" in *Eerdman's Handbook to the World's Religions* (Grand Rapids, MI: William B. Eerdmans Publishing Company, 1982), 312.

8. Caner and Caner, 72; Lothar Schmalfuss, "Science, Art and Culture in Islam" in *Eerdman's Handbook to the World's Religions* (Grand Rapids, MI: William B. Eerdmans Publishing Company, 1982), 327-328; Watt, 312-313.

9. Amin Maalouf, *The Crusades Through Arab Eyes* (New York: Schocken Books, 1984), 265.

10. Caner and Caner, 73-75.

11. Ibid., 75-78; Hopfe, 382-383; Watt, 314.

12. Bob Sjorgren and Bill and Amy Stears, *Run with the Vision: A Remarkable Global Plan For the 21st Century Church* (Minneapolis, MN: Bethany House Publishers, 1995).

13. Ibid.

14. World Jewish Congress, "Radical Islam in Europe: A United Continent Faces a Burgeoning Threat to Its Stability" Policy Dispatches, no. 83, September 2002 (online, July 3, 2003), http://www.wjc.org.ilpublicationspolicy_dispatches/pub_dis83.html.

15. R. W. Bulliet, "The Crisis Within Islam," *Wilson Quarterly*, vol. 26, no. 1, (2002), 11-19.

16. Ibid.

17. M. Vatikiotis, "A Tale of Two Madrassas," *Far Eastern Economic Review* (Hong Kong, June 27, 2002).

18. Bulliet, 11-19.

## 7. Islam in America

1. Kirk Albrecht, "Turning the Prophet's Words into Profits," *Business Week* (March, 6, 1998); Gayle Young, "Fast-growing Islam winning converts in Western World," http://www.cnn.com/WORLD/9704/14/egypt.islam/ (April 14, 1997).

2. Sharif Shuja, "Islam and the West: From Discord to Understanding," *Contemporary Review*, vol. 278, no. 1624 (May 2001), 257-63.

3. M. Ali Kettani, *Muslim Minorities in the World Today* (London: Mansell Publishing Limited, 1986), 241.

4. Bob Summer, "The Need to Understand Islam," *Publishers Weekly* (May 9, 1994), 31.

5. "Varieties of Worship: Demographic Facts, U.S. Department of State International Information Programs," http://usinfo.state.gov/products/pubs/muslimlife/demograp.htm (February 19, 2004).

6. Imam Muhammad Armiya Nu'man, *What Every American Should Know About Islam & The Muslims,* rev. ed. (Jersey City, N.J.: New Mind Productions, [1985] 1989), 53.

7. Statistics from Bureau of the Census, *Negro Population in the United States, 1790-1915*, p. 53, as quoted by E. Franklin Frazier, "The Negro in the United States" in Andrew W. Lind, ed., *Race Relations in World Perspective* (Honolulu: University of Hawaii Press, 1955): 342.

8. Sulayman S. Nyang, "Islam in the United States: Review of Sources," *Journal, Institute of Muslim Minority Affairs* 2 and 3 (Winter 1980-Summer 1981), 191; "Autobiography of Omar ibn Said, Slave in North Carolina, 1831," *The American Historical Review* 30 (July 1925), 787-795.

9. See Albert J. Raboteau, *Slave Religion: The "Invisible Institution" in the Antebellum South* (Oxford: Oxford University Press, 1978).

10. Yvonne Yazbeck Haddadd, "Arab Muslims and Islamic Institutions in America: Adaptation and Reform," in *Arabs in the New World: Studies on Arab-American Communities,* eds. Sameer Y. Abraham and Nabeel Abraham (Detroit: Wayne State University Center for Urban Studies, 1983), 65.

11. Alixa Naff, "Arabs in America: A Historical Overview," in *Arabs in the New World: Studies on Arab-American Communities,* eds. Sameer Y. Abraham and Nabeel Abraham (Detroit: Wayne State University Center for Urban Studies, 1983), 14.

12. Emily Kalled Lovell, "Islam in the United States: Past and Present," in *The Muslim Community in North America,* eds. Earle H. Waugh, Baha Abu-Ladan, and Regula B. Qureshi (Edmonton: University of Alberta Press, 1983), 94-96.

13. Naff, 19; Gregory Orfalea, *Before the Flames* (Austin: University of Texas Press, 1998): 95.

14. Kettani, 195; Naff, 25.

15. Leona B. Bagai, *The East Indians and the Pakistanis in America* (Minneapolis: Lerner Publications Co., 1967), 42.

16. Karen Isaksen Leonard, *Making Ethnic Choices: California's Punjabi Mexican Americans* (Philadelphia: Temple University Press, 1992), reviewed in *The Journal of American History*, vol. 80, no. 4 (March 1994), 1502-3.

17. Kettani, 195; Sulayman S. Nyang, "Convergence and Divergence in an Emergent Community: A Study of Challenges Facing U.S. Muslims," in *The Muslims of America*, ed. Yvonne Yazbeck Haddad (New York: Oxford University Press, 1991), 240-241.

18. Brent Ashabranner, *An Ancient Heritage: The Arab-American Minority* (New York: Harper Collins, 1991), 46.

19. B.J. Violett, "Bookshelf: Books by Faculty, Staff, and Alumni," *UCLA Magazine* (Fall 1993), 43.

20. Kettani, 196.

21. See Steven Barboza, *American Jihad: Islam after Malcolm X* (New York: Doubleday, 1993), 9n.

22. Reza F. Safa, *Inside Islam: Exposing and Reaching the World of Islam* (Orlando, FL: Creation House, 1996), 52.

23. Yvonne Yazbeck Haddad and Jane Idleman Smith, *Muslim Communities in North America* (Albany: State University of New York, 1994), 227.

24. See Safa, 52.

25. Michael Wolfe, *The Hadj: An American's Pilgrimage to Mecca* (New York: Atlantic Monthly Press, 1993), 7.

26. Carl Ellis, Project Joseph brochure.

27. R. Laurence Moore, *Religious Outsiders and the Making of Americans* (New York: Oxford University Press, 1986), 191.

28. Yvonne Yazbeck Haddad and Jane Idleman Smith, *Mission to America: Five Islamic Sectarian Communities in North America* (Gainseville: University Press of Florida, 1993), 87.

29. Clifton E. Marsh, *From Black Muslims to Muslims: The Transition from Separatism to Islam, 1930-1980* (Metuchen, N.J.: The Scarecrow Press, 1984), 51.

30. Safa, 53.

31. George Eaton Simpson, *Black Religions in the New World* (New York: Columbia University Press, 1978), 271.

32. Elijah Muhammad, *Our Savior Has Arrived* (Newport News, VA: United Brothers Communications Systems, n.d.) 36, 43.

33. Ibid., 56.

34. Ibid., 6-7.

35. "Prophet Muhammad's Last Sermon," *Alim: The World's Most Useful Islamic Software*, Multi-Media edition CD-ROM (ISL Software Corporation, 1996).

36. Alex Haley, *The Autobiography of Malcolm X* (New York: Ballantine Books, 1992), 340.

37. Elijah Muhammad, *Our Savior Has Arrived,* 61.

38. Ibid.

39. See Elijah Muhammad, *How to Eat to Live (Book No. 1)* (Newport News, VA: National Newport News and Commentator, 1967); Elijah Muhammad, *How to Eat to Live (Book No. 2)* (Newport News, VA: National Newport News and Commentator, 1972).

40. Ibid., 431-436.

41. Nyang, "Convergence and Divergence...," 241.

42. See Safa, 55.

43. Haddad and Smith, *Muslim Communities in North America,* 24.

44. "Prophet Muhammad's Last Sermon."

45. Edwin S. Gaustad, "America's Institutions of Faith: A Statistical Postscript," in *Religion in America*, ed. William G. McLoughlin and Robert N. Bellah (Boston: Beacon Press, 1968), 121.

46. Eric Lincoln, *The Black Muslims in America* (Boston: Beacon Press, [1961] 1973), xi-xii.

47. Ibid., 232.

48. E. U. Essien-Udom, *Black Nationalism: A Search for an Identity in America* (Chicago: University of Chicago Press, 1962), 83.

49. Lincoln, xi.

50. See Simeon Booker, *Black Man's America* (Englewood Cliffs, N.J.: Prentice-Hall, 1964), 116-117.

51. Safa, 60.

## 8. Monotheism: The Strength of Islam

1. Kraig Meyer, *Sharing the Gospel with Muslims* (Grand Junction, CO: Friends of Turkey, 1993), 8. See also Norman Geisler and Abdul Saleeb, *Answering Islam: The Crescent in the Light of the Cross* (Grand Rapids, MI: Baker Books, 1993), 15.

2. Lewis Hopfe, (ed.) Mark Woodward, *Religions of the World,* 7th ed. (Upper Saddle River, N.J.: Prentice Hall, 1998), 358.

3. Ibid., 1.

4. Arthur Jeffery, *Islam, Muhammad and His Religion* (New York: Bobbs-Merrill Company Inc., 1958), 93.

5. Hammudah Abdalati, *Islam in Focus* (Indianapolis: American Trust Publications, 1975), 9.

6. Badru Kateregga and David Shenk, *Islam and Christianity* (Grand Rapids: William B. Eerdmans Publishing Co., 1980), 101.

7. Faruqi, *Islam* (Niles, Ill.: Argus Communications, 1984), 9.

8. W. Montgomery Watt, *Islam and Christianity Today* (London: Routledge and Kegan Paul, 1983), 125.

9. Kenneth Cragg, *The Call of the Minaret* (New York: Oxford University Press, 1964), 42-43.

10. Ignaz Goldziher, *Introduction to Islamic Theology and Law*, trans. Andras and Ruth Hamori (Princeton: Princeton University Press, 1981), 78.

11. Geisler and Saleeb, 26.

12. Cited by Abdiyah Akbar Abdul-Haqq, "Sharing Your Faith with a Muslim" (Minneapolis: Bethany Fellowship Inc., 1980), 152, from Hughe's *Dictionary of Islam*, 147.

13. Jay Smith, "Six Muslim Beliefs (Iman), and a Christian's Response," Research Paper, 6.

14. Abdul-Haqq, 152.

15. Geisler and Saleeb, 44.

16. Smith, 2.

## 9. Beings of Light

1. Kauser Niazi, *Creation of Man* (Karachi: Ferozoono Ltd., 1975), 12. See also William A. Miller, *A Christian's Response to Islam* (Phillipsburg, N.J.: Presbyterian and Reformed Publishing Co., 1976), 45.

2. H. A. R. Gibb, *Mohammedanism* (London: Oxford University Press, 1964), 56-57.

3. Ghulam Sarwar, *Islam: Beliefs and Teachings* (London: The Muslim Educational Trust, 1989), 28. See also Miller, 46; and Geisler and Saleeb, 35.

4. Ibrahimkhan O. Deshmukh, *The Gospel and Islam* (Bombay, India: Gospel Literature Service, 1995), 23.

5. Sarwar, 28.

6. Muhammad Khouj, *The End of the Journey: An Islamic Perspective on Death and the Afterlife* (Washington, D.C.: The Islamic Center, 1988), 70, 72.

7. Abdullah Yusuf Ali, *The Holy Qur'an: Translation and Commentary* (Damascus: Ouloom AlQur'an, 1934) *1:25*.

## 10. The Role of Prophets

1. See Ghulam Sarwar, *Islam: Beliefs and Teachings* (London: The Muslim Educational Trust, 1989), 26.

2. Ibid., 27. See also Norman Geisler and Abdul Saleeb, *Answering Islam: The Crescent in the Light of the Cross* (Grand Rapids, MI: Baker Books, 1993), 53.

3. See Badru Kateregga and David Shenk, *Islam and Christianity* (Grand Rapids: William B. Eerdmans Publishing Co., 1980), 34, and Muhammad Abdul Rauf, *Islam Creed and Worship* (Washington, D.C.: The Islamic Center, 1974), 5.

4. Kateregga and Shenk, 36.

5. See Fazlul Rahman, *Major Themes of the Qur'an* (Chicago: Bibliotheca Islamica, 1980), 83.

6. Hammudah Abdalati, *Islam in Focus* (Indianapolis: American Trust Publications, 1975), 9.

7. Anis Shorrosh, *Islam Revealed: A Christian Arab's View of Islam* (Nashville, TN: Thomas Nelson Publishers, 1988), 205, 211.

8. Due to the ambiguity present in the Qur'an some sources suggest there are inferences to three other prophets in the Qur'an, which would bring the total to 28.

9. See Geisler and Saleeb, 53-54.

10. List of Arabic and biblical names adapted from Sarwar, 27.

11. Geoffrey Parrinder, *Jesus in the Qur'an* (New York: Oxford University Press, 1977), 40.

12. See Alhaj A. D. Ajijola, *The Essence of Faith in Islam* (Lahore, Pakistan: Islamic Publications Ltd., 1978), 33.

13. Abdalati, 27.

14. John Takle, "Islam and Christianity," in *Studies in Islamic Law, Religion and Society*, ed. H. S. Bhatia (New Delhi: Deep and Deep Publications, 1989), 218.

15. Shorrosh, 266.

16. Kenneth Cragg, *Jesus and the Muslim, An Exploration* (London: George Allen and Unwin, 1985), 25.

17. See William Campbell, *The Gospel of Barnabas: Its True Value* (Rawalpindi, Pakistan: Christian Study Centre, 1989), 77-87.

18. L. Bevan Jones, *Christianity Explained to Muslims*, rev. ed. (Calcutta: Baptist Mission Press, 1964), 79.

19. See Campbell (1989).

20. Lonsdale Ragg and Laura Ragg, *The Gospel of Barnabas* (Karachi, Pakistan: Begum Aisha Bawany Waqf, n.d.), 271.

21. J. Slomp, "The Gospel in Dispute," in *Islamochristiana* (Rome: Pontifico Instituto di Studi Arabi, 1978), vol. 4, 104.

22. See Matthew 20:17-19; Mark 10:32-34; Luke 18:31-34.

23. Geisler and Saleeb, 65-66.

24. See Dr. William Campbell's excellent argument in defense of "Paracletos" as a reference to the Holy Spirit, defending the criticisms made by Dr. Maurice Bucaille's work (from a Muslim perspective). William Campbell, *The Qur'an and the Bible in the Light of History and Science* (Middle East Resources, 1992), 234-248; Maurice Bucaille, *The Bible, the Qur'an, and Science*, English Edition (Indianapolis: American Trust Publications, 1979).

25. See Mark 8:22-26; Matthew 9:27-31.

26. See Matthew 8:1-4; Mark 1:40-45; Luke 5:12-15; Luke 17:11-19.

27. See John 11:1-45.
28. See Matthew 14:51-21; Mark 6:35-44; Luke 9:12-17.
29. See Matthew 14:22-33; Mark 6:45-52; John 6:17-21.
30. See Mark 1:23-27; Luke 4:33-36; Matthew 15:21-28; Mark 7:24-30.
31. Geisler and Saleeb, 232-234.
32. Ibid., 230.

## 11. The Quran: Final Word from God

1. Lewis Hopfe, (ed.) Mark Woodward, *Religions of the World,* 7th ed. (Upper Saddle River, N.J.: Prentice Hall, 1998), 363.
2. See Alhaj A. D. Ajijola, *The Essence of Faith in Islam* (Lahore, Pakistan: Islamic Publications Ltd., 1978), 104.
3. Anis Shorrosh, *Islam Revealed: A Christian Arab's View of Islam* (Nashville, TN: Thomas Nelson Publishers, 1988), 21.
4. See Ergun Mehmet Caner and Emir Fethi Caner, *Unveiling Islam: An Insider's Look At Muslim Life and Beliefs* (Grand Rapids, MI: Kregel Publications, 2002), 84-85; Norman Geisler and Abdul Saleeb, *Answering Islam: The Crescent in the Light of the Cross* (Grand Rapids, MI: Baker Books, 1993), 71; Hopfe, 360; William A. Miller, *A Christian's Response to Islam* (Phillipsburg, N.J.: Presbyterian and Reformed Publishing Co., 1976), 19-20.
5. See William Campbell, *The Qur'an and the Bible...,* 96-122; and Geisler and Saleeb, 90-91.
6. Ibid.
7. See Badru Kateregga, *Islam and Christianity* (Grand Rapids: William B. Eerdmans Publishing Co., 1980), 29-30; Maurice Bucaille, *The Bible, The Qur'an, and Science* (Paris: Editions Seghers, 1988), 134.
8. Caner and Caner, 85; Ibrahimkhan O. Deshmukh, *The Gospel and Islam* (Bombay, India: Gospel Literature Service, 1995), 70-71.
9. Caner and Caner, 90; and Shorrosh, 209.
10. Charis Waddy, *The Muslim Mind* (London/New York: Longman, 1976), 14.
11. Kenneth Cragg, *The Call of the Minaret* (New York: Oxford University Press, 1964), 55, 57.
12. C. G. Pfander, *The Mizanu'l Haqq* (Balance of Truth), revised and enlarged by W. St. Clair Tisdall (Villach, Austria: Light of Life, 1986), 264.
13. Ali Dashti, *Twenty Three Years: A Study of the Prophetic Career of Mohammed* (London: George Allen & Unwin, 1985), 48-49; and Shorrosh, 199-200.
14. Dashti, 48-49.

15. Geisler and Saleeb, 189.

16. As referenced in Shorrosh, 192.

17. See Pfander, 254; Shorrosh, 192; and W. Montgomery Watt, *Bell's Introduction to the Qur'an* (Edinburgh: Edinburgh University Press, 1970), 33-34.

18. John Glubb, *The Life and Times of Muhammad* (New York: Stein and Day, 1971), 271.

19. William Goldsack, *Muhammad in Islam: Sketches of Muhammad from Islamic Sources* (Madras, India: The Christian Literature Society, 1916), 112-114.

20. W. Montgomery Watt, *Muhammad: Prophet and Statesman* (reprint: London: Oxford University Press, 1967), 40.

21. Joseph Gudel, *To Every Muslim an Answer: Islamic Apologetics Compared and Contrasted with Christian Apologetics* (unpublished thesis, Simon Greenleaf School of Law, 1982), 72.

22. John Gilchrist, *Jam' al-Qur'an: The Codification of the Qur'an Text* (Benoni, South Africa: Jesus to the Muslims, 1989).

23. Arthur Jefferey, *Materials for the History of the Text of the Qur'an* (New York: AMS Press, Inc., 1975), 7-8.

24. Watt (1970), 60.

25. W. Montgomery Watt, *Muhammad's Mecca* (Edinburgh: Edinburgh University Press, 1988), 86.

26. Dashti, 111.

27. Ali A. Yusuf, *The Holy Qur'an: Translation and Commentary* (Damascus: Ouloom AlQur'an, 1934).

28. Geisler and Saleeb, 194-5; and Shorrosh, 195-197.

29. Ajijola, 90.

30. Edward Gibbon, *The History of the Decline and Fall of the Roman Empire,* vol. 5, ed. J.B. Bury (London: Methuen & Co., 1898), 360-361.

31. John B. Noss, *Man's Religions* (New York: The Macmillan Co., 1956), 711.

32. William Paley, *Evidences of Christianity* (London: 1851), 257.

## *12. The Day of Judgment*

1. Jane Smith and Y. Haddad, *The Islamic Understanding of Death and Resurrection* (Albany: State University of New York Press, 1981), 2.

2. Muhammad Khouj, *The End of the Journey: An Islamic Perspective on Death and the Afterlife* (Washington, D.C.: The Islamic Center, 1988), 42-43.

3. Ibid., 70.

4. Ibid., 72.

5. Ibid., 79.

6. See surahs 55:44, 11:106, 14:16-17, 69:30-32, 14:50, 22:19-21; Ibid., 85-86.

7. See Revelation 20:14; 2 Thessalonians 1:7-9; Matthew 25:46; Matthew 8:12.

8. See Khouj, 82; Smith and Haddad, 88-89; and surahs 37:42-48, 9:72.

9. See Seyyed Hossein Nasr, *Ideals and Realities of Islam* (London: George Allen & Unwin, 1975).

10. See Revelation 4–5, 21:1-7; John 14:1-4; 1 Corinthians 2:9.

11. Badru Kateregga, *Islam and Christianity* (Grand Rapids: William B. Eerdmans Publishing Co., 1980), 14.

12. Taken from Kenneth Cragg, *Jesus and the Muslim, An Exploration* (London: George Allen and Unwin, 1985), 260.

13. Muhammad Abul Quasem, *Salvation of the Soul in Islamic Devotions* (London: Kegan Paul International, 1983), 31-33.

14. Muhammad Abdul Rauf, *Islam Creed and Worship* (Washington, D.C.: The Islamic Center, 1974), 1.

15. Quasem, 45.

16. Norman Geisler and Abdul Saleeb, *Answering Islam: The Crescent in the Light of the Cross* (Grand Rapids, MI: Baker Books, 1993), 125-126.

17. Abdiyah Akbar Abdul-Haqq, "Sharing Your Faith with a Muslim" (Minneapolis: Bethany Fellowship Inc., 1980), 166-167.

18. Faruqi, *Islam* (Niles, Ill.: Argus Communications, 1984), 5.

## 14. Five Times Each Day

1. George Braswell, *Islam* (Nashville: Broadman and Holman, 1996), 63.

2. Ghulam Sarwar, *Islam: Beliefs and Teachings* (London: The Muslim Educational Trust, 1989), 47.

3. Ergun Mehmet Caner and Emir Fethi Caner, *Unveiling Islam: An Insider's Look at Muslim Life and Beliefs* (Grand Rapids, MI, Kregel Publications, 2002), 124.

4. Ibid., 124-5.

## 15. A Grueling Month

1. Ghulam Sarwar, *Islam: Beliefs and Teachings* (London: The Muslim Educational Trust, 1989), 77.

## 16. The 2½ Percent Duty

1. Ergun Mehmet Caner and Emir Fethi Caner, *Unveiling Islam: An Insider's Look at Muslim Life and Beliefs* (Grand Rapids, MI, Kregel Publications, 2002), 126.

2. William A. Miller, *A Christian's Response to Islam* (Phillipsburg, N.J.: Presbyterian and Reformed Publishing Co., 1976), 60.

### 17. Following in the Footsteps of Mohammed

1. Rym Brahimi, "Hajj stampede: 244 pilgrims dead," http://www.cnn.com/2004/WORLD/meast/02/01/hajj.stampede/ (February 1, 2004).
2. William A. Miller, *A Christian's Response to Islam* (Phillipsburg, N.J.: Presbyterian and Reformed Publishing Co., 1976), 45; Lewis Hopfe, (ed.) Mark Woodward, *Religions of the World*, 7th ed. (Upper Saddle River, N.J.: Prentice Hall, 1998), 358.
3. Miller, 36-37; Anis Shorrosh, *Islam Revealed: A Christian Arab's View of Islam* (Nashville, TN: Thomas Nelson , Inc., 1988), 69-70.
4. Hopfe, 358; Miller, 45.

### 18. Jihad and Other Muslim Practices

1. Ghulam Sarwar, *Islam: Beliefs and Teachings* (London: The Muslim Educational Trust, 1989), 81.
2. Ibid.; William A Miller, *A Christian's Response to Islam* (Phillipsburg, N.J.: Presbyterian and Reformed Publishing Co., 1976), 63.
3. Markus Hattstein, *World Religions* (Hong Kong, China: Leefung Asco Printers, undated); and Montgomery Watt, "The Way of the Prophet" in *Eerdman's Handbook to the World's Religions* (Grand Rapids, MI: William B. Eerdmans Publishing Company, 1982), 312-313.
4. Elizabeth Breuilly, Joanne O'Brien, and Martin Palmer, *Religions of the World: The Illustrated Guide to Origins, Beliefs, Traditions & Festivals* (New York: Transedition Limited and Fernleigh Books, 1997), 80.
5. Ibid.; Norman Anderson, "The Law of Islam" in *Eerdman's Handbook to the World's Religions* (Grand Rapids, MI: William B. Eerdmans Publishing Company, 1982), 322-324.
6. Anderson, 322; Daniel Pipes, "Islam and Islamism: faith and ideology," *National Interest* (2000, Spring, no. 59), 87-93.
7. Watt, 312-313.
8. Anderson, 322-324.
9. Ergun Mehmet Caner and Emir Fethi Caner, *Unveiling Islam: An Insider's Look at Muslim Life and Beliefs* (Grand Rapids, MI, Kregel Publications, 2002), 56.
10. Ibrahimkhan O. Deshmukh, *The Gospel and Islam* (Bombay, India: Gospel Literature Service, 1995), 46-47.
11. Martin Lewison, "Conflicts of Interest? The Ethics of Usury," *Journal of Business Ethics* (Dec. 1999).
12. Tom Bawden, "FSA to Look at Muslim Banks," *Marketing Week* (Aug. 12, 1999); T.W. Taylor and J.W. Evans, "Islamic Banking and the Prohibition of Usury in Western Economic Thought," *National Westminister Bank Quarterly Review* (Nov. 1987).

13. R. Aggarwal and T. Yousef, "Islamic Banks and Investment Financing," *Journal of Money, Credit, and Banking* (Feb. 2000).

14. Kirk Albrecht, "Turning the Prophet's Words into Profits," *Business Week* (March 6, 1998).

15. Mohammed Abdel-Hakim, "Principles of Islamic Banking," *Nida'ul Islam Magazine* (Nov./Dec. 1995); "Leasing According to Islam," *Airfinance Journal* (Feb. 1997).

16. Mohamed Ariff, "Islamic Banking," *Asian-Pacific Economic Literature* (Sept. 1998).

17. Abdel-Hakim.

18. Bawden.

19. Albrecht.

20. Breuilly, et al., 78-79; Caner and Caner, 152-160; Deshmukh, 51-57; David Kerr, "The Worship of Islam" in *Eerdman's Handbook to the World's Religions* (Grand Rapids, MI: William B. Eerdmans Publishing Company, 1982), 320.

21. Caner and Caner, 127.

22. Ibid., 159.

## 19. Is Islam an Anti-Christian Religion?

1. Bassam M. Madany, *The Bible and Islam: Sharing God's Word with a Muslim* (Palos Heights, Illinois: The Back to God Hour, 1981), 1.

2. Ibid., 11.

3. Reza F. Safa, *Inside Islam: Exposing and Reaching the World of Islam* (Orlando, FL: Creation House, 1996), 8.

## 20. Anticipating Muslim Arguments

1. Donald S. Tingle, *Islam and Christianity* (Downers Grove, IL: Inter-Varsity Press, 1985), 22.

2. See Norman Geisler and Abdul Saleeb, *Answering Islam: The Crescent in the Light of the Cross* (Grand Rapids, MI: Baker Books, 1993), 230.

3. Ibid., 231-234.

4. Ibid.

5. See William Campbell, *The Qur'an and the Bible in the Light of History and Science* (Middle East Resources, 1992), 96-122; and Geisler and Saleeb, 90-91.

6. See Dr. William Campbell's excellent argument in defense of "Paracletos" as a reference to the Holy Spirit, defending the criticisms made by Dr. Maurice Bucaille's work (from a Muslim perspective). Campbell, 234-248. Maurice Bucaille, *The Bible, the Qur'an, and Science?* English Edition (Indianapolis: American Trust Publications, 1979).

### 21. How to Share the Gospel with a Muslim

1. William A Miller, *A Christian's Response to Islam* (Phillipsburg, N.J.: Presbyterian and Reformed Publishing Co., 1976), 125-127.

2. See Ephesians 4:15.

3. Miller, 133.

4. Anis Shorrosh, *Islam Revealed: A Christian Arab's View of Islam* (Nashville, TN: Thomas Nelson , Inc., 1988), 41-42.

5. Forbes Robinson, *Letters to His Friends* (New York: Longmans, Green and Co., 1911), 164.

# Index

**www.understandmymuslimpeople.com**

an easy way to get supplemental materials and
to let your friends learn more about this book

**www.barclaypress.com**

on-line ordering
from the publisher

**www.gospelformuslims.com**

stay in touch with Abraham Sarker
and Gospel for Muslims, Inc.